COGNITIVE SCIENCE PROJECTS IN PROLOG

Cognitive Science Projects in Prolog

Peter Scott

and

Rod Nicolson
Department of Psychology
University of Sheffield

LAWRENCE ERLBAUM ASSOCIATES, PUBLISHERS
Hove and London (UK)   Hillsdale (USA)

Lawrence Erlbaum Associates Ltd., Publishers
27 Palmeira Mansions
Church Road
Hove
East Sussex, BN3 2FA
U.K.

British Library Cataloguing in Publication Data

Scott, Peter J.
Cognitive science projects in Prolog.
I. Title II. Nicolson, Roderick I.
153

ISBN 0-86377-182-3 (Pbk)

This book was produced directly from camera-ready copy provided by the authors.
Printed and bound by LR Printing Services Limited, Burgess Hill, U.K.

To Fiona and Margaret

Contents

Tutorial Appendix 1   A Short Prolog Tutorial

Glossary

Answers to Exercises

Figures

Exercises

Exercises in Tutorial Appendix 1

Exercises in Chapter 2

Exercises in Chapter 3

Exercises in Chapter 4

Code Appendices

Preface Notes

Cognitive Science is a newly emerged discipline which attempts to increase our knowledge of mind primarily using the technique of implementing theories on a computer. It has formed from the collaboration of a range of disciplines including psychology, artificial intelligence, neuroscience, linguistics and philosophy. Cognitive Science research is making a profound and increasing impact on theoretical developments in all of these contributory disciplines, and we believe that an awareness of cognitive science terminology and techniques will soon be a pre-requisite for students of these disciplines. Our aim in writing a book on Prolog Projects is to provide the student of cognitive science with the opportunity to 'get their hands dirty' with some reasonably complete and detailed working code. The book evolved out of two practical courses in 'Prolog for Cognitive Science' which we developed at the University of Sheffield. The first course is a cognitive science awareness course which we run for Psychology students, and takes the form of four weeks introductory Prolog followed by six cognitive science projects. The second course supports practical project work by cognitive science students who already are reasonably proficient in Prolog in which they take two topics and produce significant enhancements to our program code. In both of these courses practical laboratory based work is accompanied by background lecture material. In this book we have attempted to support both sorts of need, and so it has been written to be of interest to two distinct classes of student reader.

Aim 1. Cognitive Science Awareness for readers with little programming background.

The target reader here is a Psychologist, Linguist or Philosopher interested in examining the application of artificial intelligence techniques to modelling psychological theories in the emerging discipline of cognitive science. This reader may have a very limited experience of computing — but access to a version of Prolog and to a computer. What we feel is important in the development of this discipline is the need to "see" what the cognitive science approach looks like in an actual implementation. The details of some of the more arcane definitions will be of little interest to this reader who may be pleased to note and then ignore them. The programs we have provided here should be relatively easy to use with even the most basic understanding of the programming involved. Indeed we would argue that it is in implementing such projects as these that the real learning begins – it is only when you start **use** some technique in the context of a non-trivial application that it really takes on meaning. For this reader the book is primarily intended as a Prolog and AI applications *awareness* exercise, it is not intended that you use it primarily to learn how to program in Prolog or write AI programs. Rather it is necessary for you to learn the essential elements of Prolog programming as a tool to assist in your understanding of the real problems that confront the Cognitive Scientist. If you want to learn to program using Prolog then you should refer to the excellent sources like Clocksin and Mellish (1986), Sterling and Shapiro (1986) and Bratko (1990). We recommend that you do have some experience of Prolog before jumping into our Projects and so for those readers who have none or whose knowledge is sketchy we have provided an appendix tutorial on the Prolog language to get you started. This appendix cannot replace a full programming course or text but it should provide you with some of the background you will need if you wish to understand the detail of the projects. In fact, if you are reasonably 'computer aware' already you might be surprised at quite how much you can learn about Prolog from within our projects alone.

Aim 2. Detailed Cognitive Science Project Work for experienced programmers.

As practising cognitive scientists we have been frustrated by the difficulty of obtaining program code for many of the cognitive science 'classics', and the variety of formats and languages in which the programs are written. Our second aim is to provide a set of cognitive science 'classics' written in a consistent and approachable style for a reader such as a Computer Scientist or Cognitive Scientist who is already reasonably familiar with Prolog and who wants an interesting project to work on which will provide valuable insights into cognitive science programming.

We would suggest that even the experienced reader should skim through this tutorial appendix to see if it all makes sense to them and that they are not baffled by our use of terminology. In addition, to help in this we have provided an extended glossary of some of the most important of our technical uses of words. As for the projects themselves, this reader is more likely to skim the main chapter and to take the prototype program provided in the Code Appendix as a starting point, developing it along the lines suggested in our Advanced Exercises, returning to the chapter for explanations and context only later. A Computer Scientist may also be concerned with issues such as efficiency and elegance which in some cases we have had to sacrifice for clarity.

Many readers are somewhere between these two categories in that broad and fertile land which is becoming cognitive science. We hope that they will be able to benefit not only in terms of cognitive science awareness but also by writing their own cognitive science code.

The Organisation of the Book

The main chapters in the book give an outline of the Prolog implementation of a selection of classic projects in the development of cognitive science. They discuss their context and sketch out the most important definitions. Each major section is accompanied by graded exercises. There is no imperative to deal with the projects in the order given — however, we have arranged the chapters according to our feeling for the relative difficulty of the implementation details involved. The full programs are given in appropriate appendices. Normally there is a toy version and a more full version of each project. The toy version is typically very simple and is used to show the important aspects of the structure of the project and to give the reader an idea of how one may begin to model the problem. The full version is intended to give the project a more sophisticated interface and to concentrate on some of the more advanced features. In all cases these features are intended to be added to and refined by the reader. For each chapter we recommend that the reader load/consult the toy project program and then start reading and following the exercises as they appear.

We have often been frustrated by texts whose 'answers to exercises' are so selective that the only ones you want help on are not there. All of the questions that we pose in the exercises have answers to them. These are as complete as we can sensibly make them. The only frustration you should have is in possibly not being given enough help in the 'advanced project ideas' which we suggest at the end of each project, but in most cases spelling out the solutions would require a complete new book and quite spoil the challenge.

We intend that this work should act as a source book of project ideas that *any* level of student should be able to use as an entry point into some cognitive science work. We have only chosen projects that are well suited to Prolog and with a reasonably stimulating input-output and performance. Indeed we have explicitly excluded a number of projects in learning, perception, etc from this current book because they did not meet these criteria. We would naturally welcome comments and other projects from readers. Our hope is that in exploring our code you may be inspired to produce your own.

Peter Scott
Rod Nicolson
March 1991

Chapter 1 : Introduction

This book is not intended either as a full introduction to Prolog or as a comprehensive survey of Cognitive Science. There are now a few good books on each theme, and we hope more will emerge during the next few years. We are attempting something rather more ambitious. We are trying to make Cognitive Science 'come to life' by recreating in Prolog some of the 'classic' Cognitive Science programs. Prolog provides an excellent environment in which to illustrate these programs as it supports a declarative style of programming which can be used to highlight the logical structure of a program and focus on the representation issues. We assert that Cognitive Science is a hands-on experience, and that exploration is one of the best ways of developing interest and investigating the strengths and weaknesses of an approach. Consequently we have selected topics that have not only played a key historical role in the development of Cognitive Science, but also allow interesting explorations and enhancements. All the projects encourage the reader to play with them, adding data, making additions, seeking out weaknesses, and so on. In this chapter we present the background to both the emergence of Cognitive Science as a discipline and the rise of Prolog as a popular programming language.

1.1   What is Cognitive Science ?

Cognitive science is, as the name states, the science of cognition, where cognition refers to the broad range of the activities of the mind. The "science of mind" must be the oldest science in the world, dating back over two millenia to the timeless musings of the Greek philosophers. In its present form it is also one of the newest sciences, dating back little over thirty years to the realisation of the potential of the newly invented digital computer. In this short time workers in computer science have been very productive. In some of this work researchers in many other disciplines have seen far-reaching implications for their own work. The application of some computational techniques to disciplines like cognitive psychology, linguistics, neuroscience and philosophy promises to unite them into one common cause — a cognitive science. The main thread which unites this diversity is an interest in computational models of cognitive processes.

Let us consider the interests of two of the principal contributing disciplines, computer science and psychology. Psychologists are continually confronted with theories that claim to contribute to an understanding of the nature of human behaviour. Cognitive psychologists believe that much of this behaviour can be seen as the product of the information-processing abilities of people. So, in their explanations, cognitive psychologists tend to use mechanisms that involve the computations performed by people on information. They frame their explanations as theories on paper which they can then test in experiments with people. Computer scientists, on the other hand, are very much involved in developing mechanical devices which can implement complex information management processes. A range of work has been developed in computer science that has been broadly labelled "artificial intelligence" (AI) because it addresses information processing problems that would be said to require intelligence if performed by humans. Artificial Intelligence researchers often find that the problem being addressed is one which humans already solve very successfully! So they typically use human behaviour as the specification for their mechanical modelling. People appear to have been built to learn, communicate and solve a variety of complex problems very effectively. Any attempt to get a computer to emulate or better this performance must benefit by studying it very closely. So cognitive psychologists and artificial intelligence researchers from computer science have found that they have very much in common.

For example: how are you able to read this book?

Psychology would ask you to do things like — try to recall what was said on the last page without looking back. It is unlikely that you will be able to correctly recall many of the exact words that were used, never mind the correct order! However, you should be able to answer general questions about the information content of the page. So it seems reasonable to propose that in reading these notes you are processing the symbolic information that is represented on this paper, representing it somehow in your head and accessing it again to answer any questions. Now a cognitive scientist who wanted to implement a computer system that closely replicated your reading-recall behaviour would have to answer the same questions as any psychologist with a paper-theory, but could provide it with a very rigorous test – in essence, a psychological computer-theory.

As with any emerging science, it is often difficult to identify the key aspects in face of the diversity of applications and perspectives involved. The two major unifying themes behind cognitive science investigations are the focus on some aspect of human or abstract cognition — 'intelligent' information processing — as the domain, and the use of computer implementation as a methodological and theoretical tool. The fundamental objective of cognitive science is the development of scientific theories of human thinking via computational analysis and instantiation. The methodology used by cognitive scientists involves implementing these theories in models which represent and access human knowledge. The promise is that in attempting an implementation of a computer-theory one may gain a much better perspective on the strengths, weaknesses and omissions of the paper-theory.

Figure 1.1 The Disciplines of Cognitive Science

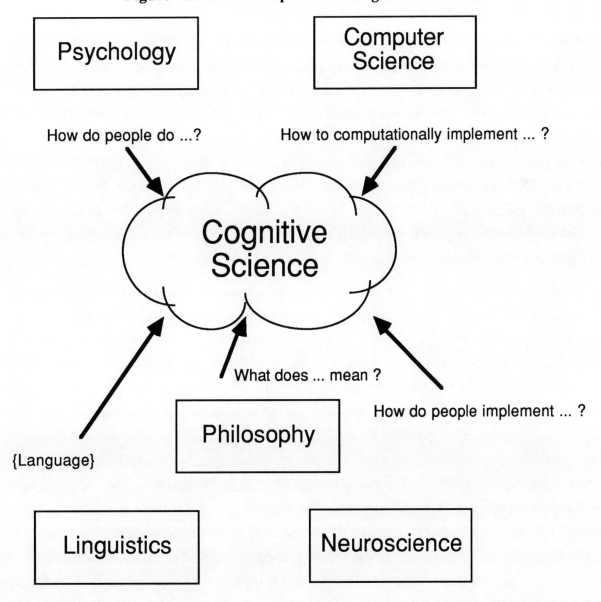

1.2   Why do Cognitive Science ?

We have already noted the interest of psychology and computer science in this enterprise, but as shown in Figure 1.1, many other disciplines have important questions to ask of a cognitive science. Linguists have a specific interest in the human language faculty. They want to know how language works, what the language mechanism is, where it comes from and how it develops. Neuroscientists want to explain how the brain supports mental behaviour, which structures are involved in which aspects of mental activity and how they function. And of course, philosophers will certainly have questions to ask about the answers that are produced by the others. The nature of intelligence, a soul, and the relationship of the mind to the body are all classical questions for philosophy.

If we consider a few real specimen cases we should see why a cognitive science is such a promising development for all of these questions. We have chosen examples from the disciplines of philosophy, neurophysiology and linguistics to show how insights from cognitive science have had a significant impact and started to provide some answers.

Philosophers over the centuries have been much exercised by the problem of the control of cognition. One early account of cognitive processing proposed that there must be a 'central executive' mechanism such as a homunculus, that somehow surveys the information coming into the senses and then decides what to do. This locates 'a ghost in the machine' that is the human mind (Ryle, 1949). Unfortunately, it must then answer the question of how the homunculus works, which leaves it prone to an infinite regress of homunculi and having explained nothing. In cognitive science John Anderson (1983) has proposed a mechanism involving a goal-directed production system architecture that provides the basis of a theory for the central control of cognition. Needless to say, the theory contains no homunculi or ghosts, but rather a very explicit combination of mechanisms and processes that could implement human cognition.

To the neuroscientist, humans are biological computational devices in which the information processed must at some level correspond to chemical and electrical activity in the brain. Unfortunately, whilst neurophysiology can provide measurements of electrochemical activity in various parts of the brain at various times, it is much harder to decide how this activity relates to cognitive activity (eg. is this measurement causal, a side-effect, or quite independent?). The only reason for taking measurements in the first place is to use them to test some mechanistic theory of the mental processes they may be related to. In short you need a cognitive science theory to know what to measure and what the results will mean. The neurophysiologists, Hubel and Wiesel (1959) caused intense scientific interest by the discovery that single cells in the striate cortex responded to very specific patterns of visual stimulation, namely 'lines' at different orientations and thicknesses. They used this result to propose that each cell could be conceived of as a primitive 'feature detector'. They further suggested that cells detecting these primitive features could be connected to higher level cells that would use them to detect composite features and so on up until a cell that would use input from all the lower ones to detect a very complex feature in the visual scene like say "your grandmother".

Unfortunately, the cortex is so complex and "noisy" that they could not find any of these "less primitive" feature detectors to support or disprove their idea.

In a cognitive science analysis David Marr (1982) provided a complete theoretical model of the vision problem which focused on the representation of information at each stage in the system. He proposed a new and important theoretical stage in the visual system, "the primal sketch", which is intermediate to the early and later processing stages. In his analysis he made explicit not only what information processing problems the visual system was solving, and how, but he also gave an alternative explanation of the role of the cortical cells. Instead of detecting fixed features from retinal stimulation, as Hubel and Weisel guessed, these cells are actually 'making measurements' which must then be fed into a further computational system. This analysis is now widely accepted and has formed the basis of fruitful interdisciplinary research, see for example Mayhew & Frisby (1984).

The linguist must account for the appearance of natural human language such as that used in everyday speech and that which you are currently reading in this book. The big problem that they face is that human language is both ambiguous and very complex. Most linguists start their analysis with a set of rules that capture some of the regularities in language. They call these rules a 'grammar'. As language is very complex the grammars that linguists tend produce are also very complex. Noam Chomsky (1957, 1965) has developed a formal account of language, based on a very sophisticated set transformations which he suggested would be needed to describe the change from different grammatical forms into others and thence into 'meaning'. We will deal with the detail of this important work later in the book, but the essential problem is that the sophistication of the descriptive theory could be masking a very simple computational mechanism. Indeed, it is though the work of cognitive scientists such as Terry Winograd (1972) who have attempted to build systems which not only processed language but acted on it in a simple simulated world that the limitations of the traditional linguistic approach became clear.

To end on a philosophical note, the origins of human knowledge — whether much was innate, derived from reason, or derived from experience —formed the focus of debate between the nativists, rationalists and the empiricists over two millenia. Recently Anderson (1989) has demonstrated that his cognitive science architecture of cognition (mentioned above) provides important insights on this central philosophical issue.

The point of these examples is not to suggest that the cognitive science analyses are correct, definitive or the only approaches to take to the these diverse problems. Far from it. They are but one perspective, which will certainly not be sufficient in itself to provide a complete analysis of the problem. The important point is that cognitive science provides an important component of any complete analysis, providing a new perspective, a valuable descriptive vocabulary and language, and a rigourous test of the sufficiency of the theoretical analysis. Familiarity with cognitive science concepts, therefore, has become essential for academics and researchers in all the fields with which cognitive science interacts synergistically, including at present cognitive psychology, computer science, control engineering, linguistics, neuroscience, philosophy and artificial intelligence. Within the next few years these interdisciplinary links will spread to other domains of psychology, education, and information science.

1.3   How should we do Cognitive Science ?

Every scientist makes a set of basic assumptions about the virtues and vices of their research paradigm. Cognitive scientists are more aware than most of the potential objections to their work. There are those who seriously question the direction and benefits of this relatively young discipline. It is important to be aware of these objections. The position that cognitive science is a futile or impossible enterprise has been argued at length by philosophers such as John Searle and Hubert Dreyfus. Rather than attempting a full examination of this very important and interesting argument here, we refer the interested reader to the critical literature (Dreyfus, 1979, 1981; Searle, 1980; Haugeland, 1981; Born, 1987). Cognitive scientists believe, rightly or wrongly, that while the philosophers debate the feasibility of the project, the researchers are steadily eroding the ground under their armchairs.

In a witty assault on standard cognitive psychological practice entitled "You can't play 20 questions with nature and win" (1973) Alan Newell convincingly demonstrated the inadequacies of the established canons of empirical science. He was instrumental in firmly establishing the need for *computational implementation* of scientific theories. The prime tool of the cognitive scientist is a computational model which reflects directly upon some psychological theory. This model should offer a good test of some of the aspects of the theory and in the process of making it work may even help us to think about the problem in a quite different way.

Let us illustrate this idea with a simple analogy after David Marr (1982). Consider the phenomenon of flight. If you were to step back a couple of hundred years and attempt to work out how things fly — clearly, you could go out and observe birds. **Birds fly**. The phenomena that might attract your attention are feathers, two wings, wing-flapping and so on. Now the question is what is the role of each of these phenomena in the mechanism which is a flying bird? Wing-flapping appears to be very important but why? Our assertion is that it is only with the attempt to model flying, in aircraft, that we can really provide answers to some of these questions. The model generates a new vocabulary — "lift", "weight to wing-size ratio", "aerofoil section" etc — and a new view of the activity of birds. Perhaps wing-flapping is not so much to thrust the bird upwards as we might naively assume, but to change the flow of air over its wing "aerofoil section" and thus change the properties of "lift" it has? Now let us extend the analogy to the phenomenon of thinking. **People think**. Psychologists spend a great deal of time observing them in a number of ways. But what is the role of all the associated phenomena that we can observe like blood, brains, self-awareness, language? The cognitive scientist is attempting to model some parts of the thinking process — in a symbol processing system. Now it is certainly possible to argue, as a philosopher might, that there is a great difference between the flight of the model, the aeroplane, and the bird. In the same way, we must be very careful about the links we make between our very limited models and people.

The analogy we have used is of course a very limited argument, for whilst we may be able to agree more or less on a definition of flight we are some way off agreeing on a definition of 'thinking'. Nevertheless, it is clear that at the very least this modelling process does provide us with some very powerful new analytical tools to bring to this problem.

Now, in the same way that we argue that an understanding of cognitive phenomena is very difficult without an implementable cognitive science, we would also argue that it is not possible to understand cognitive science without having real, experiential knowledge of the key concepts. The essential ideas and techniques — semantic networks, recursions, state space search, means-ends analysis, productions systems, and the like — can be very difficult to grasp from mere paper. Trying to understand cognitive science from a textbook is a little like trying to understand football by just watching it on the TV. That is certainly better than nothing, but it is no substitute for getting out of your armchair and having a go!

1.4 What is Prolog?

The name **PROLOG** is derived from "**PRO**gramming in **LOG**ic" – as it was originated as an attempt to provide a programming language based in the formal structure of logic. Prolog is now the best known tool in a new branch of computer science called logic programming. Fortunately, you do not have to be a logician to use Prolog, but you must get a feel for the logical style in which it functions. Prolog originated in Europe and is probably the preferred AI language for European AI researchers, though many American AI researchers use the functional and procedural language LISP.

Recent versions of Prolog have become so powerful and efficient that in 1981 it was adopted by the Japanese as **the** programming language for their 'Fifth Generation Project' which is aimed at the creation of 'intelligent' computers.

1.4.1 The Development of Prolog

Prolog has a much shorter history than even cognitive science. Work in cognitive science and Artificial Intelligence is inherently computational and bound by advances in both the hardware and languages in which to work. So it was not until the advent of a powerful computer language suited to the implementation of some of these new ideas that things could really get off the ground. The major landmark was the advent, in the 1960's, of John McCarthy's **LIS**t Processing language **LISP**. Lisp is a functional language with a rich and well defined mathematical basis. It handles the processing of symbols as elegantly as it does mathematics.

It was something like a decade before the idea of a programming language more directly based in logic began to appear on the scene. Researchers like Kowalski in the UK showed that it was possible to have a procedural interpretation of declarative logical statements and Colmerauer and his team in France first made this work on a computer. However, again it was not until the academic work became an efficient language, with Warren's compiler, that people could really take it seriously. The first real public access to the language was not until the early 1980's with the publication of the first popular textbook on Prolog by Clocksin and Mellish (1981).

1962/5	•	McCarthy publishes LISP 1.5
1971	•	Kowalski formulates the procedural interpretation of Horn clause logic.
	•	PROLOG - PROgramming in LOGic - developed (in Fortran) by Colmerauer's group at Marseilles for natural language parsing.
1975	•	Warren at Edinburgh creates efficient compiler for Prolog – DEC-10 Prolog
1981	•	Japan announces a project aimed to create the 'Fifth Generation' computer by 1992. Fundamental idea is need for Knowledge Information Processing Systems. Language adopted is Prolog 1M LIPS - Logical Inferences Per Second (100-1000M LIPS for parallel machine)
	•	Clocksin & Mellish produce "Programming in Prolog" text book.

Meanwhile the political scene had not been doing so well. In the early 1970's, academic research in the UK on artificial intelligence and cognitive science topics had been dealt a severe blow by the very negative report of one influential committee (Lighthill, 1973) to a major research funding council. Whilst UK research was struggling against severely restricted funding the rest of the world was investing great sums of money into knowledge based and computer oriented research. In 1981 the Japanese announced a major research project directed towards the 'fifth generation' computer. What was most shocking to some about the Japanese project was not so much the amount that they were investing nor the ambitiousness of their goals, but that they had chosen as the project 'core' language — the then relatively unknown and academic — Prolog. Suddenly cognitive scientists, especially those in the USA, began to take an interest in this European phenomenon. In this book we aim to give you a feel for both Prolog and cognitive science, by illustrating the one in the other.

1.4.2 The idea of Logic Programming

Question. How would you represent the relationships father, mother, male, female in your preferred conventional (procedural) language — Pascal, Fortran, Basic … ?

eg. Philip, Charles and William are all male
Elizabeth is female
Philip is the father of Charles
Charles is the father of William
Elizabeth is the mother of Charles

In particular, how would you express knowledge about relationships such as **grandfather**? You might want to represent this knowledge as a further 'fact' as above — but clearly a better idea is to make your computer language do the work where possible!

In a logical sort of English you might consider 'grandfather' to **mean** :

For all X's and Z's we can say that

X is a 'grandfather' of Z

where there exists a Y such that

X is the 'father' of Y and

Y is the 'father' of Z.

How would you express this sort of knowledge computationally? As you could see in the Tutorial Appendix 1, Prolog lets you represent simple facts and rules in a very intuitive way — with a syntax not much different from the logical form above. These logical facts and rules are statements — a logic program — which states things which are true about the world or problem under consideration.

Logic programming is a technique which essentially combines a **declarative knowledge representation** with a built-in **inference mechanism** — a method of trying to answer queries to the knowledge base from a user, (see eg. Hogger, 1984). To take an example from the database of family relationships we have already mentioned.

Given a **query** — is Elizabeth the mother of Charles? and this **knowledge base**:

---

of **facts** including such gems as
> fact 1: Elizabeth is female
> fact 2: Elizabeth is a parent of Charles
> ...

and **rules** of the form
> rule 1: X is the mother of Y **if** X is a parent of Y **and** X is female.
> ...

---

a logic program would take the query as its **goal** to be proved and would do its best to prove that the statement is true (ie. can be deduced from the facts and rules in the knowledge base). It would first find that there was no single **fact** in the above knowledge base which answered the question, but would still be able to come up with the answer by selecting a relevant **rule** and then trying to prove it was true.

In this case the proof would go as follows:

(1) find a rule that might be applicable

> in this case, rule 1 with X = 'Elizabeth' and Y = 'Charles'

(2) try to solve the first condition of rule 1

> 'X is a parent of Y' which is true (ie. the fact is in the knowledge base - fact 2)

(3) try to solve the second condition

> 'X is female.' This is also true for Y=Elizabeth (fact 1)

Consequently the whole **goal** would succeed and the program would answer

>   **Yes**   (ie. it is 'true' ie. deducible from the knowledge base)

If it had not been able to prove the goal (ie if either condition had failed) it would reply:

>   **No**   (ie. it cannot be proved from the given knowledge base, though not necessarily false

>   — it may be that a fact or rule had been omitted from the knowledge base!).

In summary, not only do logic programming languages have a powerful method of representing knowledge, they must also have a built-in method of interrogating the knowledge base.

Further examples of rules :

+---+

| X is a bird   **if**   X is warm blooded **and** X lays eggs.

| X is the child of Y   **if**   Y is a parent of X.

| X is the uncle of Y   **if**   there is an individual Z such that
| X is the brother of Z
| **and** Y is the child of Z.

+---+

Note that in the above X, Y and Z have no meaning in themselves — they could be replaced by any symbols as long as it is done consistently. They are referred to as **logical variables** and are like the 'unknown variable' used in algebra (' eg. let the speed of the car be X mph ...'), which make them quite unlike 'variables' in procedural languages — so beware!

1.4.3 Declarative versus Procedural programming languages

Most computer languages (Pascal, Fortran, Basic, C, etc) are **procedural/imperative**. Writing a computer program in an imperative language consists of telling the computer what to do at every stage. So you issue commands which are instructions for the machine to obey such as numerical or symbolic calculations. These commands can often be grouped together as *procedures* which dictate when the instructions are to be executed. So procedural languages tend to dictate what the computer is to do with data. Recently, **declarative** languages have been introduced, starting with rule-based languages such as OPS-5 and more recently knowledge representation languages. Declarative languages also tend to have 'a procedural interpretation' because they usually "do" something at some point, but they are also good at simply stating things (making declarations) about the world via the truth and falsity of data. The major aim behind a declarative language is the accurate and flexible representation of the underlying knowledge structures involved in the problem under consideration, rather than any attempt to specify exactly how the computer program is to solve the particular problem.

Procedural languages tend to say things like : DO this, next DO that, next PUT 55 into there, etc.

Declarative languages tend to say things like : This is TRUE, That is TRUE if this is TRUE, etc.

Declarative languages have several clear advantages over imperative ones:

- **emphasis** on the **representation** to be used. This is particularly important where we are trying to model complex knowledge structures such as those used in human cognition.
- **flexibility**. In general it is very difficult for an imperative program to answer any question other than the ones it was specifically designed for, whereas experience has shown that users always wish to tailor a particular system to their own requirements.

The disadvantage of a purely declarative language is that it would just sit there — you would type in all this knowledge but you would not be able to **query** the knowledge base — that is, ask it some questions and get the answers. This is where Prolog comes in. Owing to its declarative semantics Prolog is easy to read and the basic database-representation methods used are easy to understand even for non-specialists in computing (indeed, it has been claimed in that many ways it is **easier** for non-specialists because computer specialists' prior training with imperative languages can interfere).

Prolog is particularly well-suited both to :

(i) the **creation** of declarative knowledge structures — through a built-in representation of facts and rules (and through the capability of creating more sophisticated knowledge structures such as frames and scripts).

(ii) the **interrogation** of the knowledge structures in a very flexible fashion, both through its built-in search mechanism and through the capability of creating more sophisticated search algorithms.

1.5   Why do Cognitive Science in Prolog ?

The clearest formulation for how we might conduct our research was provided by David Marr. We have already mentioned Marr's work aimed at an understanding of the human faculty of vision. His view of how to conduct computational psychology (Marr 1977, 1982) is one which could be argued to apply to all science. Marr proposed that there were three levels upon which scientific study should proceed: the computational model; the algorithm; and the implementation. The first level 'the computational model' refers to something which we might normally describe as the task analysis. This is an abstract, high-level analysis of **what** is required of some mechanism that we are studying. What is the input to the mechanism? What must the mechanism do? And what is the output of the mechanism? Only after we have outlined and determined the exact nature of the task that the mechanism is performing can we begin to consider **how** it is done. This is the next stage: 'the algorithm'. An algorithm is a computational process which states how some input is transformed into some output. For any given computational model there may be a number of possible algorithms by which it could work. Finally, and only after you have considered the detail of the how is it possible to determine the **where** aspects of the mechanism — ie the machine in which the algorithm actually resides. This is the last of the stages: 'the implementation'. This analysis is simple and very top-down in nature, moving from a general specification of the **what** is nature of the process, down through to considering the detail of **how** this process might work; and on finally to **where** or in what exact hardware mechanism it may appear. Marr's analysis of scientific method for cognitive science was immensely influential — for a good discussion see Boden (1988).

So having established a general methodology for cognitive science research we can now consider how useful a tool like Prolog can be for this modelling task. To begin with we may note that people and Prolog are clearly very different in many obvious ways. Prolog is based in the logic of predicate calculus and has a built in theorem-prover which uses specific techniques of backtracking and search — which are clearly nothing to do with the the massive parallel electrochemical biological computations done by the brain. However, as Marr has demonstrated, this is missing the point. We are not suggesting that Prolog is suitable for the 'implementation level', but we do think that it is very valuable for the initial computational modelling stage. It can even help us move on to the algorithm stage — with rather more problems and care required. Marr attached great weight to deriving a sufficiently detailed representation of the top level requirement — that of specifying the computational problem that the system is attempting to solve. Only once the computational problem is specified, does it make sense to consider the range of algorithms available for solving it, and to consider the way the algorithms might be implemented in neural or electronic hardware. This brings us directly to a major strength of Prolog compared with other Artificial Intelligence languages — Prolog is a particularly good language for problem representation, with a flexible, readable method for representing knowledge and a clear dissociation between design (logic) and control. Indeed, good Prolog programming style concentrates initially on deriving a declarative representation of the problem. Its strength lies in knowledge representation, the heart of understanding cognitive science.

1.6 Implementing some Cognitive Science projects

The emergence of the discipline is best illustrated using the key projects or milestones that have shaped progress over the years. Probably the best retelling of the story of cognitive science from the historical perspective is by Gardner, (1985). Finding a start for the story is no simple task. You might select from amongst many events in the late '50s and early '60s where the influence of the ideas of information processing and the use of the computer in developing psychological theories was starting to emerge. One common choice is 1956 and a symposium on Information Theory held at MIT. This is a popular because it was one of the earliest collections of a large number of the people, like Newell & Simon, Chomsky and Miller, who were to become very influential in the later course of cognitive science research. As we are looking at this area through a few specific projects we should introduce them with a very quick sketch of some of the surrounding area of cognitive science — noting the areas that we will not have space to develop further.

In Figure 1.2 we present an outline chart which illustrates this progress under the broad headings of some of the main streams within cognitive science. The broad headings we have chosen are: Language, Cognition and Perception. Cognition is such a broad heading that it has been subdivided into a further three headings: Semantic Memory; Learning and Problem Solving. We could have included very many more projects within this figure but have chosen a very few which give a feel for the development of the discipline. The arrows between the projects mean "has had a strong influence upon". The main objective of the figure is just to give you some context for the projects which we have chosen to focus on in the remainder of the book — marked on the figure with a small blob.

Figure 1.2 A selection of landmarks in Cognitive Science

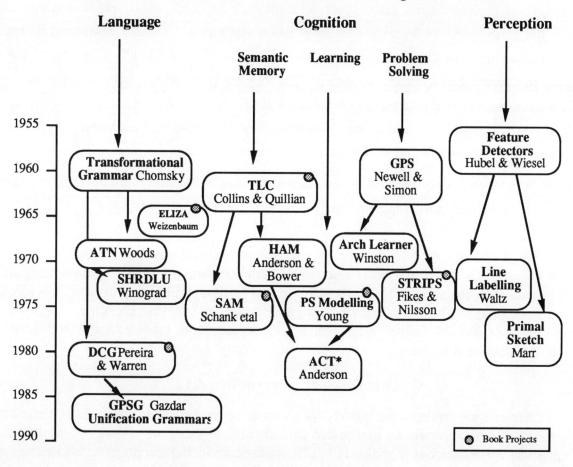

We have outlined in the boxes a selection of possible projects from which we have selected a few for this book — however it is useful to spend a few moments looking at the vast areas we have been obliged to omit. Hopefully when you have reached the end of the book you may be tempted to return here to do something on the remaining projects for us!

The biggest stream of cognitive science which we have illustrated above and not provided a project for is 'perception'. The perception heading of Figure 1.2 shows three major projects. The first, Hubel and Wiesel's (1959) work on the physiology of the visual system is shown as an early influence on the two later computational vision projects. As we have discussed already, Hubel and Wiesel investigated the visual system seeking a physiological correlate of simple visual "features", such as lines — at various thicknesses and orientations. The earlier computational project by Waltz attempts to process a scene using very simple features. It uses a line drawing representation of simple objects and concentrates on the junctions of the lines. The lines are interpreted as part of some object using knowledge about how the junctions of lines can appear in the real world. Marr's work (which we have already mentioned) is only slightly later, and yet very much more sophisticated. We have avoided a perceptual project in this book for the excellent reason that the vehicle we are using —

Prolog — is less ideally suited to this problem than many other more procedural and numerical computer languages.

Looking under the 'Cognition' stream Newell and Simon's GPS, General Problem Solver, was the first major effort in the problem-solving and planning area to provide some general purpose techniques with a psychological basis. It was an inspiration for much subsequent research including work in the general area of learning such as Winston's program. Winston developed a program which learned simple structural descriptions (like what makes up an "arch" — eg a lintel and two uprights, etc) by using near-misses to teach it. The STRIPS program is a more direct derivative of the GPS work as it is based on a technique called Means-Ends Analysis that was the prime technique explored originally by Newell and Simon. The remaining landmarks are mentioned in the following chapters — when we provide a more detailed context for each individual project.

The main purpose of this book is to help you examine a range of "classical" cognitive science topics. Each topic is introduced as a complete project to implement in Prolog.

A model of semantic memory.

In Chapter 2 we consider what a semantic network looks like and examine some of the properties which caused theorists like Collins and Quillian (1969) to propose it as a model of human memory. These properties included inheritance and cognitive economy. This work was very influential on further work which has explored the representation and access of representations of memory.

A pattern based conversation, ELIZA.

In Chapter 3 we implement a 'parody' of a non-directive therapist produced by Weizenbaum (1966). This was quite an impressive performance at the time. However, whilst able to produce some snatches of dialogue which appear convincing the program was clearly very narrow and superficial. The deficiencies of ELIZA as a model of a conversationalist serve to indicate the overall complexity of the problem and some of the areas requiring a much more detailed analysis. Whilst it is an essential and important lesson for cognitive scientists it is not in itself a work of cognitive science!

Following on naturally from this parody of a human conversationalist we examine two attempts to analyse natural language understanding from two different theoretical perspectives. The first seeks to examine the structural complexities of the language's Syntax. The second seeks to capture the Semantics underlying natural language stories.

Understanding Natural Language : Syntax.

In Chapter 4 we develop a Definite Clause Grammar parser for natural language sentences in English. The syntactic school of natural language work was highly influenced by the work of Noam Chomsky who dramatically altered the view and scope of linguistics. The parser is a mechanism for bringing to bear the syntactic rules of language — the grammar — on a sentence. Its objective is to check that the sentence is legitimate in the language and to show how its components are structured. The DCG parser we implement has much in common with the earlier procedural transition networks such as Woods' Augmented Transition Network. The ATN was the core of a very famous and influential system SHRDLU produced by Terry Winograd.

Understanding Natural Language : Semantics.

The Yale analysis of the role of Memory, Context & Language in understanding how sentential segments may be connected together, is considered in Chapter 5. Schank's use of Conceptual Dependency primitives and memory structures called 'scripts' was implemented in the program SAM. In the project we explore the role of slot-filling, script triggers and defaults in the context of understanding stories of visits to eating establishments. The Yale team have been very productive in this general approach to language understanding.

Cognitive Modelling.

In Chapter 6 we examine a simulation of learning using production systems developed by Richard Young in 1976. This system implements the use of production rules to model the development of seriation performance in children. Various additions and deletions to the production rules cause changes in the seriation activity of the system. Young proposed that children could be seen as extending their own rules about a task in the same way. This modelling of cognition using production rules has been a common theme of much influential work — culminating in the recent ACT* work of John Anderson and the SOAR architecture developed by Alan Newell and his colleagues.

Problem solving and Planning.

Search is the key to understanding much existing AI research. In a complex situation where many actions are possible, intelligence helps agents to choose to do one thing rather than any other. Search is about comparing alternative things to do and choosing to do just one for some reason.

In Chapter 7 we examine brute-force methods of search and consider how they could be improved with the use of context specific heuristics. Finally we examine a robotics micro-world where the robot was able to act intelligently from a limited knowledge about the effects of its actions and its eventual goals. This is called MEANS-ENDS analysis, and was used in both the GPS and STRIPS projects.

An overview of the Core Contents of this book

	Project	Main Technique discussed
Chapter 2	Collins & Quillian's TLC	Semantic Networks
Chapter 3	Weizenbaum's ELIZA	Pattern Matching
Chapter 4	DCG Parser	Grammar Rules
Chapter 5	Schank's SAM	Scripts
Chapter 6	Young's Seriator	Production Systems
Chapter 7	STRIPS	Means-Ends Analysis

1.7 Further Readings

Cognitive Science

1. Posner M.I. (ed). **Foundations of Cognitive Science.** MIT Press, 1989.

   A superb technical overview of 21 key areas of Cognitive Science. Not for the beginner, but a major resource for researchers. Expensive, but good value.

2. Stillings, N. A., Feinstein, M. H., Garfield, J. L., Rissland, E. L., Rosenbaum, D. A., Weisler, S. E., & Baker-Ward, L. **Cognitive Science: an introduction**. MIT Press, 1987.

   One of the few good overview texts on Cognitive Science not just AI.

3. Gardner, H. **The mind's new science: A history of the cognitive revolution**. Basic Books, New York, 1985. *Very interesting and chatty historical / philosophical perspective.*

4. Boden, M. **Artificial Intelligence & Natural Man.** OU Press, 1977 / 87.

   The first edition was a classic, but the second edition is now somewhat dated. Insightful analysis and critique of many '70s AI programs.

Prolog

1. Clocksin, W. F. & Mellish, C. S. **Programming in Prolog**. (2nd ed). Springer-Verlag, Berlin Germany, 1986.

   1st edition was the first good Prolog text. New edition not much different.

2. Sterling, L. & Shapiro, E. **The Art of Prolog**. MIT Press, 1986

   Superb style and clarity. Interesting Cognitive Science programs.

3. Bratko, I. **Prolog programming for artificial intelligence**. Addison-Wesley, UK, 1986/90.

   Good. Written from computer science viewpoint. Lots of search trees. Tendency to focus on cunning but rather opaque definitions.

Chapter 2 : Modelling Semantic Memory

The first Prolog project involves two areas that are of central importance in the enterprise of Cognitive Science research: memory and knowledge representation. These issues are presented via two mini-projects. The first is an implementation of the classical work of Collins and Quillian (1969) on modelling semantic memory. This is set in the context of the development of psychological theories of memory. The second mini-project reimplements this work in the now standard AI knowledge representation notation of 'frames' (after Minsky, 1975).

2.1 Background: Semantic Knowledge

The first steps towards modern analyses of cognition were inspired by analogy with information transmission along telegraph wires and the like. Early versions of 'information processing theory' (Broadbent, 1958), provided information flow diagrams of the 'human information processing system'. This approach attempted to describe human cognitive architecture in terms of structures (self-contained modules) and processes (methods of recoding information and transmitting it between the structures). These so-call 'box models' peaked in the late 1960s with Atkinson and Shiffrin's model of memory shown schematically below. Information passes from the environment into the first module (the 'sensory register') which holds it for a short period of time, sufficient for the 'central executive' to select the important aspects for further processing within the 'short-term store'. This serves the dual role of central executive (deciding what to do next) and short-term storage system with around seven 'slots' for storing information. Information held long enough in the STS may be transferred to the long-term store where it will remain indefinitely (though it may be hard to retrieve).

Figure 2.1   The Atkinson & Shiffrin (1968) Multistore Model of Memory

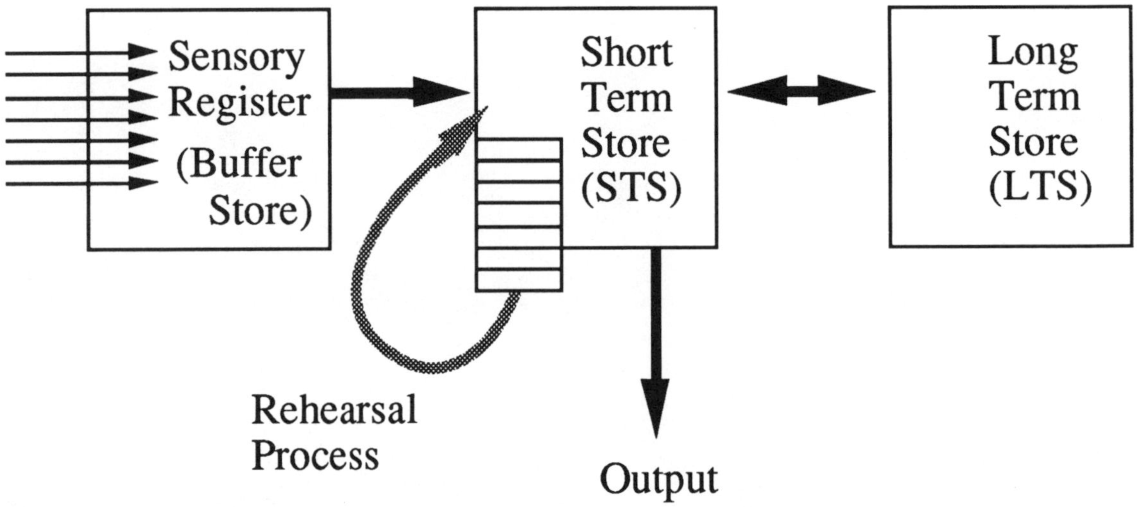

The next decade saw a fundamental reassessment of this type of model, when it was acknowledged first that information flow diagrams were at an inadequate level of detail, and second, that the type of processing involved depended crucially on the existing knowledge of the organism. The problem with level of detail was that it was necessary to be explicit about how the information was represented within each structure, since otherwise it was impossible to empirically compare different theories. Furthermore it was difficult to know how to test any model that was not 'complete' - that is, a model that accounts in detail for each stage of analysis, from the input of the words to the construction of a reply. Following Tulving (1972) it is customary to divide knowledge into two: 'episodic' knowledge, relating to relatively isolated events, often autobiographical; and 'semantic' knowledge, knowledge for structured information - from the meanings of words to common-sense knowledge of the world. Experiments in the '60s showed that memory for semantically related information was qualitatively different from that of meaningless information, and that consequently an understanding of how human semantic knowledge was organised in memory was a pre-requisite for any real understanding of the full system. Early and influential attempts to build complete models of human cognition were provided by cognitive theorists like Anderson and Bower (1973) and Norman and Rumelhart (1975). All these workers were inspired by the research of Quillian in the 1960s into representing semantic knowledge in a model of human memory.

2.2   Simulating Human Semantic Memory

It is appropriate to begin the main cognitive science projects with a partial re-implementation in Prolog of Collins and Quillian's (1969) Teachable Language Comprehender (TLC) because TLC, despite its many limitations was one of the first attempts to model human knowledge on a computer, and its success proved the catalyst for the subsequent explosion of computational modelling of cognitive processes. TLC represents an early milestone in cognitive science which grew out of attempts by Quillian in the '60s to implement an artificial model of memory that was able to answer simple questions by semantics alone (an antidote to the then current emphasis on syntactic parsing) and also to 'learn' by adding semantic facts to its network.

A flavour of the approach may be obtained from the diagram below which represents a fragment of the semantic network for animals.

Figure 2.2   An Animals Hierarchy (After Baddeley, 1982)

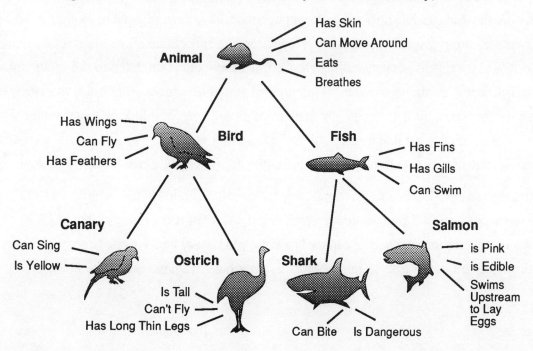

It may immediately be seen that the representation makes a number of assumptions:

(i) facts may be organised in a **hierarchical network** with nodes linked by class inclusion to nodes representing more and more general classes, ie. a concept is linked to at least one

superordinate concept (eg. sprint --> run --> go --> do or mallard --> duck --> bird --> animal --> living_thing etc.). Concepts correspond to a semantic entity and have associated **properties** which take **values** - eg. canary has_colour yellow

(ii) there are at least two types of links:

(a) **class inclusion** links which link the classes of semantic entries together. So a canary is a bird and a bird is an animal etc.

(b) **attribute** or **property** links which label the semantic entries as having various features. So that a canary is yellow, a bird can fly and an animal has the property of having skin.

All the links are all-or-none (ie. have no strength values) which is to say that either a canary is a bird or it isn't.

(iii) attributes are stored at the highest possible level in the hierarchy in order to avoid duplication. Nodes lower in the hierarchy may be inferred also to possess a higher level property by **inheritance**. So a canary has not only the features that are immediately attached to it but can inherit ones from above: it can fly because it is a bird; it eats because it is an animal and so on.

This technique, known as the **cognitive economy** principle has proved a valuable tool for hierarchical network representations though its applicability to human semantic memory remains controversial.

In addition to this declarative knowledge representation, TLC had a procedural mechanism for parsing and answering simple questions. The basic idea was that, if a node in the network was activated (ie. the node token appeared in the input stream), 'activation' spread along the network like a 'harmless spreading plague'. Activation spread along all links in an all-or-none fashion, and in due course it would meet activation spreading from some other node, which led to the establishment of a semantic link between the two nodes. This type of semantic processing could, in principle, parse "The canary the shark bit had wings" by semantics alone, correctly linking canary with wings and shark with bit.[1] TLC also had a mechanism for learning semantic facts in that if a sentence was parsed the information was automatically added to the network (hence the "Teachable" soubriquet).

Arguably, the reason TLC had such a major impact was that Collins demonstrated that TLC mirrored human performance in a simple sentence verification task. Human subjects (and TLC) were given a series of simple questions such as 'a canary is a table'; 'a canary has wings'; 'a shark is an animal' to which they had to answer true or false as fast as possible. Human results are in Figure 2.3 shown below.

---

[1] Unfortunately TLC failed with statements of the type "He hated the landlord so much that he moved into the house on Brunswick Street" in that landlord would incorrectly be associated with house. Much more sophisticated syntactic and semantic parsing would be needed for that type of sentence.

It may be seen that each extra level in the hierarchy appears to add an extra 100 msec or so to the decision time. Collins and Quillian interpreted these data as supporting their hierarchical architecture, with activation spreading at the rate of 1 link per 100 msec. Subsequent research has demonstrated that the data may be explained in a number of other ways, but nonetheless this apparent correspondence with human performance generated great interest in the model.

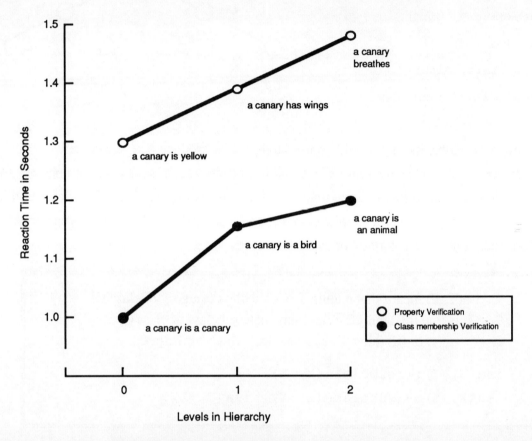

Figure 2.3 The relationship between mean verification time and hierarchical separation (after Collins & Quillian, 1972)

In summary, the Teachable Language Comprehender was one of the most influential models in early cognitive science, introducing a number of key issues which much subsequent work on knowledge representation has refined and elaborated.

2.3 A Prolog Semantic Network

In this project we will make no effort to implement the TLC semantic parsing mechanisms (in any case they now seem rather primitive compared with more recent semantic parsers — see Chapter 5). However, we shall attempt to reconstruct and query a hierarchically organised semantic memory network built on the principles pioneered by Collins and Quillian. We can define a semantic tree using the relation **subclass** to say that one category is a subclass of another category of thing. In the following definition, both canary and ostrich can be seen as subsets of the class bird. Similarly, bird is a subclass of animal, etc.

```
% subclass(T, C) means that thing T is a subclass of Class C.
```

```
subclass(animal, living_thing).

subclass(bird, animal).

subclass(fish, animal).

subclass(canary, bird).

subclass(ostrich, bird).

subclass(shark, fish).

subclass(salmon, fish).
```

Clearly this set of subclass facts could be used together to produce a semantic network such as that shown next to it. But what we require is some definition which works on the subclass facts and effectively says how they may be seen together as a network of this kind. This definition is called **isa**. You should recognise it as a simple recursive predicate. (If you do not then you should read the section on recursion in the Tutorial Appendix 1).

```
%   isa(T, C) means that a thing T is a subclass category of class C.
%     It is true if (i) thing T is an immediate subclass of class C,
%              or (ii) thing T has a subclass which itself isa C.

isa(X, Y):- subclass(X, Y).
isa(X, Z):- subclass(X, Y), isa(Y, Z).
```

This definition is elegant, recursive and very powerful. It takes a little thinking about!

Essentially, it is the same as almost all of the recursive predicates in this book: the first clause is the stopping-check or success condition of the definition; and the second clause is the main recursive body of the definition which recurses on a (hopefully simpler) version of the same query. So the stopping check trivially defines 'isa' in terms of the 'subclass' database entry, ie you know that an X isa Y if it is immediately connected to that Y in the subclass definition. The recursive bit says that X can still be connected to some Z in the subclass definition if there are an intermediate subclass link via some Y that will get to Z. Now Y does not have to be connected directly to Z (via subclass) but uses 'isa' again and can add another intermediate node into the link and so on indefinitely - or at least until we find Z or run out of tree. Compare this to the **parent/2** definition in the tutorial appendix to see how very similar they are.

We can also use the **isa** access to the subclass hierarchy to store a thing's physical properties at the highest common point in the tree and access them via inheritance. So if we define the relation **property(X,Y)** to mean that a thing X has the property Y we would have something like this :

```
% property(Thing, P) means that a class of Thing has the immediate property P
```

```
property(animal, breathes).              property(bird, warm_blooded).
property(animal, has_skin).              property(bird, has_feathers).
property(animal, eats).                  property(bird, can_fly).
property(animal, can_move).              property(bird, has_wings).

property(canary, can_sing).              property(ostrich, size(tall)).
property(canary, size(small)).           property(ostrich, cannot_fly).
property(canary, colour(yellow)).
```

Then we can define a program that inherits these properties via the isa definition:

```
%  has_property(Thing, P) means that a Thing has a property P
%      and these properties can be found directly or
%      can be inherited via the 'isa' relation and the properties of its superclass.

has_property(Thing, P):-

                property(Thing, P).
has_property(X, P):-

                isa(X, SuperClass),

                property(SuperClass, P).
```

This is a particularly cunning definition which states that a property of a thing can **either** be found as stored explicitly in the property definition; **or** that a thing can 'inherit' the properties of anything of which it **isa** subclass.

Exercises 2.1 Collins & Quillian

Exercise 2.1.1 Try the following queries. What do they mean?

(? i) isa(canary, animal).

(? ii) isa(canary, shark).

(? iii) isa(canary, X). {all solutions}

(? iv) isa(A, bird). {all solutions}

Exercise 2.1.2 Run & explain these queries.

(? i) has_property(canary, can_sing).

(? ii) has_property(canary, swims).

(? iii) has_property(canary, Property).

(? iv) has_property(Creature, size(Size)).

(? v) has_property(Creature, breathes).

Exercise 2.1.3 Add further facts to the network.

i) Add that a robin is a kind of bird.

ii) Where would you add a fact to say that robins lay eggs. HINT : remember cognitive economy.

iii) Add mammal to the network.

iv) Add a property of mammal eg. bear_live_young

v) Add that a dolphin and rat are kinds of mammal.

Type in all the data necessary to complete the C & Q network given (see Figure 2.2) and try some more queries. Add some more subclass entries of your own.

Exercise 2.1.4 Timing memory access in the model with `speed/3`.

We have provided a predicate called `speed` which takes three arguments. The first is a query which the `speed` predicate will run and time how long it takes. The second and third arguments are always variables, the second will return the time it takes to run the query and the third will return its success or failure. The idea is to simulate the predictions for human recall performance of Collins & Quillian's theory.

(i) Try to generate the data to draw the standard categorisation time graph. eg.

```
(? i)      speed(isa(canary, bird), TimeTaken, YesOrNo).
(? ii)     speed(isa(canary, animal), T, YN).
(? iii)    speed(isa(canary, living_thing), T, YN).
(? iv)     speed(isa(canary, shark), TimeTaken, T, YN).
(? v)      speed(has_property(canary, colour(yellow) ), T, YN).
(? vi)     speed(has_property(canary, breathes ), T, YN).
(? vii)    speed(has_property(canary, swims ), T, YN).
```

(ii) How do the simulation data compare with human data? Note that this raises the question of **functional equivalence** - at what level should the data parallel the human data for a successful simulation. Obviously not at the level of the actual times - this is dependent entirely upon the speed of the computer in question. Indeed, you might have to slow down execution speed (as we suggest in the appendix definition) to prevent these queries being answered in less time than your machine can count. As we note with the appendix code for this definition, the use of computer speed to provide timings is very problematic — to make the same point you could use "network distance", which is just a direct measure of how many links the search must traverse.

(iii) Try timing some queries of your own - predict relatively how long they should take before you try them.

Exercise 2.1.5 Limitations of the model

Try to find a few things that are wrong with this program as a model of C & Q. Eg.

(i) Is it fair to say that fish breathe?

(ii) Can an ostrich fly or can't it ?

2.4   Subsequent Developments

Not surprisingly, given the simplicity of the TLC model, subsequent research identified some serious problems for it.

(1) Even their own data were inconsistent with the model. The reaction times for falsification were faster the greater the semantic distance (eg. 'a canary is a tulip' is rejected quicker than 'a canary is a robin'). TLC would predict that the former would require a search through the whole network before rejecting it and thus it should be slower.

(2) Eleanor Rosch (1975) showed that 'a robin is a bird' is verified faster than 'a chicken is a bird'. She demonstrated this could be attributed to the difference in **typicality** between the two (ratings on a 1--7 scale for typicality for robin--bird, and chicken--bird were 1.1, 3.8 respectively). Try substituting 'robin' and then 'chicken' for 'bird' in the sentence 'a *bird* sat on a branch near my window'! These findings cannot be handled by TLC since its links are all-or-none, rather than having an 'associative strength' attached to the links. So the model clearly needs some way of accounting for the finding that robins and sparrows are in some ways "better birds" than chickens and penguins.

(3) The only support TLC had left is the sentence verification times. Carol Conrad (1972) demonstrated that even these results could be explained just as well by typicality. She claimed that in C&Q's experiment 'canary is yellow' is more typical of canary than 'canary has wings' and so on. She constructed a hierarchy where typicality was controlled and demonstrated that then there was no evidence for cognitive economy.

An example of a completely different approach which contested the very idea of a hierarchically organised semantic network was **Feature Theory**, which was put forward by Smith, Shoben and Rips in 1974. This theory suggested that, rather than being hierarchically organised, semantic memory might be better seen as a series of essentially unorganised concepts, each represented by a bundle of features. It is best seen as a *performance* model rather than a *competence* model, attempting to account for the results of the categorisation time experiments started by Collins & Quillian, without making any assumptions about the underlying organisation of semantic memory.

The model had two essential components: first that there are two types of features - defining features and characteristic features - and second that subjects employ a 2-stage decision strategy for categorisation experiments. Defining Features for a concept are features necessary for any exemplar of that concept whereas Characteristic Features, though usually associated with the concept, are not strictly necessary. The table below gives examples of the two types of features for the concept 'bird' and the concept 'robin'.

	Defining Feature (DF)	Characteristic Feature (CF)
Bird	biped	can fly
	has wings	builds nests
	warm blooded	6-9 inches long
	has feathers	perch in trees
	lays eggs	undomesticated
Robin	biped	perch in trees
	has wings	undomesticated
	warm blooded	about 6 inches long
	has feathers	builds nests
	lays eggs	
	red breast	
	can fly	
Chicken	biped	lives on farms
	has wings	we eat the eggs
	warm blooded	doesn't fly
	has feathers	about 12 inches long
	lays eggs	clucks

The second assumption of the feature model gives rise to the performance predictions. Smith *et al* proposed that in doing sentence verification task of the 'X is a Y yes/no' variety, people adopt a 'two stage decision strategy'. The first stage is a 'Quick Overall Match' in which all features (ie both DFs and CFs) are compared *in parallel*. If there is a large overlap then one responds 'true', or if there is a large mismatch one responds 'false'. Otherwise one has to go through stage 2, a 'Slow Exhaustive Search' in which all the DFs of the Y concept, are checked one at a time. If all Y's DFs are satisfied by X, respond 'true' whereas as soon as one is found to be false, reply 'false'. Examples of responses to different questions are shown in the table below.

Question	Decision Process	Decision	Speed
A robin is a bird	OK from stage 1 since large overlap	True	Fast
A chicken is a bird	Large stage 1 overlap so need stage 2.	True	Slow
A table is a bird	Little stage 1 overlap	False	Fast
A bat is a bird	Large stage 1 overlap so need stage 2.	False	Slow

Feature theory handles all the empirical results very well. Rejections are handled in exactly the same way as confirmations, using the same decision model. Typicality has a natural explanation in that a more typical X will have more features in common with Y and so is more likely to be satisfied by stage 1 of the comparison process. Errors (ie saying true when false and vice versa) are handled by saying that, under time pressure, people sometimes respond before stage 2 is finished. Support for this proposal derived from the facts that errors were more frequent for the longer responses and that people generally realise when they have made an error (presumably upon completing stage 2).

Unfortunately, Feature Theory suffered from several problems and limitations. Arguably the most severe problem is that of *defining* the Defining Features. For instance, is a 1-legged, green-dyed, dead robin still a robin? A limitation (which was a deliberate decision for Smith *et al*) is that of incompleteness. Unlike TLC it is not a complete model, for instance it makes no assumptions about how input is parsed, or how the semantic representation is accessed, or how the bundles of semantic features are organised. Consequently, the decision strategy can be 'bolted on' to a variety of other models. Furthermore, the model has restricted scope in that it only works for class-inclusion (eg. a shark is a fish) and doesn't handle obscure statements like 'Richard Nixon contains molecules' which would normally be answered by 'Richard Nixon is a real object', 'real objects are made of molecules'.

The whole issue of Hierarchical Semantic Networks versus Feature Models was thrown into confusion when it was demonstrated (Hollan, 1975) that feature models can be translated directly into network models, and so there's not necessarily a real dichotomy between networks and features. Whether one writes it as features or a semantic network is merely a matter of convention. Probably the main contribution of feature theory was to demonstrate (once again) the inadequacy of the cognitive economy assumption and to add a performance model to the underlying semantic representation.

The issue of semantic representation was the subject of very active research throughout the '70s. The idea of spreading activation as a method of accessing information has been highly influential, both in elaborations of the TLC model (Collins and Loftus, 1975) and in general architectures for cognition (Anderson, 1983). While it is possible to represent spreading activation in Prolog, it is not particularly natural to do so, and further discussion is beyond the scope of this book. Further readings are provided at the end of the chapter.

While the idea of purely semantic parsing was enthusiastically championed by influential researchers such as Roger Schank (see Chapter 5 for his approach), it is fair to say that most theorists now believe that a combination of syntactic and semantic parsing is needed for satisfactory scope. The basics of syntactic parsing are outlined in Chapter 4.

By far the greatest contribution of TLC to cognitive science was that it inspired researchers to attempt to develop a methodology for representing and using knowledge, and it is to this we now turn.

2.5   The Representation of Knowledge using Frames

From the viewpoint of good declarative programming style the knowledge representation we used in our TLC reconstruction suffers from an over-reliance on just one way of representing semantic information — in terms of class hierarchies. This gives it good performance on a small subset of possible queries (eg. is a canary a bird?) but the commitment to hierarchies reduces performance on other types of relationship. For instance, no support is given for relationships such as 'has_as_part' eg. `has_as_part(animal, head)`, a relationship which also allows some (but not all) property inheritance, and no support is given for other inheritance possibilities, such as:

run -- walk -- locomote -- move, etc.

Young children are able to answer a whole range of questions about things, like for instance, dogs. It is unlikely that they "inherit" the features of the class of dogs from the class of "mammals" or "living-things". Nevertheless their knowledge can really be quite rich. In other words, it is likely a hierarchical 'isa' link is only one of many possible relationships that might be employed in semantic memory, and so a more neutral notation for memory representation should be used. From the viewpoint of declarative programming methodology, our TLC reconstruction represents a failure to distinguish clearly between Data and Logic (processes acting on the data). Consequently, we shall attempt to re-reconstruct TLC using the more neutral, and more powerful, knowledge representation of a 'frame'. This method was introduced during the '70s and is at the heart of much subsequent AI work.

The idea of a **frame** was introduced by Marvin Minsky in 1975 to allow a multi-level representation of knowledge, with inheritance working in appropriate directions on appropriate relationships. Consider the appropriate knowledge representation for a house. As any house buyer knows, a house can be represented succinctly in terms of the values of relatively few attributes — say a detached, brick built, Victorian, four bedroom house in Hampstead with a large garden, price £1 million. This top level structure would need to be unpacked if one were interested in a more full description. For instance, one might wish to know the size and layout of each bedroom and within each bedroom one might want to note the type of door construction, about the windows, and so on. A schematic top down representation is shown in Figure 2.4.

Figure 2.4   Partial frame representation for a house

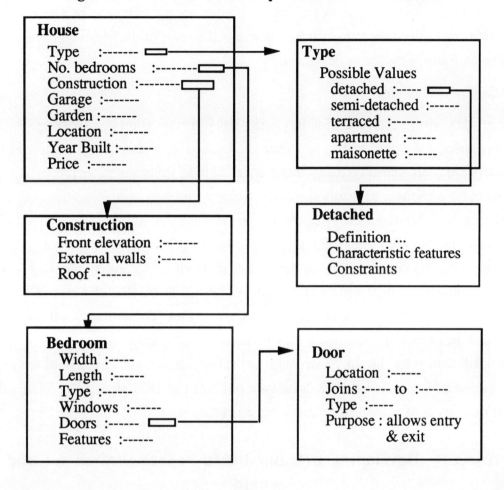

It is worth highlighting three aspects of the representation:

- **Slots and fillers**

It can be seen from the above figure that, at each level, there are a number of 'slots' (ie. attributes that require a value). For the top level house description the slots are: Type, No. of bedrooms, Construction, Garden, Garage, Location, Year Built and Price. For a given house, each of these slots will have a specific 'filler'. In our example above the fillers would be Detached, Brick and so on. Note that this slot/filler notation is extremely powerful, and may be used either to 'comprehend' information (by discovering an appropriate frame and assigning the information given to fill appropriate slots therein) or to help retrieve information (by identifying all the possible slots, and trying to find the appropriate filler for each slot). Consider how an architect could use a structure such as that shown in Figure 2.4 to elicit information from a client. Starting from an 'empty frame' in which none of the 'slots' has been 'filled' the architect can ask the client the necessary questions - what type of house do you want, how many bedrooms, and so on, gradually filling in all the slots with values such as 'Type=detached', 'No. of bedrooms=4' and so on.

- **Frames within frames**

One of the most powerful features of a frame representation is that a slot filler can also be a frame itself. Consequently, implicit in a single filler can be a great deal of information, and so the representation achieves a remarkable degree of economy. This feature also allows techniques such as data summaries to be achieved naturally and easily. Furthermore, a frame can be a part of many other frames — for instance the door frame outlined above will be part of the bedroom frame, the kitchen frame, any room frame, a car frame, and so on.

- **Reasoning with Frames**

The power of a knowledge representation lies in its ability to support problem solving. In particular, as one might expect, one would wish to be able to use knowledge within the system to be able to find suitable fillers for slots sensibly using techniques such as inheritance, defaults or constraints generated from the information already specified. Three commonly used inheritance techniques are subclass inheritance (inheriting values from higher up the hierarchy, as in TLC), part-kind inheritance (inheriting some, but not all, values from higher up), and default inheritance (inheriting values from higher up, but with less certainty then in the former methods). A further technique is known as procedural attachment in which a particular procedure or rule is attached to a part of a frame. The attached procedures are often referred to as "demons" as they are like little sprites that can be woken up to go off and do something when and if they are needed. An example from the house frame might be an 'if-needed' demon for the slot 'Year Built' in the form of the rule 'if you need to find the year built, and 'Victorian' is mentioned, then the answer lies between 1837 and 1901'. We shall develop methods for these types of reasoning in the project we outline next.

2.6   Project - Developing a frame-based representation for the TLC world

The Basic Knowledge Representation

As noted earlier, it is advisable for declarative programming to adopt a neutral representation for representing facts, and to have a separate inference mechanism for reasoning about the knowledge. We shall adopt the standard approach of 'Object, Attribute, Value' triples where Value represents the value of the relationship Attribute for the given Object . For instance, rather than the relationship subclass(bird, animal) we shall use the triple <bird, subclass, animal>. The value of the relationship 'subclass' applied to the Object 'bird' is 'animal'. Alternatively, in frame notation the filler for slot 'subclass' of object 'bird' is 'animal'. We shall use the terminology value(Object, Attribute, Value) to represent these triples[2]. They correspond to independent facts.

---

[2] Value is a rather unfortunate predicate name in that it presupposes that we shall be using the predicate to find the value of an object-attribute pair, whereas one might equally use the triple to find the object which had a given attribute-value pair. However, we shall later need to bring in default values for Object-Attribute-Value triples, so it is important to distinguish actual values from default values.

Typical entries for our database are:

```
value(animal, slot, habitat).
value(mammal, a_kind_of, animal).
value(animal, has_as_part, head).
value(bird, fly, yes).
value(ostrich, fly, no).
```

The first value clause states that the Object animal has a slot with name habitat. The remaining clauses are very similar to the TLC program above. The slot clause is given so that we can explicitly state what slots are sensible for a certain frame and (if we can inherit slots) for those frames below it. So in the case of animals, it makes sense for animals in general and for anything that is a kind of animal to have a habitat slot.

Value Inheritance

This also essentially the same as in TLC. Here however we allow the database builder to explicitly specify which attributes (or which Object-Attribute pairs) allow inheritance. The first clause looks for an explicit value, and the second clause allows inheritance on permitted attributes (through **inherits/3**).

```
has_value(Object, Slot, Value):-
      value(Object, Slot, Value).
has_value(Object, Slot, Value):-
      inherits(Object, Slot, Relation),
      value(Object, Relation, SuperClass),
      has_value(SuperClass, Slot, Value),   % note the recursive call
      not_explicit(Object, Slot).
```

The final line is to prevent erroneous inheritance in exceptional cases. For instance, 'bird can fly' is stored at the bird level, whilst the exception 'ostrich cannot fly' is stored at the ostrich level - so we need to exclude the inheritance 'ostrich is bird so ostrich can fly' by ruling out inheritance where an explicit value is given.

```
not_explicit(Object, a_kind_of):- !.
not_explicit(Object, has_as_part):- !.
not_explicit(Object, Slot):- not(value(Object, Slot, _)).
```

Note that we could not simply have used `not(value(Object, Slot, _))` because we must make a special case of the `a_kind_of` and `has_as_part` slots. After all, almost all objects will have an explicit value for the `a_kind_of` slot but must still be able to inherit by it. Similarly, objects can have numerous entries for `has_as_part` and still want to inherit parts from parent frames. So we have provided a simple definition called **not_explicit/2** which simply covers these three cases: first the exception for a_kind_of ; secondly the exception of has_as_part; and thirdly the case which states that it must **not** be true that the value is present at the Object Frame's own level. The cuts (!) here simply ensure that this definition is only true once - ie not resatisfied on backtracking for the same values. So, if the `Slot` is either `a_kind_of` or `has_as_part` then the cut (!) says that this should succeed and there is no need to look any further for a solution - if you come back to here, don't bother to try the other clauses in this definition.

The definition of inherits is very straightforward. The first clause simply says that all possible slots may be inherited via the `a_kind_of` relation. It uses member to generate all possible slots in turn. In principle it is possible to exclude any slots from this list and prevent them being inherited via the `a_kind_of` link. As it is we have only excluded the name slot - simply because we couldn't think of a sensible case for inheriting it.

```
inherits(_, S, a_kind_of):-
    member(S,[ a_kind_of, age, bite, breathes, breed, circulation,
        coat, colour, energy_source, family_name, fly,
        food_source, habitat, has_as_part, locomotion,
        makes_noise, owned_by, part_of, reproduction,
        run, size, skin_covering, slot, swim, weight]).
inherits(S, part_of):-
    member(_, S, [ part_of, age, colour, owned_by ]).
```

The second clause states that there are only a few slots that may be inherited by a part of the object. Permitting inheritance via links other than a_kind_of is only sensible if it is done with great care. If we have the knowledge that my dog fido has a head which is a part of him then it is sensible to infer that his head is the same age as he is. Similarly, if we were to go as far as representing his eyes as a part of his head then the same would go for these. Properties like colour are more tenuous but we have left it in the definition to give you a feel for the issues. Perhaps this distinction looks more sensible if you think about representing things like motor cars which are often considered structurally. I own my car and therefore I own my car's engine and all the parts thereof.

Adding a Demon : If-needed

Often it is valuable to be able to apply (procedural style) rules in certain situations. For instance, it is sensible to enter the date of birth of an animal into the database —

```
value(tweety, date_of_birth, 1989).
```

but it might be inefficient to enter a value for the current age —

```
value(tweety, current_age, 1).
```

since that would need to be updated each year. A better idea would be to use the following definition **if_needed**/3 to work this out for you when and if it was needed.

```
if_needed(Object, current_age, Years) :-
    value(Object, date_of_birth, DoB),
    current_year(ThisYear),      % this has to be entered into the database of course
    Years is ThisYear - DoB.     % do the necessary subtraction
```

It is then possible to add a further clause (make it the last) to the **has_value**/3 predicate:

```
has_value(Object, Attribute, Value) :-
        if_needed(Object, Attribute, Value).
```

This means that if one needs to know something like the current_age value for something then it can be calculated as required from other information. This clearly reduces the explicit knowledge that needs to be stored at the cost of having to work it out when it is needed. Note that this 'procedural attachment' strategy, although necessary and useful in some cases, destroys the clean declarative style of the program, and can make it difficult to predict how programs will run in more complex situations. We have included the feature as it is a standard method in frame-based work, but would suggest that it is better to avoid such procedural attachments if at all possible and preserve the declarative meaning.

Default Rules

Many of one's decisions or ideas are based upon stereotypical judgements. For instance, a typical dog is friendly, about 3 foot long, has brown hair, a long tongue, runs fast, likes fetching sticks and so on. Particular dogs may differ substantially from these stereotypes, and most will differ on at least one attribute. Nonetheless, it is valuable to include this stereotypical information, as long as one is clear that it is not certain to be correct. It may be seen that this information corresponds to the 'characteristic features' proposed by Smith et al in their feature comparison model of semantic memory. Normally in frame-based representations this information is known as default information, and may be entered in a way analogous to the value information entered earlier.

eg.

```
default(dog, disposition, friendly).
default(dog, length, 3).
```

and so on.

This information may be made accessible through modifying the has_value predicate again by adding a further clause:

```
has_value(Object, Attribute, Value) :- default(Object, Attribute, Value).
```

It is also possible to build in inheritance into default values. However, this should be done with care, and we have not attempted it in this project. Maybe one's default animal is a dog, but it would be a nonsense to inherit dog-like defaults for non-mammals such as fish, or worms ... ! Nevertheless, as soon as you start to consider inheritance via defaults in your model you may wish to reconsider some features like those which state that birds fly and don't swim. Looking at the other features which we have given for birds in the appendix - most of them are incontrovertible like laying eggs, breathing air and being warm-blooded. Surely it could not be a bird without these features, whilst there are quite a few birds who don't fly and many birds that are good swimmers. So, whilst you do want them to be inheritable they may actually seem to be more appropriate as defaults. We offer no solution here - but the challenge of Cognitive Science is to make you think about whilst trying to do it & make it work.

Different Control Strategies for Inheritance

One of the advantages of the neutral, uniform data structure adopted is that it is possible to adopt different control strategies for different purposes. The control strategy adopted here for inheritance is shown below - summing up some of the changes we have suggested.

```
has_value(Object, Slot, Value):-
     value(Object, Slot, Value).
has_value(Object, Slot, Value):-
     inherits(Object, Slot, Relation),
     value(Object, Relation, SuperClass),
     has_value(SuperClass, Slot, Value),
     not_explicit(Object, Slot).
has_value(Object, Attribute, Value) :-
     if_needed(Object, Attribute, Value).
has_value(Object, Attribute, Value) :-
     default(Object, Attribute, Value).
```

In effect this goes up the hierarchy one level at a time checking whether the new class has the required attribute filled explicitly. If that fails, it starts again at the bottom checking whether there is an if-needed clause available or if there is default information available, and then goes up the hierarchy checking each new class for if-needed or default information. This in fact falls between the two standard inheritance control strategies, known as N and Z. The N strategy involves first checking explicit values for each level in the hierarchy, starting again and checking if-needed values for each level in the hierarchy, then starting again if necessary and checking default values for each level in the hierarchy (N is used because its up-down-up shape reflects the strategy!). The alternative Z strategy involves checking explicit values, if-needed values and default values for each level up the hierarchy in turn. Again the across-up-across shape of the Z reflects the strategy.

Exercises 2.2   Frames

Easy Exercises

E 2.2.1 Exploring the frame-based version of semantic memory.

  (i) Go through the inheritance exercises E 2.1 from TLC checking that the appropriate results are obtained in the frame version.

  (ii) Introduce some human interest by adding slots for people, maybe ending up by classifying your family and friends.

E 2.2.2 Implement a Z inheritance strategy.

E 2.2.3 In fact, this whole approach to inheritance is rather unsatisfactory. It is quite important to know whether the value was explicitly present for the object, whether it was calculated by an if-needed rule or whether it was a default. Probably the best way to maintain this information is to add a fourth argument to the `has_value` definition.

Eg. `has_value(Object, Attribute, Value, Reason)` where `Reason` reflects the reasoning used, such as: `explicit`; `calculated`, `default` etc. Augment the `has_value` definition appropriately. One thing that this might help you ask is which Object-Attribute-Value's are calculated? The inherited `Reason` is slightly harder, but for now just get it to tell you that inheritance is involved.

Rather Hard Exercises

E 2.2.4 As a further refinement, try to give the system a rudimentary explanation facility, by augmenting `Reason` to store which node provided the necessary information. It would then be possible to construct a predicate `explain(Object, Attribute, Value)` which writes out the reason. For instance in response to the query:

```
(?)  explain(tweety, breathes, A).   should write something like:
                tweety breathes air
                  because
                    it is a_kind_of canary and
                    it is a_kind_of bird and
                    the property is explicit for bird
        YES   Where A = air
```

E 2.2.5 Write a predicate for inferring everything that is known or may be inferred about a particular concept. Note that the program should check what all the necessary slots are, and then return all the slot fillers that can be inferred.

Possible Advanced Projects on Frames

Project 1. (Easy) Write a predicate for adding a new fact to the database. This predicate should identify all the necessary slots and then ask what the values to fill them are, allowing the possibility of not filling them. It should then ask whether the new concept has any new slots of its own, and what the appropriate fillers should be (if anything).

Project 2. (Medium) Take your own favourite hobby (ornithology, stamp collecting, rock music, cars ...), and try to decide on a sensible semantic representation for the facts involved and implement them as a semantic net. You might start to cobble together a natural language interface to it after reading the next chapter.

Project 3. (Hard) Consider causality. We can certainly use a frame based representation to capture the relationships between the components of any simple system. For example, we could easily take a motor car and represent is as a collection of integrated subsystems like the braking system; the cooling system; the engine; the electrics etc. Each system will have its own subsystems down to whatever level of nuts and bolts that you like. This representation tells you the structure of the systems involved, but not necessarily how they combine to make the thing function. So spend a little time thinking about how you might represent the idea that it is the engine that turns the wheels - through a variety of physical connections. You might start off with some "applies physical force to" links where some part causes some other part to move. How might you represent the notion that depressing the accelerator causes the wheels to turn? Or that turning the key in the ignition causes the wheels to turn (if the clutch is "in"!) ? If you feel that this problem is too hard for you because it is too complex then start off with a much simpler mechanical device such as, say, a lead propelling pencil - that is actually still quite a challenge!

2.7   Further Reading

Semantic Memory. It is hard to know what to include within this section since most recent developments in cognitive modelling can be traced back to TLC's contributions. An immediate development of TLC was made by Collins and Loftus (1975) who outlined a much more powerful model, still based on spreading activation, but without strict hierarchical organisation. The concept of spreading activation has received wide support from empirical studies, and is probably best developed in the ACT* model of cognition (Anderson, 1983). As noted earlier, the concept of semantic parsing was developed much more fully by Schank and his colleagues (see chapter 5). Any recent textbook on cognitive psychology will give a reasonable overview of theories of semantic memory. It is fair to say that interest in the field has waned in the 1980's owing to a growing belief that it is not really possible to distinguish between different models of semantic memory by direct experimentation.

Knowledge Representation. The field is now very complex. Good sets of relevant papers are collected in Aitkenhead and Slack (1985) and in Brachman and Levesque (1985). It should be noted that explicit knowledge representation languages such as KRL have been introduced, and that an alternative methodology for creating such systems is provided by object oriented programming environments such as Smalltalk. It is possible to buy commercial packages for knowledge representation. The Flex™ expert system toolkit provided by Logic Programming Associates is one of the most powerful Prolog-based packages.

Chapter 3 : Eliza Project

The project introduced in this chapter is important because it is NOT a good model of human cognition. It was actually never intended as a model of human cognition – so the comparison is rather unfair. However, it is actually quite instructive to start off our examination of language with a project that is clearly inadequate as a model of human language understanding. This requires us to consider exactly how it fails as a model and to propose models which are clearly better.

Joseph Weizenbaum's ELIZA program is a parody of a conversationalist rather than a serious psychological theory. Nevertheless, it represents a landmark in the use of unaided pragmatics; it provides an interesting test-case for the examination of machine intelligence; and the technique involved can actually prove valuable in low-cost approaches to question answering in restricted domains.

3.1 Overview – Natural Language Understanding

As social intelligent agents we communicate with each other all the time. This communication takes place through a number of channels and on a number of levels. If we just look closely at two individuals having a conversation, they are communicating through the clothes they are wearing, the way they are standing or sitting, the tone of their voices, gestures with their hands and so on. All of these things count as communication if they are transmitting a message – that has meaning – to the other party in the interaction. One of the richest channels of communication which is available to humans is language (often called natural language or NL to distinguish it from artificial languages like a computer programming language). The cognitive activity of producing and understanding natural language is something that seems intrinsic to human intelligence and thinking. The most obvious appearance of this ability is in conversation. Whilst the two participants in a conversation are communicating in many ways, the channel over which they have the most conscious control is the linguistic one. We tend to generate language sounds freely and easily as speech and regularly expect other intelligent agents around us to hear the message and understand its meaning.

Even leaving aside language generation and the understanding of spoken language, the understanding of written language by computer has proved a surprisingly difficult problem. It has become clear that the main reason for the difficulties involved in natural language understanding by computer (NLU) is that language communications are extremely knowledge-rich and situation-dependent.

3.1.1 Aspects of Natural Language Understanding

There are a number of conventional divisions that are usually made in evaluating the contribution of any model of natural language. These divisions relate to different aspects of any given utterance. When considering any possible model it is important to consider its contribution to each aspect.

Consider these two sentences:

1a. John gave the ticket to Mary.

1b Mary gave the ticket to John.

They have different meanings, of course, and the meaning is determined by the order of the words and their relationship to each other. The rules about the relationships between these words is captured in the **syntax** of English sentences. Syntax determines that in sentence 1a John is the giver whereas in 1b Mary is the giver. Now consider the next pair of sentences:

2a. John gave the ticket to Mary.

2b. Mary was given the ticket by John.

The syntax of the two sentences is very different, but the underlying meaning, the **semantics** is very similar. Interestingly, even after only a few seconds, people apparently forget the precise form of words used in a sentence, remembering only the underlying semantics (eg. Sachs, 1967). It is also clear that people do a lot of 'extra' work with this input to give it meaning. Quite possibly, you have already interpreted 'ticket' as some sort of "entrance voucher" or "permit" and would not be unduly surprised by further sentences which assumed this interpretation - eg. where Mary planned to board a train or enter a theatre. Now consider this sentence:

3. The traffic cop gave the ticket to Mary.

In this case knowledge of the world - **pragmatics** - allows us to infer that the ticket is in fact a notification of a traffic offence rather than the more "default" interpretation of voucher/permit. An adequate model of NLU requires all three sources of knowledge - syntax, semantics and pragmatics, but owing to initial decisions to develop each separately and to explore how well each could function independently of the others, early NLU programs tended to be aggressively unidimensional in terms of approach. The next three projects examine natural language understanding systems which all take a different perspective. The first project actually uses none of these sources of knowledge!

3.1.2 The Turing Test

One view of cognitive science research is that it is an attempt to replicate human intelligence on a machine. Indeed, this is evident from the term 'artificial intelligence' which is often used synonymously with cognitive science. In current AI research this is a model of human cognition on a digital computer. The first metric that we may use to judge any model is how closely it appears to resemble the complex system that it is attempting to replicate.

Alan Turing is mainly remembered for two specific ideas : his "Machine", a theoretical device that is often used as a standard against which to gauge computational power, and his "imitation game." The imitation game was presented as an intuitively appealing test for artificial intelligence in the October 1950 issue of the journal MIND. Turing proposed that the simplest way to test a machine 'simulation' of human cognition was to ask someone to try and tell it apart from the real thing. If a human is unable to distinguish the artificial from the human response, we have a prima facie simulation of intelligent behaviour, and therefore it is appropriate to attribute intelligence to the machine behaviour. Given that computer technology was then (and still is) incapable of a convincing replication of a human voice or face, he suggested that the experiment be constrained to a conversation conducted via a 'teletype'. The teletype was the interface which was used to the computers of that time, permitting a line by line interaction with the machine to be printed out.

The conversation idea was that a human 'interrogator' would have access to two individuals, one a person and the other a machine simulating a person. The interrogator would be asked to conduct a conversation with these individuals to determine which was which. Because of the teletype making the interaction look the same superficially, the interrogator would have to rely on what was 'said', and how, to make the distinction.

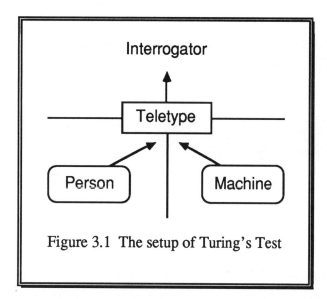

Figure 3.1 The setup of Turing's Test

The rationale for the task is intuitively plausible: if you could not distinguish between them then surely the machine must be acting intelligently? However it is also rather informal: we do not know the details of how the interrogator is to go about making this decision; we do not know for how long or how often we would require before we were prepared to assign the label 'intelligent'; nor indeed does the machine need to be in any way like the human to simply perform (for a short time) like one.

The first real candidate for an attempt at the Turing test was a program devised by Joseph Weizenbaum in 1966 which he called ELIZA. The program played the role of a therapist conducting a teletype conversation with the user/patient.

3.2   The Project - Weizenbaum's ELIZA

The program ELIZA should be treated as a parody of a Natural Language Understander. It is a conversationalist that can respond to input with an appearance of 'understanding'. The usual scenario is that she represents a non-directive (Rogerian-type) psychotherapist. A non-directive therapist typically refrains from direct questions and leading lines of inquiry, preferring to be patient-driven, attempting to draw out their problem in their own words.

A sample dialogue might go like this (See Boden 1977, or Greene 1986) :

USER:	Men are all <u>alike</u>.
ELIZA:	In what way?
USER:	They're always bugging us about <u>something</u> or other.
ELIZA:	Can you think of a specific example?
USER:	Well, <u>my boyfriend made me come here</u>.
ELIZA:	Your boyfriend made you come here.
USER:	He says <u>I'm depressed</u> much of the time.
ELIZA:	I am sorry to hear you are depressed.
USER:	It's true. <u>I am unhappy</u>.
ELIZA:	Do you think that coming here will help you not to be unhappy?
USER:	<u>I need some help</u>, that much seems certain.
ELIZA:	What would it mean to you if you got some help?
USER:	Perhaps I could learn to get along with my <u>mother</u>.
ELIZA:	Tell me more about your family.

...

Figure 3.2 An example dialogue with the ELIZA therapist

In the sample dialogue of Figure 3.2 the therapist is apparently asking questions and emphasising points of possible (therapeutic) interest so as to help the patient to speak freely about what they are feeling. In fact, ELIZA is doing no such thing – it is very much more shallow. The program is actually making no effort to 'understand' the user's input at all, but is simply looking for key words or sequences in the user's input to deliver an appropriate conversational reply. The probable 'trigger' words or phrases in the user's input are underlined in the above conversation. The program responds to key words & patterns such as "mother" which are used as triggers for plausible replies like "Tell me more about your family". This triggering process can be seen as simple rules where the rules map input patterns onto the plausible replies. eg.

```
I am  X ----> Why are you  X ?
```

In this example the input must begin with "I am" for the rule to be appropriate. If it does then the rule dictates that whatever comes after this (called X) is to be 'echoed back' to the user in the reply. So if the user said "I am sad" then ELIZA's reply would be "Why are you sad?" If we permit the system to allow a flexible matching process, where X could be quite complex then it could handle: "I am very sad and lonely" with the reply "Why are you very sad and lonely?"

This echoing is clearly very simple but effective, particularly as it is expected of a non-directive therapist. However it cannot always be used so blindly. The most obvious problem is that some words would change in a natural echo. So for example the system will need rules to look through the echo to detect and change patterns like 'you are' into 'I am' and 'me' into 'you' etc. Consider this example:

```
USER :      I am sure you are against me.

ELIZA :     Why are you sure I am against you?
```

In addition the program may make use of a small amount of context. ELIZA can store some interesting keywords which it can return to later if stuck. If none of the patterns is suitable the program might use the fact that the keyword "mother" was given earlier in the conversation to continue the dialogue with:

```
ELIZA :     You mentioned your mother ...
```

The best insight into what something is doing and how it claims to do it, is to explore it yourself, so on you go. You can easily write your own simple version of this program.

3.2.1 Defining a toy ELIZA

For a rapid prototype of the ELIZA program we will represent both the user's input and ELIZA's replies as Lists. Each word of the input is an element of one list and the plausible reply is another list. Basically, you can start by defining a relation 'pat' (short for pattern) with two arguments, where pat(In, Out) means that if the input to the relation is the list In then an appropriate ELIZA-like pat reply is Out. So the database definition of the ELIZA patterns will look something like:

```
(i)        pat([bye], [bye]).
(ii)       pat([hello | _], [hello, there]).
(iii)      pat([i, am | Rest], [why, are, you | Rest]).
(iv)       pat([i | Anything], [why, do, you, say, that, you | Anything]).
(v)        pat(Anything, [tell, me, more]).
```

You can interact directly with this simple relation one query at a time, giving a specific input and a variable to match with the suitable output. You should note that, for uniformity, we have made all the words in the patterns lower-case letters, and so will conduct the toy conversation entirely in lower-case also. So the query:

```
(?)  pat([hello, there, eliza, you, clever, program], Reply).
```

will reply;   Reply = [hello, there]

The first clause (i) simply states that if the user says [bye], then ELIZA should also say [bye]. The second clause (ii) in the definition above says that if the first element of the Input list is 'hello' then the ELIZA 'pat' reply would be [hello, there]. The last clause (iv) is a "catchall" which will match any Input. It is used as a form of default reply - when no earlier (more specific) reply could be found. The clauses in between are more complex in that they make use of part of the input list to produce the output list (echoing). We have used the list guillotine 'I' to state that the input must begin with specific words, but anything can come after these. In clause (ii) we have used the "don't care variable" underscore because if the first word is 'hello' then we can safely ignore the rest of the input and reply [hello, there]. However in patterns (ii) to (iv) we have given the tail variable of the guillotine a name so that we can use it in the echoed reply.

When querying this definition you are only interested in the "**first**" match Prolog makes. This is because the definition relies on the implicit ordering built into the Prolog pattern-matcher to capture the fact that earlier clauses are 'more specific' and therefore better replies. This means that the 'catchall' clause (v) above "[tell, me, more]" will be an appropriate reply to *any* input, however as it is the last clause in the definition it will only be sought after Prolog has already tested all those above it and failed to find one suitable.

Exercises 3.1

E 3.1.1   Implement this pat/2 definition of ELIZA. Try a variety of queries to it. Remember that you are only interested in the first match Prolog makes. These two queries would make a good start:

```
(?)  pat([i, feel, that, noone, is, really, listening], X).

(?)  pat([i, am, sick, of, computers], X).
```

(Note that it is easy to get this simple version to reply something silly - eg. it can't exchange 'i' for 'you' or 'you' for 'me' in anything echoed !)

E 3.1.2   Extend the definition to cope with other simple matches. You extend the program by adding further clauses in between the 'hello' clause and the 'catchall'. For each added clause, try a query to see if your addition works properly.

(eg) add this pattern

```
pat([i, need | Something],
    [what, would, it, mean, to, you, to, get | Something]).
```

E 3.1.3   If we extend the definition with some **rules** we can add some much more powerful messages. Extend the pat/2 definition of ELIZA with the rule:

```
pat(List, [tell, me, more about, your, family]):-

              member(father, List).
```

This means that if the word 'father' is to be found (anywhere) as a member of the input List then the appropriate reply is [tell, me, more about, your, family]. NB. This will mean that you will have to provide the program with a definition for the list-processing predicate member/2 - maybe your version of Prolog has one built-in or maybe not.

E 3.1.4   Add some more rules for specific words. Eg. What should pat/2 say to 'depressed', 'computers', etc. HINT: use the same method as for 'father' above.

E 3.1.5   Define the relation family_member(X). This should mean that X is a word referring to families. This relation can replace the rule you added in (iii) to find father, and will respond appropriately if the input list contains any reference to a 'family_member'.

HINT: One definition might read X is a family_member if X is a member of the list [father, mother, ... etc]

E 3.1.6   Depending on your creative imagination (especially regarding suitably "vague" replies) you could extend this simple ELIZA very much more. Eg should ELIZA be able to spot the presence of a 'badword' (foul language) in the input list and respond indignantly. How ?

If you want to provide a better interface to your ELIZA, to make it more conversational (a smoother turn-taking interaction), it's not technically difficult and depends upon input/output (i/o) procedures such as those given in Code Appendix 1. We provide an i/o solution via the predicate liza/0 which depends upon the predicate rap/1 which in turn calls the i/o predicates `talk/2` & `say/1`. The call to `talk(Message, UserInput)` prompts the user with a Message and permits them to type their response without the need for the list format. The code for `talk/2` and `say/1` in Code Appendix 1 is rather obscure so don't worry unduly if you don't yet understand it! As with many other things, you don't need to fully understand how it works in order to use it - unless it doesn't work properly with your version of Prolog.

% liza/0 starts off the toy-eliza conversation

```
liza:- rap(['Hello, Please tell me about your problems']).
```

% rap(MessageToOutput) just keeps the conversation going until the user says bye.

```
(i)        rap([bye]):- say(['Goodbye, I hope you have found our chat useful']).

(ii)       rap(Output):-
                talk(Output, UserInput),
                pat(UserInput, NewOutput),
                rap(NewOutput).
```

The predicate which organises all of this is called **liza** because it may be thought of as a shortened 'e-liza' program for the toy program. Similarly the predicate which organises the conversation is called **rap** and is the core of a later predicate which does a more complete job of 'the-**rap**-y'. In fact the `rap/1` call takes in a message which is to be output to the user via `talk/2`. The `talk/2` predicate handles the interaction, printing out its first argument to the user and returning their reply as its second argument. The user's reply is used by the `pat/2` definition as above to find an appropriate reply which is then handed on recursively to `rap/1` to go around again. This process will continue indefinitely until the user says 'bye'. This will match with the first pattern above in `pat/2` to give a reply of 'bye'. This reply will match with the first clause of `rap/1` and the predicate `say/1` will deliver a parting shot before the call to the 'rap' definition succeeds. When `rap/1` succeeds - so will `liza/0`, and the program will finish with a 'YES'. If this all sounds rather confusing, don't worry. Just implement the program above and step slowly through the above explanation referring to the code.

3.3   Implementing the ELIZA project

As can be seen from Figure 3.3 the model for the complete program for the ELIZA project is actually not much more complex than the toy example just seen. Again `talk/2` can handle the input/output side, taking freely typed-in continuous input and segmenting it into a list of separate words. But now a more sophisticated pattern matcher will use this list to find a suitable pattern list for a reply. This reply list is then given back to `talk/2` to output to the user.

Figure 3.3   The Architecture of ELIZA

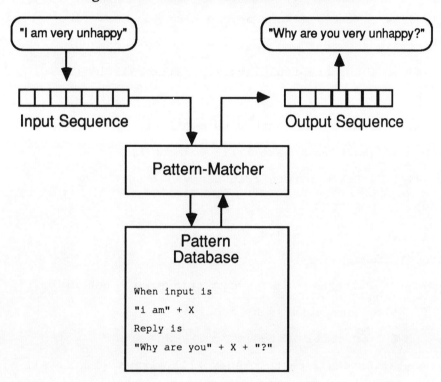

3.3.1   The ELIZA Patterns

Let us look first at these more sophisticated patterns. In the following definition of `pattern/3`, the call *pattern(N, In, Out)* means that conversational patterns are numbered *N*, and that *In* is the input from the user and *Out* is the plausible ELIZA reply. The first argument *N* is either a unique integer or the word `'x'`. The use of the unique number will enable the program to keep track of the things it has said. The patterns labelled with the word `'x'` can be repeated as often as necessary - as they may come out differently each time. However, if the pattern has a number it will be possible to check that this number pattern has not already been used in the conversation. This can then be used to prevent the program repeating exactly the same fixed comment twice. As with the toy definition the most specific patterns come before the more general ones because Prolog will look at each in turn until it finds a match, and we are only interested in the first clause which matches. So the very first clause is the 'stopping' pattern - if the user says "bye" then ELIZA should just say "bye" in return.

```
%  the 'quit' pattern
pattern(x, [bye], [bye]).

%  echoing patterns - will not be repeated
pattern(10, [i, X, my | Rest], ['Do you often have these feelings of ', X,

        ' towards your ', Rest, '?']):-  feelings(X).

pattern(40, [this, is | Rest], ['Why do you say that this is', Rest, '?']).

pattern(50, [my | Rest], ['Your', Rest, '?']).

%  general patterns with some echoing - can be repeated

pattern(x, [i, am | Rest], ['How long have you been', Rest, '?']).

pattern(x, [i, like | Rest], ['Does anyone else you know like', Rest, '?']).

%  Patterns triggered by just one word - not to be repeated

pattern(100, [X|_], ['Cut the foul language, slimeball !']):-

      badword(X).

pattern(170, [X], ['Dont be so short with me!', nl,

        'What does', X,' mean here?']):- yesorno(X).

pattern(180, [X|_], ['Do computers frighten you ?']):-

      important(X, computers).

pattern(190, [X|_], ['How close are you to your', X, '?']):-

      important(X, family).

        %  Default Patterns - if nothing triggered - not to be repeated

pattern(250, [], ['Tell me about your family']).

pattern(260, [], ['I am still listening ...']).

        %  General Catchall pattern that will always work if all else fails

pattern(x, [], ['Tell me more ... ']).
```

The first point of note is the use of quotation marks to delimit long atoms in the output lists which may contain spaces and punctuation. So ['Tell me more ... '] is actually written here as one long quoted word. The words 'Tell' and '...' would have to be quoted anyway to prevent Prolog treating the former as a variable and the latter as a mistake. We could have written something like ['Tell', me, more, '...'], but the single long-word format is easier. In the same vein you will note that the word 'nl' appears in the output list of pattern number 170. Now as you may know nl/0 is a built-in Prolog primitive to make output appear on a new line – but it is not actually called as Prolog here. Neither is it intended to be printed out to the user as a word - rather it is intended as a flag to indicate that there should be a 'new line' inserted in the text at this point. This will make the next item in the list, 'What does', appear on the line beneath the previous items. This 'nl' formatting flag is picked up by the predicate which is responsible for taking this list and printing it on the screen (see definition 1.3 in Code Appendix 1).

Now most of the patterns in this definition are facts, and resemble the facts in the toy definition. However, some of the clauses in the definition are rules and thereby insist that a little more work is done before the pattern may be considered to be an appropriate match. The most simple extensions are where the rule simply adds an extra test to the pattern, where the test is defined elsewhere. One instance of this is pattern 10, which states that: if the input matches the list [i, X, my | Rest], then the appropriate reply is ['Do you often have these feelings of ', X, ' towards your ', Rest, '?'], but that this is only true where the query feelings(X) is true.

```
pattern(10,

        [i, X, my | Rest],

        ['Do you often have these feelings of ', X,

         ' towards your ', Rest, '?']):-  feelings(X).
```

So if the definition of feelings/1 is something like the following:

```
feelings(hate).
feelings(love).
feelings(fear).
```

Then given an input like [i, hate, my, pet, squirrel] then this pattern would match binding X with 'hate' and Rest with [pet, squirrel] which would indicate that the appropriate ELIZA pattern to reply would be ['Do you often have these feelings of ', hate, ' towards your ', [pet, squirrel], '?'].

The whole rule only succeeds because the word matched with X in the pattern is provably a 'feeling'. Also, because its first argument is a unique integer the inference procedures that use this definition will be barred from using it again. Other examples of such tests include badword/1, yesorno/1, & important/2. The definitions of badword/1 is obvious – it defines all known words that are 'not nice' – you may have implemented a definition in the previous exercises. The definition of yesorno/1 defines the words "yes" and "no" and any other ways of expressing them. The final test, important/2, keeps definitions of other keywords that are important in a variety of contexts. The first argument to important/2 is the keyword, the second argument is the context. So important(X, family) means that X is an important keyword in the context of the family, like "mother", "sister" or "home". Similarly, important(X, computers) may mean that X is a word like "byte" or "Prolog". Unfortunately, ELIZA does not have even the most simple general rules about English grammar - such as the addition of 's' to the end of a noun to make a plural. So if you want both 'computer' and 'computers' to be recognised in the "computers" context they must both explicitly be there in the database!

3.3.2 The ELIZA control programs

The top-level predicate : eliza/0 only tidies up after any previous conversations and then hands over to therapy/1 giving it a suitable message to present to the user to start the therapeutic ball rolling. The need to tidy up with the tidy/0 predicate is explained shortly, and talk/2 we met in the toy program.

```
eliza :-
    tidy,
    therapy(['Welcome to ELIZA.  What seems to be worrying you ?']).
```

The main definition is clearly therapy/1. The definition of therapy/1 is given a therapeutic output pattern as its one argument. It has two clauses: the first is a simple stopping check; the second is its main recursive body. The first clause is only appropriate in the circumstance where the output pattern is the list [bye]. In this case the program is to output a goodbye message and can then succeed. The predicate writel/1 is one which we have produced to print out its list argument in a flexible way.

```
(i)       therapy([bye]) :-
              writel(['Goodbye. I hope you feel better !', nl,
                  'Have a nice day.']).
(ii)      therapy(Output):-
              talk(Output, Input),
              match(Input, Reply),
              exchanges(Reply, Reply1),
              therapy(Reply1).
```

Clause (ii) does all the real work. If the message to be output is not just [bye], then the message is handed on to talk/2 which is responsible for printing it out and taking in what the user inputs as a list Input. (See Code Appendix 1 : D 1.4). It then hands this Input to match/2 which attempts to find an appropriately "therapeutic" Reply. On finding a suitable Reply it then makes any appropriate exchanges ('i am' for 'you are', etc) in the message. This ensures that any part of the Reply which is an 'echo' is correct. Then it calls itself recursively with the new output message and the recursion continues.

The two definitions in this which require explanation are match/2 and exchanges/2. The definition of match/2 is fairly simple. As can be seen it checks whether the current Input matches with any of the patterns, and if so whether that pattern is still 'do-able'. Before returning the Output this definition calls add/1 with the number of the pattern used so that it can be added to the database and doable/1 will ensure that is is not used again. Again, the standard recursive template of stopping check and recursive body is clearly recognisable.

```
(i)        match(Input, Output):-           % picks up empty list and multi-word matches

               pattern(P, Input, Output),   % picks up empty list and [i,am | Rest] etc

               doable(P),

               add(P).                       % flag that pattern P has been used

(ii)       match([_ | T], Output):-         % otherwise throw away first word

               match(T, Output).             % and recurse on the tail
```

Clause (i) attempts to match its input argument with the input part of a pattern in the pattern/3 definition – if it matches then the Output is appropriate and it does some of the work already mentioned and succeeds. However, if the direct match is unsuccessful, the matcher will proceed on to clause (ii) which instructs it to throw away the first word in the input list and try again. It guillotines the input list calling the tail part T which it hands on to a recursive call. The variable Output is simply passed on down the recursion in clause (ii) unchanged. It will eventually be bound by the pattern/3 part of clause (i) and acquire a value. Do not be overly distressed if you find this confusing at this stage, try tracing a call to it: you will see the user's input getting shorter and shorter, as words are stripped off the front, until some pattern matches. Alternatively you can leave this and come back to it later – when you may be able to spot some serious problems with this approach to pattern matching.

Other simple parts of the match/2 program are the complementary definitions of add/1 and doable/1 which incidentally explain the call to tidy/0 in the eliza/0 program. The add/1 program, as has been noted, takes the number of a pattern just used in the conversation and if it is an integer adds it to the database as 'done'.

```
add(x).
add(N):- integer(N), assert(done(N)).
```

If the argument given is the word 'x' then it does nothing, otherwise if it is an integer then this uses the built-in predicate assert/1 to add to the definition of done/1 with the integer number of the pattern. In a similar way the definition doable/1 simply checks to see if the number of the pattern it is given is in the database as done/1.

```
doable(x).
doable(N):- integer(N), not(done(N)).
```

It is like add in that it will only succeed if it is given the word 'x' or an integer number that is ' not' in the done/1 definition. This makes the need for the tidy/0 call in the initial eliza/0 definition apparent. Clearly when this conversation is over, the database may have a large definition of add-ed numbers for patterns which have been 'done'. Before the next conversation begins this definition must be erased so that these patterns can be used in the next conversation. The cut (!) here ensures that this will not be resatisfied on backtracking.

```
tidy:- retractall(done(X)), assert(done(0)), !.
```

The next easiest definition to understand is `exchanges/2` which is called from the `therapy/1` definition and handles all the exchanges of "me" for "you" etc in any part of the input which is to be echoed as output. Consider this example:

eg. (?) exchanges([i, am, unhappy], X). YES. Where X = [you, are, unhappy].

The definition of exchanges takes two arguments: the first is the Old list and the second is the New list with all exchangable words exchanged for the appropriate counterparts.

```
(i)         exchanges([],[]).
(ii)        exchanges([X, Y | T], [X1, Y1 | T1]):-
                exchange([X, Y], [X1, Y1]),
                exchanges(T, T1), !.
(iii)       exchanges([X | T], [X1 | T1]):-
                exchange([X], [X1]),
                exchanges(T, T1), !.
(iv)        exchanges([X | T], [X | T1]):-
                exchanges(T, T1), !.
```

The definition uses `exchange/2` to tell it what the words and their counterparts are. So the definition of `exchange/2` could look like this:

```
exchange([i, am], [you, are]).
exchange([you, are], ['I', am]).
exchange([i], [you]).
exchange([you], [me]).
```

This example definition of `exchange/2` says that the sequence "i am" should be exchanged for "you are" and vice versa, whereas "i" on its own should be turned into "you" and "you" alone should become "me", etc. So the definition of `exchanges(Old, New)` above simply states that (i) if the Old list is empty then the New list will also be empty and you can finish exchanging. Otherwise (ii) look for two word exchanges via `exchange/2`; then (iii) look for one word exchanges; finally (iv) assume that the word cannot be exchanged and simply pass it on to the New list. The definition is a very simple recursive predicate in which an element is guillotined off a list, something happens to it and then it is guillotined on to a returning list. So in (iii) one element is guillotined off the list, `exchange/2` is checked to see if this word needs to be exchanged, if it does then the new word is guillotined on to the second argument New list, but this will only happen after the rest of the Old list has been processed via the recursive call and the tail list T1 has a value. The clause (ii) of the exchange definition is much the same as (iii) except that it deals with two elements at a time. Also clause (iv) is similar except that the word is not exchanged (it would have matched at either (ii) or (iii) if it needed to be changed) but is simply guillotined back onto the New list - after recursion has dealt with the remaining tail of the Old list.

In principle, whilst the above definition can only deal with exchanges of two words, it could be extended to changing sequences of three words by simply adding another clause to the definition (eg [X, Y, Z | T]). In practice this is rather more difficult. The current definition cannot exchange [i, really, am] for [you, really, are] because it is a three word sequence. The first problem is that "really" could be many things (eg "certainly", "probably", "sure", etc). The second problem is that the same sort of pattern can be arbitrarily long - not just three words (eg [i, really, really, am], etc). But this problem is just one case of the infinite patterns that we use in English, and which would require very many "special case" patterns for ELIZA to match.

An astute reader might foresee a possible problem arising from the fact that the exchanging of words happens after the matching of patterns in the definition of therapy/1. The match/2 predicate provides an output pattern to say to the user and *all* of this pattern will be checked for suitable exchanges. Now we only really want to exchange bits of 'echoes' in the pattern. Note that the only legitimate exchanges in the first argument of exchange/2 are lower case single words - this prevents exchanges/2 changing anything in the message that is not part of an 'echo' because the output patterns are usually 'funny words' in Prolog (ie. enclosed in single quotes and including spaces etc). The things that are part of an echo will have been delivered by talk/2 as single words converted to lower-case, and as such will be checked through for a match with the 'exchanges' patterns given here. This is a "feature" of this definition that could easily be a "bug" if you are not careful in how you write the output patterns. Eg. the single word "my" as an item in the output pattern list would always get exchanged and printed as "your" unless it was enclosed in some funny word.

Exercises 3.2

E 3.2.1   The first range of exercises that can be done with this prototype are to do with improving the range of patterns given. The version of the program given in Code Appendix 3 is rather more verbose than the one discussed here, but could still be very much extended with clever patterns to fool the user that the program was reacting intelligently to their input. You will notice that the program uses a number of new definitions that it can refer to, such as **uncertain**/1 and **negative**/1, in addition to further **important**/2 entries.

E 3.2.2   A sensible extension to the competence of this ELIZA prototype would be to provide her with some simple method of bridging between response patterns that refer to the same context. In other words it may help the dialogue if ELIZA could be seen to be 'talking about' a specific sort of thing across a few utterances. The clause **important**/2 already consists of important words that are organised around specific contexts where "mother", "father" and "brother" are important in the family context, whereas "mate" and "boyfriend" are important in the context of friends. So whenever one of the responses keyed to a particular context was used it would be possible to make a note of the name of this context. If ELIZA was stuck for a more specific reply at a later point she could find out which context was last referred to and use some sort of 'bridging' pattern to stimulate further discussion. An example pattern using this might look like the following:

```
pattern(99, X, ['I am asking the questions !', nl,
                'Tell me more about your ', Context]):-
        question(X),
        context(Context).
```

It will need a predicate 'change_context' that takes the new context and retracting the old one adds the new one. Clearly the same mechanism that is currently employed for the 'done' predicate could be appropriate here. The context should be changed whenever ELIZA comes across a word that is **important** in some new context. Do not forget to augment the `tidy`/0 program to reset any flags that you use, before beginning a new therapy session. The therapy session should obviously start with a specific context. Try changing this start context to see how it changes the direction of an interaction.

3.3.3 Evaluation of ELIZA

The ELIZA program is 'smart' in that it can robustly cope with mistakes and always has a reply - it doesn't just crash or say "I don't understand" when the user does something unexpected. However this is actually because it is able to completely **ignore** most of what it is told - reacting 'blindly' to a very few words. ELIZA searches for known patterns in the input and has a response when it finds one. So if one of the database patterns instructed it to just look for the word "hello" at the start of the input, then the reply "Hello there. How are you?" might, in some circumstances, be appropriate.

```
User  :  Hello eliza.
Eliza :  Hello there.  How are you?
```

This gives it a good tolerance for the flexibility of Natural Language.

```
User  :  Hello doc! Howya doin ... eh?
Eliza :  Hello there.  How are you?
```

but a poor tolerance for the conversational context. Indeed, utter rubbish would also cause ELIZA to respond in exactly the same way.

```
User  :  hello cdsf xxx 2d rt @£%cds eee sdsds
Eliza :  Hello there.  How are you?
User  :  I xxx 2d rt @£ they me you me you.
Eliza :  Why do you say that you xxx 2d rt @£ they you me you me?
```

As a program it clearly doesn't "understand" in any sense. It won't object if you misspell a word or make a grammatical mistake or don't even stick to the normal rules of grammar. It has **no** model of syntax, semantics, pragmatics, nor even conversation. Indeed it only has plausibility if you 'play the game' of therapist-patient. It works only because people are able to anthropomorphise - to attribute intention and intelligence to a performance that has some outward features that they can identify with.

According to McCorduck (1979), Daniel Bobrow tells this tale:

The Vice President of TeleComp Computing arrives at Bolt, Beranek & Newman in Boston 1968 on a Saturday morning at 9 am. He is hoping to talk to Bobrow but cannot find him in his office. However there is a note attached to a teletype computer terminal saying : "Type all messages into this teletype and end them with a Period.' Apparently, the Vice President assumes that this is connected with Bobrow, wherever he is.

Vice :   Can I use the computer this morning?
Com :   Why do you ask?
Vice :   I might be able to make some additional TeleComp sales.
Com :   Why aren't you sure?
Vice :   My prospective customers have never seen a demonstration of the system.
Com :   Does this mean very much to you?
Vice :   Of course it does.
Com :   You seem very positive about that.
Vice :   This is ridiculous.
Com :   What do you mean ridiculous?
Vice :   Is there any reason why I can't use the computer now?
Com :   Tell me more about your prospective customers.
Vice :   Please dial me up on 491-1850
            << Omits Period so no reply - VP phones Bobrow at his home>>
Vice :   Why are you being so snotty to me?
Bobrow :   What do you mean, why am I being so snotty to you?
...

Figure 3.4 Bobrow's Tale

Of course, the terminal was running a version of the ELIZA program, and true or not it is a very good story.

3.4 Beyond ELIZA

The programs BASEBALL & STUDENT were more serious attempts to get on without Language Understanding. BASEBALL (Green et al, 1963) had a database of facts about baseball games. It used pattern query 'templates' to 'understand' a question about the database.

Where did the dodgers play on June 7th ?

would be recognised as a query to the database of baseball games giving a team name and a date as entries and requiring the "PLACE" database entry because it associates the word "where" with the "PLACE" entry. Similarly it would associate "when" with the "DATE" and "who" with the "TEAM" entries.

Another pattern-matching program STUDENT (Bobrow, 1968) could match the standard elements of algebra problems (written in English) to work out what mathematical calculation was involved. So given the following problem:

"The gas consumption of my car is 15 miles per gallon. The distance between
Boston and New York is 250 miles. What is the number of gallons of gas used on
a trip between New York and Boston?"

the program would use patterns to extract the salient information from each sentence.

Eg.   1. The pattern "Xs per Y" refers to division where $X / Y = 15$ and $X =$ mile; $Y =$ gallon;

2. Something is 250 X's ; so the value for $X = 250$

3. So if it is safe to assume that the unknown is Y then use an algebra rule to work out from $250 / Y = 15$ that:

$$Y = 250 / 15$$

Clearly, it would be utterly trivial to confuse both of these programs. For example in STUDENT you could use 'per' not meaning division, or 'is' not meaning equation (as in 'per capita' and 'is interesting'), or introduce irrelevance such as the cost of the petrol and this would really ruin the simple assumptions that it needed to work. Again neither program is doing "understanding". They are like reading algebra and answering questions in a foreign language where you look for a few familiar patterns and ignore all "difficult" words.

The program PARRY by Colby, Webber & Hilf (1971) and Parkinson, Colby & Faught (1977) was more sophisticated again in that it included elements of "emotion" and other complex features. Where ELIZA was the doctor, PARRY was an attempt to model a "paranoid" patient. Again, the role was carefully selected to be one in which some "unusual" conversational features could be accepted. (Who expects a paranoid person to talk completely 'normally'?). Human paranoids have a delusive belief system and a feeling of persecution. Colby and others used the computer to examine how a paranoid conversation might work. The program was basically a pattern-matcher like ELIZA but it made some attempt to work on the patterns - to identify verbs and noun phrases for example. It changed verbs of different forms and tenses into a standard format so that they could be handled more generally.   On the other hand PARRY also had a limited model of itself and the other conversationalist. The program had sets of ratings like "self-esteem" which it could adjust according to whether the conversation 'went well' or not from its viewpoint, so it could even become "more (or less) paranoid" as the conversation progressed. The interviewer in the conversation could also be rated depending on what they said as friendly, hostile, dominating etc.

The following is an extract from a dialogue between a Psychiatrist Interviewer (I) and a very 'strongly paranoid' model of PARRY (P).

I :   Why are you in the hospital?
P :   I shouldn't be here.
I :   Who brought you here?
P :   The Police.
I :   What trouble did you have with the police?
P :   Cops don't do their job.
I :   What do they do instead?
P :   Cops arrest the wrong people.
I :   They arrest the right ones sometimes.
P :   The law should get those Italian crooks.
I :   Are you Italian?
P :   My background is British but I was born in this country.
...

Figure 3.5 An interview with the PARRY paranoid

The PARRY designers ran a set of Turing-like tests on psychiatrists, who were asked to rate the degree of paranoia of the 'patient'. In these tests 8 psychiatrists performed the interviews via teletype of 3 real patients and 2 models of PARRY (a strong and weak paranoid version). Later on 33 psychiatrists rated these transcripts. Now they were not told that a computer was involved as 2 out of 5 patients and they generally rated the PARRY interviews as reliably as the human interviews. That is, that they agreed with each other about how each 'patient' should be scored on various clinical scales. None actually stated that any patients were 'unusual' in any way.

In a later study, Colby (1973) explicitly asked a set of psychiatrists to identify the 'computer' transcripts from the human ones and found that the PARRY model was indistinguishable from the human patients. It is probably worth noting that a "normal paranoid" conversation is at best rather strange anyway!

Possible Advanced Projects on Pattern-Matching

Project 1.   Implement a different ELIZA.

An ELIZA program can make a convincing non-directive therapist - but how convincing could it be in some other roles you might imagine? Try to build a simple set of patterns for some other conversationalist. How about a computer-buff ELIZA, that can churn out lots of computer jargon and insists on talking about bits, bytes and floppy disc drives. Alternatively, how about a pop-music bore that insists on talking about the current hits and fashions in music?

The potential range of "one-sided conversationalists" to think up patterns for is endless - but you will find it very hard to make any conversation with them really convincing. If you try to extend ELIZA into another domain you will see just how good a choice of conversationalist the Rogerian non-directive therapist really is. There can be few better domains for features like 'echoing'.

Project 2.   Implement STUDENT, BASEBALL or PARRY.

It would be a mistake to invest too much time in developing any of the above projects in the name of cognitive science as the pattern-matching approach is very clearly limited. However one possibility is to take one program as a basis and attempt to re-implement it in a more principled way. PARRY is a good case in point in that the original program has developed subsequently with less and less reliance on the pattern-matching core and more on an approach to the syntax and semantics of the problem. The next two chapters may provide you with ideas for this.

Project 3.   The provision of 'cheap' database front-ends.

Whilst cognitive scientists tend to disparage pattern-matching alone as a principled method for natural language analysis it is worth noting that it has advantages as an easy and powerful technique in database front-end systems. In an application where there are only so many sensible things that can be done and only so many sensible ways to do them a pattern matcher can be easy to implement and robust, whilst more complex NL systems are rather experimental and fragile. If you were to implement a front-end system that communicated with a simple adventure-game for example a pattern matcher might be a good start. In a world where you can only PICK UP SWORD or KILL ENEMY or RUN AWAY then it may make more sense to look for these sorts of words in the input and ignore any of the detail or accompanying input. Unfortunately as the world gets more and more complex then this approach gets less and less satisfactory.

3.5   ELIZA Summary

Weizenbaum (1976) says that he has subsequently been very surprised (if not shocked) by the seriousness with which his experiment was treated. He now advocates that we be very wary of the risk of computers **dehumanising** some of the tasks to which they may be applied. For example, the idea of seriously replacing a human psychotherapist with a computer is an anathema from this point of view. Nevertheless, the reason that his program received such notoriety is simply because it could achieve a semblance of human dialogue with almost no theoretical effort.

So, could ELIZA pass Turing's imitation test for intelligence. Probably not. The system discussed is so inherently flawed that Turing's interrogator is unlikely to be fooled for very long. Having no model of a conversation the system cannot really keep track of what it is talking about and inevitably will jump wildly from issue to issue. Even adding a complex "context" mechanism as suggested in one exercise will not help it much. ELIZA doesn't actually "know" about anything, so any question asked by the interrogator would remain unanswered. Subsequent attempts to remedy some of these faults have used pattern-matching as a basis for answering database queries (BASEBALL), solving problems (STUDENT) and even to attempt a more serious model of the conversation and language (PARRY). A program like PARRY may well be able to perform much better in Turing's imitation test - and Colby may even assert that PARRY already has passed a version of this test through his experiments with Psychiatrists. However, this is missing the point. Even if a very sophisticated program based on the ELIZA-like matching of patterns was to consistently fool a human interrogator for some time could it really be classed as "intelligent"? That is, what would a 'pass' on the Turing Test really tell us about intelligence? The answer is of course, nothing much – in an ELIZA-like case it says more about the problem solving abilities of the human interrogator than the system on test! An ad hoc collection of rules and patterns is intrinsically flawed in that it does not have the necessary human **competence**. It does not solve the same problems that human intelligence **must** solve. The programs which came after ELIZA were advances in as far as they attempted to take on board the principled analyses of important features of human communication. Indeed PARRY's improved abilities arose through the adoption of techniques from parsing - such as identifying noun phrases and subordinate clauses. The real lesson of this work to an emerging cognitive science discipline is a warning that **performance alone is not sufficient**.

The obvious final experiment is to have the ELIZA computer therapist (E) converse directly with the PARRY computer paranoid (P), (reported by Berry, 1983).

```
P :   In my opinion you have a one-track mind.
E :   What makes you think I have a one-track mind?
P :   I used to go to the tracks every week.
E :   What does that suggest to you.
P :   I avoid racetracks now because the races are fixed.
E :   Is that the real reason?
P :   I'd rather not discuss it.
E :   What else would you like to discuss?
P :   That's something I don't want to go into.
...
```

Figure 3.6   The ELIZA therapist and PARRY paranoid

In this absurd example of the blind leading the blind, no "cure" is reported to have been effected.

3.6   Suggested Readings

Weizenbaum, J. (1966) ELIZA - a computer program for the study of natural language communication between man and machine. **Communications of the ACM**, 9, pp36-45

Greene, J. (1986) **Language Understanding - A cognitive approach**. OU Press. See Section 3

Boden, M. (1977 / 87) **Artificial Intelligence & Natural Man**. OU Press. See especially Section 3

Barr, A. & Feigenbaum, E. (1981) **Handbook of Artificial Intelligence**. Pitman, London.

Turing, A. M. (1950) Computing Machinery and Intelligence. In Feigenbaum, E. A. & Feldman, J. (eds) **Computers and Thought**. McGraw-Hill, NY. pp 11-35

Colby, K. M., Webber, S. & Hilf, F. D. (1971) Artificial Paranoia. **Artificial Intelligence**, 2, 1-26.

Parkinson, R. C., Colby, K. M. & Faught, W. S. (1977) Conversational Language Comprehension Using Integrated Pattern-Matching and Parsing. **Artificial Intelligence**, 9, 111-134

Chapter 4 : A Syntax Project

'Twas brillig and the slithy toves did gyre and gimble in the wabe'
(Lewis Carroll, Jabberwocky)

It often seems as though there are two different and irreconcilable positions that are taken by language understanding researchers, one advocating the primacy of syntax, the other arguing for the primacy of semantics. It seems obvious that both approaches need to be integrated in some ideal scheme, but in practice they can lead to some very different research themes. This chapter is concerned with the Syntactic approach and how something may legitimately be expressed. It begins by looking at the individual words in a sentence and how they may be combined. The purpose of syntax is to provide a decomposition structure which can show useful 'chunkings' in the parts of the sentence – which words and clumps of words go together.

4.1 Background - Chomsky and Syntax

In 1957 Noam Chomsky started a revolution in our understanding of the study of the Psychology of Language with the publication of his book "Syntactic Structures". The detailed implications of his work do not concern us here but the theme of the movement he started, emphasising the role and power of language **Syntax** has been very influential. If you read Lewis Carroll's famous poem about the Jabberwocky you will see that it contains many individual words that are patently nonsense and which you may never encounter in any other context than the poem. Our knowledge of English syntax however is not hopelessly confused by this novelty and imposes sufficient structure on it that it can be read and some interpretation placed upon it. For example, it is our knowledge of syntax which suggests that *toves* means that there was more than one *tove* in the above line and that these *toves* could be described as being *slithy* - even if we are unsure about exactly what this means!

The influence of syntax is just as apparent even if we only deal with words that do have a well known meaning. Consider Chomsky's famous example sentence **"Colourless green ideas sleep furiously"** which he used to demonstrate the **productivity** of language. He argued that noone would ever previously have used that sequence of words before, and thus destroyed almost at a stroke the behaviourist view of language learning expounded by Skinner (1957) which assumed that language was learned by the reinforcement of associations between words heard. Clearly, according to Skinner it should be impossible to create novel word juxtapositions, whereas Chomsky demonstrated that this is in fact an everyday feature of language production. Chomsky's demonstration sentence appears at first to be semantically very confusing — What does it mean for ideas to have colour? Can you do such a thing as "sleep furiously"? Could something be both colourless and green? However, it is actually only possible to ask such questions because the sentence has an interpretable structure due to the syntax of the English language which is automatically imposed upon it by the reader. In contrast, it is infinitely more meaningful than "ideas furiously green colourless sleep" or any other of the many random permutations of these words. Chomsky and many subsequent researchers have taken such a position to argue that the first point of entry into an understanding of human language was to determine the rules and regularities of natural language syntax. Chomsky's analysis has evolved and changed significantly over the years, but we take the view that such cumulative, evolutionary progress can only really be understood if its origins are understood. Consequently, we will consider only a simplified view of Chomsky's (1965) 'classic' views on syntax for the current project. Such was his impact on the field that these early ideas provide an essential overview of the syntactic position and form an essential prerequisite for understanding later developments. Chomsky noted that language understanding must proceed on a number of levels - moving downwards (as it were) from the symbols that we perceive to our understanding of their 'underlying' meaning. Two of the most important levels on the way towards meaning in this 'understanding' process are the 'Surface Structure' and the 'Deep Structure'.

Given any sentence, such as "John hit Mary", the first problem encountered by a language understander is to provide an initial structure for this sequence of symbols. This structure can be provided by the regulations of legitimate English syntax which can be represented as a set of rules (called a 'grammar'). A grammar states that some sequences of words are legitimate and that some are not. So if we compare "John hit Mary" with both "John kissed Mary" and "John green Mary", it is clear that 'kissed' is similar to 'hit' in a way which 'green' is not. Of course 'kissed' and 'hit' are verbs whereas 'green' is an adjective.

Chomsky used a grammar of English represented in a set of rules called **phrase structure rules** to capture the initial chunking of these words into phrases. A 'phrase' here is used to denote a collection of words which are grouped together based on their syntactic class. For instance, the sentence "The dog bit the man" comprises two phrases: "the dog" (which is called a noun phrase) and "bit the man" (a verb phrase). Each phrase can be further split into constituent parts according to a fairly small set of grammar rules, as described in the following section. This initial phrase structure, based only on the syntax of the language, he described as **Surface Structure**. Clearly the surface structure is not directly related to the meaning of the sentence — for instance a variety of surface structures (eg. "The man was bitten by the dog yesterday", "Yesterday the man was bitten by the dog", "The dog bit the man yesterday") can have essentially the same underlying meaning. In an attempt to capture the relationship between these surface structures of language and the meaning of the phrases Chomsky proposed that there was a level below the surface syntax (but above the semantics) which he called **Deep Structure**. All three sentences above would have the same deep structure, which may therefore be thought of as a 'canonical form' for that expression. The deep structures would act as syntactically based intermediaries between the logical meanings of the phrases and their appearance in the syntax of the language. So in summary : the 'meaning' level would capture the semantics of basic elements in language (eg 'a dog' being "an animal I saw in the street" and 'bite' being related to "teeth sinking into something" and so on); the 'deep' level would capture the relationship between these elements (eg where I mean to say that "A dog bit me yesterday"); and finally the 'surface' level would capture any legitimate syntactic expression of this (eg. "A dog bit me yesterday" or "I was bitten by a dog yesterday" or "Yesterday I was bitten by a dog" and so on). The basic process of generating legitimate natural language expressions then simply involved transforming the product of one level into another level. Chomsky proposed a set of complex rules which were called **Transformations** to capture the movement between these levels (a common transformation would be to transform from active to passive voice). Some of these Deep to Surface 'transformational' rules proved to be very complex and difficult to represent, so later workers based in the syntactic tradition have sought to eliminate the need for them and to include them directly in the 'surface' grammar. In this project we show how these simple surface grammars can be implemented and discuss how they may be augmented to directly capture some of the linguistic knowledge normally associated with the 'deeper' levels.

4.2   The Project - Augmenting a Phrase Structure Grammar

A sentence in any language can be considered to be made up of a sequence of *grammatical constituents* (see Figure 4.1 for some example English language constituents). These constituents can only be combined in a very few ways to make sequences that are legitimate in that language. The combination of constituents is governed by a set of **Grammar** rules that are described as the rules of the **syntax** of that language.

Figure 4.1   Example Constituent Phrase Structures of English Grammar

Sentence	(S)	the puppy found the child
Noun Phrase	(NP)	the puppy / the big bad wolf / an apple / life / he
Verb Phrase	(VP)	found the child / slept / flew the kite in the park
Prepositional Phrase	(PP)	in the park / on top / by the puppy
Noun	(N)	child, puppy, honesty
Verb	(V)	find, have, sleep, bite
Adjective	(Adj)	green, smart, lazy, big
Pronoun	(Pro)	it, he, she
Preposition	(Prep)	at, in, on, to, with
Determiner	(Det)	the, a, an (also known as Article)
Adverb	(Adv)	slowly, quickly, crucially

Each word in a language has a well defined 'role' or set of roles and these roles define the most primitive constituents (eg adjectives, nouns, verbs etc). The constituents can be combined into larger constituents or 'phrases' in only certain ways. So in English for example the sequence "sleeps he" breaks these rules whilst "he sleeps" adheres to them. The process of taking a sentence and analysing it as a sequence of more primitive constituents is known as **parsing**. The result of breaking down a sentence into its constituents can be drawn out as a tree-like structure to help illustrate the decomposition. This drawing is known as a **parse tree** or a phrase structure tree. It is an unambiguous representation of one decomposition of the sentence.

Figure 4.2   A parse tree

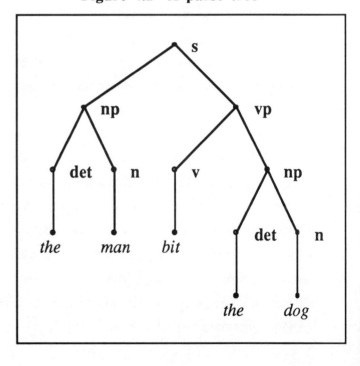

The parsing process can be described as the application of grammar rules which are sometimes called **phrase structure grammar** rules, **PSGs**, or **rewrite** rules. These grammar rules state which linguistic constituents can legitimately be combined with which other constituents and give this combination a name as another constituent. So in some sense the rules define macro-constituents. For example, a fundamental rule of such a grammar might be that :

sentence --> noun phrase then verb phrase.

This states that a sentence is a linguistic constituent which may be re-written as two separate (more primitive) constituents. eg. a sentence like "the man bit the dog" can be rewritten as

sentence([the, man, bit, the, dog]) --> noun_phrase([the, man]), verb_phrase([bit, the, dog]).

Furthermore, both the noun-phrase and the verb-phrase given can be re-written further into yet more primitive constituents. These rules are set out more formally in Figure 4.3 below, using the conventions that:

--> means *'may be rewritten as'*

(Constituent) means that the Constituent is *optional*

*Constituent** means that Constituent *may occur one or more times consecutively*

Figure 4.3   Phrase Structure Rules (rewrite rules)

(1)	S	-->	NP	VP		A sentence may be a noun phrase followed by a verb phrase.
(2)	NP	-->	Det	(Adj)*	N	A noun phrase may be a determiner followed by 0, 1 or more adjectives, followed by a noun.
(3)	VP	-->	V	(NP)	(PP)	A verb phrase may be a verb, which is optionally followed by a noun phrase, and/or an optional prepositional phrase.
(4)	PP	-->	Prep	NP		A prepositional phrase may be a preposition followed by a noun phrase.

It is possible to translate rules of this form fairly naturally into a Prolog-compatible form as shown below in Figure 4.4. The most primitive of the constituents - the words themselves - are normally considered to be separate from the rules and are represented in a lexicon or dictionary. The lexicon would state that a determiner was a word like "the" or "a"; that a noun was a word like "woman" or "cat" and so on. In the following Figure 4.5 the lexicon is written in the form of the rules themselves - for simplicity. The convention used here to show that a right-hand side constituent of the rule cannot be further decomposed (technically known as a **terminal**) is that it is enclosed in square brackets.

It must be noted that while the rules of Figures 4.4 & 4.5 are described as a "Prolog form" they are not "pure" or "raw" Prolog, because they do not correspond directly to the standard Prolog rules and facts that we have used so far. However the writing of grammars in this form is such a generally useful thing to do that it is better for the programmer to be able to write programs in this stylistic format and have a separate Prolog program which turns these rules into 'proper' Prolog later. One of the powerful features of Prolog is that we can write 'meta-interpreters'. These are Prolog programs which take Prolog programs as their input. The meta-interpreter here must take the parser rules and convert them into an executable set of 'raw' Prolog rules.

Figure 4.4   The Prolog form of the Phrase Structure rules of Figure 4.3

1		sentence	-->	noun_phrase ,	verb_phrase .
2	a	noun_phrase	-->	determiner ,	noun_phrase2 .
	b	noun_phrase2	-->	noun .	
	c	noun phrase2	-->	adjective ,	noun_phrase2 .
3	a	verb_phrase	-->	verb_phrase2 ,	prepositional_phrase .
	b	verb_phrase	-->	verb_phrase2 .	
	c	verb_phrase2	-->	verb .	
	d	verb_phrase2	-->	verb ,	noun_phrase .
4		prepositional_phrase	-->	preposition ,	noun_phrase .

Figure 4.5   A lexicon for the rules of Figure 4.4

5	a	verb	-->	[bit] .
	b	verb	-->	[sat] .
6	a	noun	-->	[man] .
	b	noun	-->	[dog] .
	c	noun	-->	[tree] .
7	a	adjective	-->	[big] .
	b	adjective	-->	[lazy] .
	c	adjective	-->	[green] .
8		determiner	-->	[the] .
9		preposition	-->	[by] .

System Note : It is important to remember that the grammar rule syntax is not "standard" Prolog. In fact it should be seen as a form of 'syntactic sugar' that makes writing and reading grammars easy. For example, it uses a rewrite arrow operator '-->' which is clearly different to the normal if-rule syntax operator ':-'. Your Prolog interpreter should treat them just as facts - based on the unusual predicate '-->' with two arguments (the right & left hand sides of the rewrite). It is the special feature of Prolog operator syntax which allows the system to understand the predicate and arguments combination in this easier to read form.

This operator syntax is controlled by the Prolog built in predicate op/3.

Using the grammatical rules and the lexical rules of Figures 4.4 & 4.5 sentences such as (S1) would be seen as legitimate.

(S1) The man bit the lazy dog by the big green tree.

As you can see the rules 2 & 3 from Figure 4.3 have been expanded into a number of separate rules for the Prolog form. This is because the summary phrase structure form in Figure 4.3 allowed optional and repeated components. In the rules given in Figure 4.4 the exact meaning of 'optional' and 'repeated' has been made explicit. In the case of rule 2 this could be read from Figure 4.3 as saying that a noun phrase NP may be rewritten as a determiner Det followed by an optional number of adjectives Adj and then a noun N. In this reading there may be either no adjectives or any number of adjectives in the noun phrase. In Figure 4.4 the bracket and star notation is not used, but the same meaning is written as three rules rather than one. Rule 2a states that a noun phrase must consist of a determiner followed by something which has been called noun_phrase2. This is a convenient name for a constituent which is entirely internal to the noun phrase rules and its definition is made up of the further two rules 2b & 2c. The rule 2b says that a noun_phrase2 may be simply a noun on its own, (which covers the case of no adjectives). However, if not then the rewrite rule 2c permits a noun_phrase2 to be made up of an adjective followed (recursively) by another noun_phrase2. Consider the example noun phrases from sentence (S1) as they would be parsed by rule 2 from Figure 4.4 :

(NP1) "the man"

Rule 2a would look for a determiner followed by a noun_phrase2. As we can see that "the" qualifies as a determiner by lexical rule 8 then what remains is for the rules to rewrite 'man' as a noun_phrase2. Rule 2b can rewrite from just a noun and as "man" is a noun by rule 6a this will succeed. So (NP1) is easily a legitimate noun phrase.

(NP2) "the lazy dog"

If we try to parse (NP2) as a noun_phrase we will again use rule 2a to find a determiner ("the" will do) and then must rewrite 'noun_phrase2' as "lazy dog". This time rule 2b will fail as "lazy" is not a noun, but rule 2c will find it as an adjective (by rule 7b) and must then find another noun_phrase2 as the word "dog". This is clearly recursive so 2b will be tried again - to find just a noun on its own, as "dog" is a noun by rule 6b.

(NP3) "the big green tree"

For noun phrase (NP3) rule 2c will recurse on itself twice, to find two legitimate adjectives, before finding a 'noun_phrase2' that is 'only' a noun. In this way these three sub-rules in the definition of rule 2 will cope with any number of repeated adjectives. Now if these rules were used generatively, to produce sentences, then this rule would be dangerous in that it is clearly open to the risk of infinite recursion. Fortunately however it is not intended to generate sentences but to parse existing ones.

Rule 3 for verb phrases uses this technique again to allow one optional prepositional phrase after a verb_phrase2 and to allow the verb_phrase2 to either be a verb on its own or to have one following noun_phrase.

>   (VP1) "bit the lazy dog by the big green tree"

This verb_phrase would be parsed by rule 3a using the following decomposition:

>   3a --> 3d and 4,   (ie the second type of noun_phrase2 and a prepositional_phrase)
>   3d --> 5a and 2a,   (ie a specific verb and a noun_phrase)
>   5a is the verb "bit" &
>   2a is the noun_phrase "the lazy dog" already discussed above as (NP2)
>   4 --> 9 and 2a   (ie a specific preposition and a noun_phrase)
>   9 is the specific preposition "by" &
>   2a is the noun_phrase "the big green tree" discussed as (NP3) above.

As complex as it may seem at the moment it is actually very simple when get the general idea. Having explained some of the important sub-pieces of the decomposition you should now see that the sentence given above as (S1) may be seen a a rewrite of rule 1, a noun_phrase which was discussed above as (NP1) followed by the verb_phrase just considered (VP1).

4.2.1 A Meta-Interpreter for Grammar Rules

We have already noted that the Prolog form of the grammar rules are actually just rather unusual looking Prolog facts (thanks to Prolog's operator definition mechanism). What is required is some means of translating these grammar-rule facts into a 'raw' Prolog that you can execute. There are two ways that this can be done: the first is to have a Prolog that has the grammar rule interpreter already built in; the second is to build a grammar rule interpreter of your own that will take these facts as input and output a more proper (but less easy to read) set of Prolog clauses.

1. If you are lucky then your version of Prolog has a grammar rule interpreter already built-in. These grammar rules may then automatically be turned into 'raw' Prolog rules by your Prolog system when it comes across them (during a 'consult' or similar or whenever it compiles the program). For example, in LPA MacProlog™ on the Apple Macintosh™ this happens automatically before you 'run' a Query, but you can force it to happen with the 'Check Program' item from the 'Eval' menu. The grammar rule interpreter takes each grammar rule and "expands" it into a "proper" Prolog form. The expanded form of the rules tells Prolog what to do with the words it is given in a list. That is, how to consume the constituent elements in the input list - and what is left over after they have been consumed.

The translated rules are normally accessed via a predicate such as `phrase/2`. Its first argument is usually a non-terminal word (eg. 'sentence') and a list or string of words to parse. The phrase predicate will then see if it can use the grammar rules to legitimately decompose/rewrite the non-terminal into the given list or string.

```
eg.    phrase(sentence, [the, man, bit, the, dog]).

       phrase(noun_phrase, [the, dog]).

       phrase(verb, [kicked]).
```

These should all succeed according to the rules above.

As we are primarily interested in parsing only whole sentences we will mainly use a predicate parse/1 which calls this `phrase/2` primitive. To begin with it may be defined very simply:

```
parse(L):-
    phrase(sentence, L).
```

2. If you are less lucky you must refer to Code Appendix 4.1 and build your own grammar meta-interpreter to do the above. You should diligently scour your Prolog system manual for references to things like 'Definite Clause Grammars' , 'grammar rules', 'special operators' and suchlike. If there is no help for you in your manual and no sign of your Prolog coping with the above grammar rules, eg. you try to load the above rules and get worrying error-messages, then you must implement Code Appendix 4.1 before trying again.

When you have eventually succeeded you will naturally be curious to see just what has happened to these nice clear grammar rules so that Prolog can directly execute them. To see what the 'raw' Prolog of these rules actually looks like query the built-in predicate **listing**. This should output to the screen a listing of all that Prolog has in its current database. Look at the rules that are printed out - can you recognise anything of the grammar rules that we had above? (Remember that underscore-number is Prolog's own internal format for variables). Basically the 'sentence' rule is translated into this:

```
sentence(XYZ,  Z) :-  noun_phrase(XYZ,  YZ), verb_phrase(YZ,  Z).
```

You should think of the two arguments to each predicate as standing for (i) the whole list to look at & (ii) what remains in the list after the phrase concerned has been found and "consumed". So this rule essentially means that the whole list of words XYZ is a sentence if you find a noun_phrase at the front of it and hand what is left - call it YZ - on to find a verb_phrase.

So if we recall the essentials of what the `phrase/2` query will be doing :

```
(?)   phrase(sentence, [the, cat, bit, the, dog]).
```

Its job is to construct a new query to be executed along these lines:

```
(?)   sentence([the, cat, bit, the, dog], []).
```

Which clearly means: find a sentence phrase in this list - leaving no constituents left over.

So if you think what some dictionary entries would look like:

```
noun([dog | T],  T).

verb([bit | T],  T).

det([the | T],  T).
```

then the input-output format and list-processing is quite evident. The first fact states that a noun is found where the input first argument is a list whose head is "dog", and that what remains to be considered is the tail of the list T. This clearly shows the idea of "consuming" constituents during the parse - as the noun "dog" (or verb "bit"; or determiner "the") can be consumed from the input leaving the output as the second argument.

This should be clearer if you consider what happens when you trace an example of this parser at work. You don't particularly need to do it, just look at the following example. The sample output is given below in a somewhat simplified and clarified format, in particular the noun and verb phrase2 rules have been replaced with ... to make it easier to see what is happening.

```
(?)    parse([the, man, bit, the, lazy, dog])

call: sentence([the, man, bit, the, lazy, dog], [])
    call: noun_phrase([the, man, bit, the, lazy, dog], _993)
       ...
    exit: noun_phrase([the, man, bit, the, lazy, dog], [bit, the, lazy, dog])
    call: verb_phrase([bit, the, lazy, dog], [])
       ...
            call: verb([bit, the, lazy, dog], _1160)
            exit: verb([bit, the, lazy, dog], [the, lazy, dog])
            call: noun_phrase([the, lazy, dog], _1170)
               ...
            exit: noun_phrase([the, lazy, dog], [])
       ...
    exit: verb_phrase([bit, the, lazy, dog], [])
exit: sentence([the, man, bit, the, lazy, dog], [])
YES.
```

The trace above is in the form of nested call/exit pairs. Your own version of Prolog may have a slightly different tracing mechanism, but the idea will be the same. In this simple form we can see what is given to Prolog as a call, often with uninstantiated variables, and anything that the call may itself need to call on before it can succeed. Eventually, if the call does succeed, it will have a matching exit message printed out to indicate the success, with any variables (hopefully) given a value. Do not be alarmed by the unusual symbols such as _1160 which are simply our Prolog's internal format for variables that it is using. For each new variable it generates a new number to keep track of the value of that variable, so any numbers which are the same in the above simply denote the same (currently unknown) thing.

You will note that after our initial query to parse/1 the main call is to sentence/2. This is the 'raw' Prolog form of the grammar rule noted above. The call to sentence takes two arguments: the first is the list of words to be parsed; the second states what should be left over after this list is 'eaten up' in the parse. In the case of the sentence we do not want any words to remain after the sentence has been consumed - so the second argument is [] an empty list. As we have indicated in the indented trace of this call there are two direct sub-calls from sentence (as the rule itself dictates), one to noun_phrase/2 and one to verb_phrase/2. The second argument to noun_phrase/2 is handed on as the first argument of verb_phrase/2 and represents what is left over from the original sentence after the `noun_phrase` has been 'parsed' - all of which should be a verb phrase. In the above trace our version of Prolog has replaced the variable names that we used in the rule with the internal underscore-number format : look for `_993` which eventually gets bound to what is left after the first `noun_phrase` is found; and `_1170` which eventually gets bound to what is left after the second `noun_phrase` is found, (ie `[]` - nothing).

Exercises 4.1

First we will work on the **Parser 0** program, a complete listing of which is given in Appendix 4.2. Make sure you have read the preceding pages and have either your own meta-interpreter for the rules from Code Appendix 4.1 or one which is already built-in to your version of Prolog.

Look at this basic set of grammar rules (as they are given in Figure 4.4 & 5 or from Code Appendix 4.2). Notice particularly the rules about specific words numbered 5-9 in Figure 4.5. Enter a few more nouns and verbs in the appropriate places (ie. enter new noun-defining rules at the bottom of the noun rules, verbs at the bottom of the verb rules etc). Make sure that the following words are classified as they are needed for the queries in the next question:

>   bit,   bought,   man,   dog,   kite,   shop,   red,   purple,   the,   a.

Now to try to parse some sentences! Try the following queries (note that the input sentence must be in list format - each list element separated by a comma).

>   (a?)   parse([the, man, bought, the, red, kite]).
>   (b?)   parse([a, man, red, bought, kite]).
>   (c?)   parse([a, man, bought, the, purple, kite, from, the, shop]).
>   (d?)   parse([the, man, bit, the, dog).
>   (e?)   a legal sentence of your own invention ...

You will notice it's not very exciting, answering **Yes** if the input sentence was parsed OK, **No** if it wasn't. Nor is this very informative. A 'Yes' answer doesn't tell us what roles were assigned to the words to make a legitimate parse. A 'No' could mean either that the lexical entry for one of the words is missing or that the sentence doesn't fit our current rules.

E 4.1.1 Enhancements. These phrase structure rules are by no means complete. Try modifying them so that the parser can parse the following queries:

>   (a?)   parse([he, bought, the, red, kite]).
>   (b?)   parse([she, walked, quickly]).

Hint. For the first query you need to parse **pronouns**. The appropriate rule will state that a noun phrase may be rewritten as a pronoun on its own. (You can't have either a determiner eg "the she" or any adjectives eg "green she"). Modify the sentence parser appropriately, then try the sentence.

For the second query you need to parse **adverbs** for which the rules are less easy - can you work it out for yourself? It could have something to do with verb_phrase2.

Do you understand why you cannot use this definition for this rule?

    verb_phrase2   -->   verb_phrase2, adverb .

E 4.1.2 Now try to find the limits of the phrase structure rules by constructing grammatical sentences which it fails to parse. How many different types of limitation can you think of?

4.3   Implementing a Definite Clause Grammar parser

The parser implicit in the phrase structure grammar rules above can be relatively easily **augmented** so that it can do a little more than just report on the legitimacy or not of a set of sentences. In this section we greatly improve the parser interface to make it easier to experiment with. In doing so we will also increase the power and potential complexity of the parser.

The rules we have considered so far are very simple because none of the constituent phrases in the parse are affected by any of the other constituent phrases around them. For example, the legitimacy of a noun-phrase cannot be affected by any features of a preceding verb-phrase - or indeed any other part of the sentence. However, many linguistic phenomena require that phrases are sensitive to their current context. Some features of phrases do affect the parsing of quite separate (and even very distant) phrases. You should note that in the examples given here and in the exercises that we will use the linguistic convention of marking phrases we consider grammatically illegitimate by following them with an asterisk. Consider these example phrases.

    (a) the dogs swim
    (b) the dog swims
    (c) the dog swim *
    (d) the dogs swims *
    (e) the dog that peter loves very much swims
    (f) the dog that peter loves very much swim *
    (g) a dogs ... *

Now, in phrases (a-d) above the *form* of the verb and the noun-phrase do affect each other, because whilst (a) and (b) are fine, neither (c) nor (d) is legitimate. To show that this effect can be quite distant, consider examples (e) and (f) in which the noun-phrase "the dog" and the verb "swim(s)" are far apart and could be separated very much further. In the same way, even within the noun-phrase the form of the determiner and noun affect each other as the illegitimacy of (g) indicates! The critical feature here is the number - *plural* or *singular* - relating to many or just one thing. For instance, whilst the determiner "the" can be either, the determiner "a" must be *singular* and cannot accompany a *plural* noun like "dogs". In English the agreement of plural or singular is important. There are many features of this sort like case, tense, gender, person and so on. In this section we introduce some augmentations to the simple grammar that makes it much easier to cope with these features. In the exercises at the end of the section we challenge you to use the new grammar to solve problems of transitivity and agreement.

Augmentations to provide such sensitivity include features such as extra arguments and curly brackets. The addition of arguments to the rules allows them to pass flags to each other or even more complex structures - like parts of a tree. The curly brackets can be used to enclose arbitrary pieces of 'pure code' that are not part of the rule itself. A parser augmented in this way is called a **Definite Clause Grammar (DCG)** parser. A full listing of a simple DCG program is given in Code Appendix 4.3. The new parse rules are computationally very different from the simple rules above in that they are very much more powerful. Power here refers to the ability to do things which the earlier type of rule could not do *even in principle*.

One useful feature of the DCG form is that it can store the roles of individual words in a separate set of dictionary definitions - the lexicon. This means that instead of a new grammar rule for each new word that is say a 'verb' - the curly bracket notation in the following single rule covers all verbs that are in a separate database definition.

```
eg.            verb   -->   [X] ,   { v(X) }.
```

This definition says that a verb is a phrase consisting of one thing which is primitive, called X, where the X is true of the Prolog query `v(X)`. In fact, the curly brackets contain 'raw Prolog' which can be executed when the rule is used. This code can be any Prolog code to perform any task - so whilst the example given is very simple - it could be anything. What happens is that the meta-program (written by you or built-in) does not try to "expand" the code in the curly brackets - it just adds it directly into the Prolog rule that it creates from the grammar rule.

Some augmented rules are shown in Figure 4.6, numbered for convenience. We have provided rules for pronouns (#2c) and adverbs (#4a, 5a & 5c). Note first that all the relations now take **arguments**. These arguments will initially be uninstantiated variables but once the parse for a phrase has been completed, the argument will be instantiated via recursion to the code for the constituent elements of the phrase.

Figure 4.6   A Prolog form of Definite Clause Grammar rules

```
1     sentence(s(N, VP))              -->    noun_phrase(N),   verb_phrase(VP).

2a    noun_phrase(np(D, N))          -->    determiner(D), noun_phrase2(N).

 b    noun_phrase(np(N))             -->    pronoun(N).

3a    noun_phrase2(np2(N))           -->    noun(N)

 b    noun_phrase2(np2(A, N))        -->    adjective(A), noun_phrase2(N).

4a    verb_phrase(vp(A, VP))         -->    adverb(A),   verb_phrase(VP).

 b    verb_phrase(vp(VP, PP))        -->    verb_phrase2(VP),
                                            prepositional_phrase(PP).

 c    verb_phrase(vp(VP))            -->    verb_phrase2(VP).

5a    verb_phrase2(vp2(V, A))        -->    verb(V),   adverb(A).

 b    verb_phrase2(vp2(V, N))        -->    verb(V),   noun_phrase(N).

 c    verb_phrase2(vp2(V, N, A))     -->    verb(V),   noun_phrase(N),
                                            adverb(A).

 d    verb_phrase2(vp2(V))           -->    verb(V).

6     prepositional_phrase(pp(PREP,NP)) -->    preposition(PREP),
                                              noun_phrase(NP).
```

% there are a set of rules about individual word roles and related definitions in the lexicon

```
7    verb( v(X) )            -->    [X],   {  v(X)   }.
8    adjective( adj(X) )     -->    [X],   {  adj(X)   }.
9    determiner( det(X) )    -->    [X],   {  det(X)   }.
10   noun( n(X) )            -->    [X],   {  n(X)   }.
11   pronoun( pron(X) )      -->    [X],   {  pron(X)   }.
12   preposition( prep(X) )  -->    [X],   {  prep(X)   }.
13   adverb( adv(X) )        -->    [X],   {  adv(X)   }.
14   conjunction( conj(X) )  -->    [X],   {  conj(X)   }.
```

Figure 4.7   A Lexicon for the rules of 4.6

det(the).	adv(quickly) .	pron(i).	adj(red).
det(a).	adv(carefully).	pron(it).	adj(very).
det(an).	adv(powerfully).	pron(he).	adj(good).
v(drove).	prep(by).	n(car).	conj(and).
v(was).	prep(to).	n(park).	conj(but).
v(sang).	prep(on).	n(jim).	
v(said).	prep(with).	n(lawn).	
v(hit).			

Don't forget that Prolog isn't using these rules directly as they are written. First the rules are translated by a meta-interpreter program into a 'raw' form of code that Prolog can understand directly, but which is rather harder to read. All that is required is that the meta-interpreter knows what to do with these extra features that we have introduced. What happens with the contents of the curly brackets is that the meta-interpreter must just take the bracket contents and treat it as 'raw Prolog' already - simply inserting it directly into the new rule that it creates.

The most obvious problem with **Parser-0** was that, although it did actually parse a sentence, it didn't show us the parse that it was doing. Now that the rules are allowed to have arguments it is very easy to get it to build a tree structure for us as it goes along. We can then print this out at the end to see what it found during the parse.

The parse tree that the rules return is a set of embedded clauses such as :

```
S =  sentence( np(pron(he)), vp( vp(verb(took), np(det(the),
            np(adj(big), np(adj(red), np(noun(kite))))))),
            pp(prep(from), np(det(the), np(noun(store)))))))
```

This is only readable if you can easily count brackets! The outermost brackets enclose the arguments to the predicate **sentence**. The sentence clause has two arguments: the first is **np** and the second is **vp**. Similarly both the **np** and **vp** predicates are quite complex clauses with arguments that are themselves further clauses. This form is used for the parse product because the clause form produced can be read as a 'tree' representing the structure of the parse.

So `sentence(A, B)` means that sentence is the root node of a tree with two branches.

Where `Branch A = np( pron(he) )`

&

Where `Branch B = vp(vp(verb(took), np(det(the), np(adj(big), np(adj(red),`
`np(noun(kite)))))), pp(prep(from), np(det(the),`
`np(noun(store)))))`

If we focus on branch B of **sentence** we can see that the same thing applies. In this case vp(C, D) states the vp is a node with a further two branches

```
Branch C = vp(verb(took), np(det(the), np(adj(big), np(adj(red),
        np(noun(kite))))))
```

```
Branch D = pp(prep(from), np(det(the), np(noun(store))))
```

In this way we could use this clause-tree form to draw out the 'upside-down' trees which we introduced as grammar parse trees above, (see Figure 4.2).

It is relatively easy to write a predicate that actually draws this clause out in a form which is more visually appealing. The program must simply take the clause-tree, take it apart, and print the predicate out to the computer screen with its arguments suitably indented.

Figure 4.8 A text printout of a parse tree clause

```
(?)   test_sentence([he, took, the, big, red, kite, from, the, store], S)

| sentence
    | np
        | pron
            | he
    | vp
        | vp
            | verb
                | took
            | np
                | det
                    | the
                | np
                    | adj
                        | big
                    | np
                        | adj
                            | red
                        | np
                            | noun
                                | kite
        | pp
            | prep
                | from
            | np
                | det
                    | the
                | np
                    | noun
                        | store
```

Note that this parse tree is printed on its side - with the root on the left hand side of the page and the branches growing from left to right. It takes a bit of getting used to, but is easier to follow than the underlying value of the parse tree (see S = ... above). Join the branches and leaves as appropriate (eg. join sentence to np and vp etc).

Technical Note :   The UNIV built-in predicate

This tree printing program will work with any Prolog that supports the built-in predicate '=..' (equals-period-period) which is commonly known as 'UNIV'. It takes two arguments: the first is a clause and the second is a list, where the general format is :

$$P(A, \ B) \ =.. \ [P, \ A, \ B]$$

so specifically :

```
fred(a, b, c) =.. X.       YES.   Where X = [fred, a, b, c].

X =.. [ hello, there ].    YES.   Where X = hello(there).
```

This enables the ready manipulation of clauses and their predicates. For example, clauses must always have a known number of arguments whereas lists can have an arbitrary number of elements when they are handled using the list-guillotine.

Some modern versions of Prolog will support sophisticated graphics that enable the output of much more tree-like versions of the sentence clause. These are very much easier to read and so we will use these in further discussions. The trees of Figure 4.9 below were produced by LPA MacProlog™ on the Apple Macintosh™.

A typical parse tree produced from the DCG rules given above will have a number of branches that may not be strictly necessary - that is, do not aid legibility. This is because the tree is a direct product of the path of the parser through the rules and some of these rules are pragmatically partitioned to prevent infinite loops. If we contrast the two trees in Figure 4.9 for example we can see that tree A was produced directly from the rules above whilst tree B is identical save that it is missing the 'extra' **vp2** & **np2** nodes.

Figure 4.9 Graphical versions of a parse tree

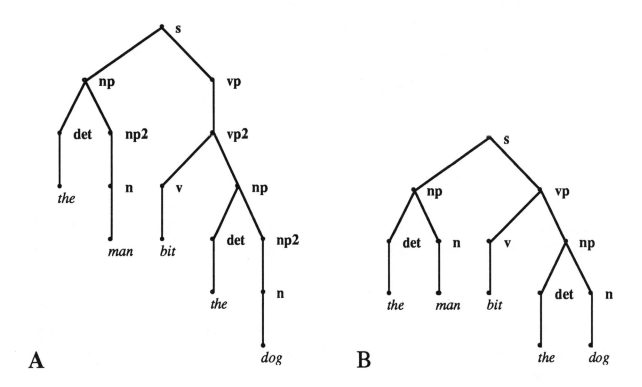

A

B

Exercises 4.2

E 4.2.1 Write down on paper the (non-Prolog) parse trees for the following sentences. You may use the simplified form illustrated in Figure 4.9 (B).

a)   the dog bit the man

b)   the man hated the cat

c)   he took the big red kite from the store

d)   the colourless green ideas sleep furiously

(Note in (d) we insist in our rules that nouns must have determiners!)

Now we will work on the **Parser 1** program from Code Appendix 4.3. Using the 'parse' query obtain the Prolog parse trees equivalent to the 4 sentences that you have just drawn by hand - you may have to type in the lexicon entries. Compare them with your hand-drawn trees.

E 4.2.2 Add some rules for Proper-nouns (ie names like "rod" and "peter"). Some entries in the definition **pn** (proper noun) already exist in the lexicon. The rule may look rather like the pronoun rule you already added - but don't forget the rule which tells it where to look for the lexical definition. It should now parse these:

a)   rod built the house.

b)   peter went up the hill

E 4.2.3 You may think that the trees produced are rather unnecessarily ugly with all these stray **np2**'s and **vp2**'s in them. There is a predicate (see definition D 4.4.4 in Code Appendix 4.4) that was written to condense the trees produced by this grammar into more attractive ones. Change the definition of the predicate 'parse' so that it uses `condense/2` to print a more compact tree.

Now that we can print out the parse trees produced the next simplest improvement to **Parser-1** is to allow you to type in sentences in normal sentence format rather than as list in the query. The required definition is as follows:

```
% parse/0 : reads in a sentence from the user and hands it on to parse/1
% put this clause just above/before the existing database definition of parse/1

    parse :- talk([please, type, in, your, sentence], S), parse(S).
```

This definition uses the predicate `talk/2` (see definition D 1.4 in the utilities Code Appendix 1) to read in a sentence, pick out the individual words and put them in a list format suitable for `parse/1`.

All you do is evaluate the query (?) **parse.** (no argument needed) and an interface is provided for you to type in.

E 4.2.4 Conjunctions are hard - so why not start with some simple rules that may only handle a very few cases ie Try to handle cases such as (a) and (b) below :

   a) rod **and** peter drowned slowly
   b) rod and peter drowned slowly **but** shouted loudly

   HINT : If your Prolog gives a message like "Out of Memory" then you have probably written a rule which is infinitely recursing upon itself! You may need quite a few new rules (that duplicate existing ones) that do not recurse.

E 4.2.5 Try to add some rules to cope with auxiliaries of verbs. These are in the lexicon under the definition of **aux**. The auxiliary is a word like "was" or "is" in a verb-phrase such as "was shouting" or "is singing". The verb parts in these cases are "shouting" and "singing" respectively, being a past participle of the verbs "to shout" and "to sing". You can't get the grammar to insist on a past participle yet - so don't try. Just make a rule that can put an optional auxiliary before a verb on its own (NB no following Noun Phrase is allowed).

Advanced Exercises 4.3

You can hack around with the set of grammar rules for quite some while - adding more and more rules to handle more and more legitimate phrases of English. However, for every legitimate structure that the addition of a new rule permits - it may well be allowing the grammar to handle dozens of illegitimate phrases also! Some of the advanced exercises suggest that you start to constrain some of the rules.

E 4.3.1   Improving the interface

As you've no doubt discovered, it's very irritating to have a parse fail merely because the word is not in the lexicon, and it's also fairly tedious to have to type in the lexical definition. A better parser would get around these problems by, before it tries to parse an input sentence, checking whether all the words are in the lexicon. If a word is missing it should ask you what its grammatical class is, and insert it automatically in the lexicon. This done it should get on with the parsing in the usual manner. Improving the interface to a parser to assist in its evolutionary development is an on-going commitment for, as in the next two exercises, once you improve the quality of the rules you may have to return to re-jig your helpful interface!

E 4.3.2   Verb restrictions

* The dog slept the man

Slept in this example is a specific type of verb known as 'intransitive' because it cannot take an object noun-phrase. If you consider a simple transitive verb such as 'bit' in a sentence like "the dog bit the man" we say that "the dog" was the subject of the verb whilst "the man" was the object of it. So a transitive verb requires both a subject and object, whilst an intransitive insists on only having a subject. Although the dog may sleep, it may not (as it were) sleep AT anyone or thing! This restriction about verbs can be seen as an extra piece of information stored with each verb entry in the lexicon. When the verb definition is checked in the parse this transitive/intransitive entry must force an appropriate rule to be used to either forbid or insist on an object noun-phrase.

E 4.3.3   Agreement

* A dogs ran away.

The problem with this example is that there is a lack of 'agreement' between the determiner and the noun in the subject noun-phase. The word "dogs" is plural (meaning more than one dog), whilst the determiner "a" is singular (meaning that there was only one thing). So whilst it is legitimate to have "the dogs" or "the dog" because the determiner "the" may be either singular or plural, it is only legitimate to have "a dog". As with the verb restriction noted above the word "a" must have a 'singular' restriction added which must be used by the rules to force the noun after "a" to be 'singular' also. This restriction means adding an extra argument to the definitions of all the determiners and nouns in the database - flagging each as either 'sing' or 'plural'.

Ideas for Advanced Projects

One possible advanced project would be to implement this parser for another language apart from English.

Another idea is to produce a parser that can make fragmentary parses. It is very frustrating to have a parse fail and just report NO without any indication of what it cannot cope with. In the above exercises we suggested that you attempt to implement a mechanism to trap 'new' words that are not in the lexicon. But how about parses which cannot be coped with by the current rules? It will almost certainly be the case that some fragment of the input can be dealt with by the existing rules. One idea for a project would be to consider how you could return a fragmentary parse for an illegitimate sentence, ie with some of the constraints of the grammar rules relaxed in some way. The first challenge here is think of what to relax and how. If the idea is to spot parts of an illegitimate sentence that the rules can deal with - in order to show which bits it cannot - then you might consider a strategy which searches for specific things in the input. For example you might look for noun-phrases first before attempting to combine them with surrounding constituents, and so on.

4.4 Summary

This project will not be more fully developed due to the excellent coverage of matters linguistic in Cognitive Science in the existing literature. For the general linguistic and Chomskian background Smith and Wilson (1979) is still a good read.   Allen (1987) is an excellent general text which provides a complete and detailed overview of the computational perspective of language understanding. A collection of original important readings, largely taken from the AI Journals, is provided by Grosz et al (1986).

We have covered only a tiny fraction of the linguistic tasks which would be required of a robust language understander. However, linguistic complexity is not the only problem which stands in the way. Here we have only considered a system that verifies the legitimacy of some very simple phrases and returns their syntactic structure - but an NL understander must also provide a semantic structure for the linguistic phrases. In the next chapter we examine a project that provides a radically different perspective on parsing. But before we leave the more "traditional parsing" we should note that much recent work has focused on the provision of a semantic structure alongside the syntactic structure produced in the parse. One common semantic structure used is the notion of the "logical-form". The logical form is a logical template attached to the phrase rules and in the lexicon. It can be combined into a logical expression during the parse (in the same way that the parse tree is constructed) and then evaluated according to some database definition. The program CHAT-80 (Warren and Pereira, 1982) is a classic DCG based example of a natural language front-end to a complex database of facts about world geography. The tutorial text by Pereira and Sheiber (1987) helps you build a simple CHAT-like system using logical form semantics. The text can be quite difficult to follow - but is very rewarding.

Finally, on the programming side we would highly recommend Gazdar and Mellish (1989) which provides a wide-ranging survey of NLP techniques. They have written a multi-lingual series on NLP in LISP, POP-11 and Prolog. The Prolog NL programming book is excellent, but rather sophisticated for the reader who has only got this far in our book.

4.5 Recommended Readings

Allen, J. Natural Language Understanding. Benjamin/Cummings, California, 1987.

Gazdar, G. & Mellish, C. Natural Language Processing in Prolog. Addison Wesley, 1989.

Grosz, B. J. & Sparck-Jones, K. & Webber, B. L. (eds) Readings in Natural Language Processing. Morgan Kaufman, Los Altos California, 1986.

Pereira, F. C. N. & Sheiber, S. M. Prolog and Natural Language Analysis. CLSI, Stanford, 1987.

Smith N, & Wilson, D. Modern Linguistics. Penguin, 1979.

Chapter 5 : A Semantics Project

The main aim of this project is to illustrate Schank's concept of a **script** by showing how a simplified model of **SAM** - the Script Applier Mechanism - could be implemented in Prolog. SAM shows how semantic, script-based knowledge can be used to put story events into a rich contextual framework. You should consider how well the computer theory, as it is implemented here, compares with the contextual knowledge actually used by people. The model also illustrates Schank's method of representing the underlying semantics of language as **conceptual dependency** relations.

5.1 Background - Representing Concepts and Dependencies

Over the years Roger Schank and his colleagues at Yale have developed a set of programs which emphasise the semantic nature of natural language processing. There are (at least) three aspects of the Yale approach which are of significance to us: minimal-syntax parsing; representing sentence meaning in semantic primitives; and emphasising memory structures as a context for understanding. These issues are actually independent of one another and each is theoretically interesting in its own right, but as we shall see the Yale team has bundled all three together in a very productive research programme.

The first aspect arises from the relatively slow progress of the syntactically driven parsing methods discussed in the last chapter. Syntactically driven research has tended to focus on the complexities of human language and has been forced into searching for increasingly complex linguistic rules. Semantically driven research suggests that it may be possible to move directly from the sentence to its meaning with the minimum of intervening syntactic effort. As language understanding is all about finding the meanings of sentences perhaps our parsers should focus on this first. Schank's team argues that in order to represent the **semantics** underlying language the meaning of a sentence should be represented in terms of the *primitive* concepts involved and the dependencies between them. The notation that they have suggested is therefore called **Conceptual Dependency**, (CD). Schank took the view that a primary need for understanding language is to determine what happened - what **actions** took place - and so actions or acts have a crucial role in his analysis. Consider for example the sentence **"The man took a book"**. Schank (1973) represented the essential underlying relationship visually as a "conceptual dependency diagram" as illustrated in Figure 5.1. This states that the act 'take' is connected to the main agent 'man' and that it is in the past, (from 'took'). Also we know that the object of the taking was the 'book'. One very desirable feature of this representation is that a sentence of equivalent meaning (eg. "A book was taken by the man") will have exactly the same concept and dependencies. In order to process this sentence the parser does not bother to build any intermediate structure like the parse trees discussed in the last chapter - instead it does the minimum syntactic work necessary. It can find the verb and must work out the 'primitive action' involved and then simply assigns the nouns either side of it to the appropriate roles for that action. In the case of the original (active) sentence - the agent is the noun to the left of the verb and the object is the noun to the right of it. In the case of the latter (passive) version (with "... taken by ...") the parser uses "by" to note the simple reversal of these roles! All that is constructed is a semantic parse - of the concept and its dependencies.

Now while the CD diagram seems to convey graphically the concepts involved and the dependencies between them, it is clearly possible to add further information simply from what we know about the 'take' verb as an act. So we could add, as in Figure 5.2, that the meaning of the verb 'take' includes the knowledge that the object of the act is transferred from somewhere to the agent of the act.

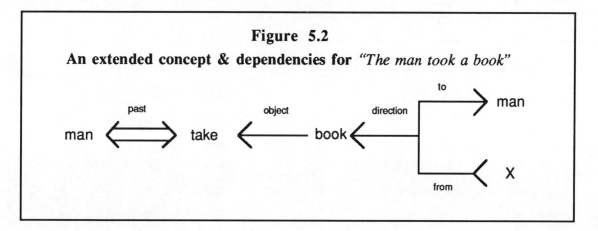

Figure 5.1 A simple concept & dependencies for
"The man took a book"

Figure 5.2

An extended concept & dependencies for *"The man took a book"*

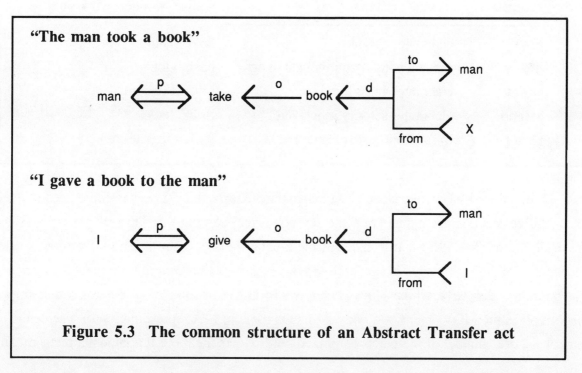

"The man took a book"

"I gave a book to the man"

Figure 5.3 The common structure of an Abstract Transfer act

In the added semantic information of Figure 5.2 the X is an unknown as we cannot say from our knowledge of taking - or from the syntax of the sentence where the book was taken from. Were the sentence to be "The man took the book from the shopkeeper" then the role X in the above conceptual diagram would be filled by the word 'shopkeeper'.

Schank noted that many different verbs seem to be highly related at some conceptual level. So for example, he would argue that the verbs 'give' and 'take', whilst they are used syntactically quite differently, both involve a common semantic act, the transfer of possession of something. In the two diagrams of Figure 5.3 he would suggest that the verb forms "give" and "take" should be replaced by the single semantic act that they both share in common. Schank would call it some sort of Abstract **TRANS**fer, or **ATRANS** for short, as it is the transfer of of an abstract thing - possession. This then would also be true for our understanding of many other verbs such as "steal" or "borrow" and so on. (NB In Figure 5.3 The "past", "object" and "direction" cases are shortened to "p", "o" & "d" respectively). Schank has suggested that almost all actions can be interpreted in terms of (one or more) of these **primitive actions** as discussed in Figure 5.4 below.

Figure 5.4   Eleven primitive actions, Schank & Riesbeck (1981)

	CD	Means		Examples
1	**atrans**	Abstract **TRANS**fer	(possession)	give, take, receive, sell, buy
2	**ptrans**	Place **TRANS**fer	(location)	go, walk, move, fall
3	**mtrans**	Mental **TRANS**fer		read, tell, forget, teach, promise
4	**ingest**	to take inside		eat, drink, breathe
5	**propel**	apply force to		hit, kick, pat, push
6	**mbuild**	Mental **BUILD**		realise, wonder, work out
7	**grasp**	elaborates acts like		hold, snatch
8	**move**	move a body part, involved in eg.		push, kick
9	**speak**	elaborates verbs like		say, tell, shout
10	**attend**	elaborates sensory inputs like		listen, look
11	**expel**	to send out (esp. of body)		puff, spit, sneeze

Acts 7-11 are labeled 'instrumental acts' by Schank and Riesbeck (1981) as they are used to qualify the 6 primitive acts (ie. they explain *how* the act took place). So the verb "to see" can be considered as basically an MTRANS in that it involves the mental transfer of information from the world to someone's mind, but it clearly also generally involves the ATTENDing of that person's eyes to the visual stimulus. Similarly, whilst a kick is clearly a PROPEL of something towards something else, it also involves the MOVEment of a body-part such as 'foot'. A representation of a sentence may often consist of a number of these acts combined, with 1-6 as the more fundamental ones, modified by the rest.

Further modifications of the CD may well be required to represent the variety of other aspects of the information contained in a sentence. This information may refer to simple syntactic details such as the tense and time of an act. It may also include complex semantic information: about any *states* that are involved, eg that "kill" is a state changing act which turns alive into dead; or whether any of the roles involved have any *features* mentioned eg. the noun phrase "John's dog" refers to a 'dog' which has the feature of being possessed by 'john'; or if any *causal* links are necessarily implied eg. that X happened "because" of Y; and so on. Schank suggests that much of this information, particularly the semantic implications of an act, can be embedded in the dictionary entries for each verb-as-an-act.

The semantic richness that this adds to the parser is easily illustrated by looking at an example. Consider the simplified dictionary entry, shown in Figure 5.5, for the verb "hit" as it might be understood as a PROPEL act. This basic entry states that the Agent of the act is doing a PROPEL. The small 'o' arrow indicates that what is being propelled is the Object and that the direction of the act (the 'd' arrow) is from the Agent to some Recipient. However, in this example we have shown an extra "causal" arrow (marked using three lines in the arrow) which indicates that a necessary inference of the verb "hit" as a PROPEL is that the roles for the cases Recipient and Object come into PHYSCONT - ie physical contact!

Now consider how one might represent the 'meaning' of the sentence such as **"Mary hit John"** according to the CD dictionary entry in Figure 5.5 for 'hit' as a PROPEL. This is shown in Figure 5.6. The agent of this PROPEL act is the noun-phrase to the left of the verb: 'Mary', ie the one doing the hitting. We might hope to find what she is using as the hitting object, perhaps after a word like "with ..." but cannot. So as we cannot say what is being propelled, it is labelled as an unknown (variable X) in the diagram. However we can say that the direction of the act is from 'Mary' towards an individual named in the sentence as 'John'. In addition we can also bring along a causal inference in the lexical entry - that a consequence of the act will be that the individual 'John' and whatever was being propelled X will come into physical contact.

If you examine the diagram in Figure 5.7 representing the meaning of a very similar sentence, "Mary punched John" you can see that the dictionary entry for the verb "punched" as a PROPEL act insists that the object of the act is a 'fist' which means that we also know what comes into physical contact with 'John'. Because this type of PROPEL act is so much more specific than a general "hit" we can add that the **instrument** ("i") of the act is itself as a **further** act which typically involves Mary MOVEing a part of her body, ie her fist.

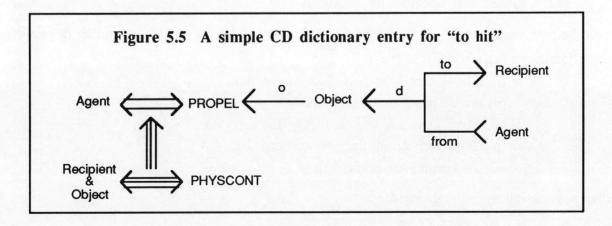

Figure 5.5   A simple CD dictionary entry for "to hit"

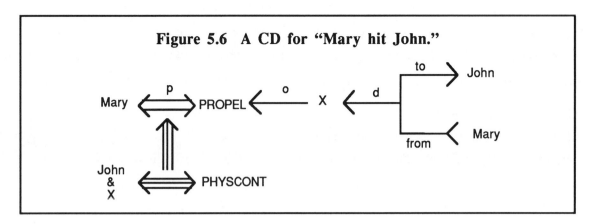

Figure 5.6 A CD for "Mary hit John."

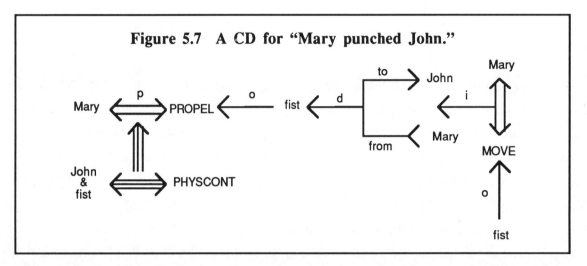

Figure 5.7 A CD for "Mary punched John."

The early work of the group led by Schank was presented in the system MARGIE (Memory Analysis Response Generation and Inference in English). The MARGIE system included a semantic parser which made an attempt to render an English language sentence into the semantic notation of Conceptual Dependency. This parse produced a semantic parse like the arrow diagrams illustrated above. Next the system added even more knowledge to the CD representation based on plausible inferences about the motivations and effects that are often attached to primitive acts like 'hitting'.

So for example the sentence,

Mary kissed Bill because he hit John

could be represented as a set of PROPELs and MOVEs and it could have a number of plausible (causal) inferences attached to it such as :

    (i) Bill's hitting John caused John to be hurt.
    (ii) John's being hurt pleased Mary.
    (iii) Mary's pleasure was caused by Bill's action.
    (iv) Mary feels positive emotion towards Bill.
    (v) This causes her to kiss him.

Other possible inferences might include :

    (vi) John may fall to the ground.
    (vii) John may become afraid.

Unfortunately for this approach it is very difficult to know where this chain of inferences may reasonably be extended and how far you can go. Indeed one of the many other possible inferences that may be attached could even be that :

<blockquote>(viii) Bill may receive an Olympic Boxing medal.</blockquote>

The essential difficulty is that the system is vulnerable to an **inferential explosion**. That is that it cannot easily tell when to *stop making inferences* to add to the initial parse. Subsequent work attempted to contain this explosion by providing an explicit story context which can inform the system about the range of inferences that are reasonable in certain types of situations.

5.2   The Project - a Script Applier Mechanism

In this project we are going to focus primarily on the role of the story **context** in understanding sequences of natural language sentences. We will show how this context can be represented as a human **memory** structure and can be used to state explicitly which inferences are legitimate ones to make - and thus avoid an inferential explosion.

Consider the the following short story:

Story 1:   Zoe walked to Pizza Hut. She had a Deep Pan Vegetarian. Then went to the cinema.

Adults easily make the inferences necessary to answer questions such as:

> *What sort of place is "Pizza Hut"?*
> *What did Zoe eat?*
> *Who took Zoe's order?*
> *What other events most probably took place?*

and so on.

Schank has argued that people can do this because we have knowledge relating to **stereotyped** situations which: (a) organises the knowledge necessary for comprehension of stories; (b) indicates what behaviour is appropriate; and (c) allows us to fill in omitted details. Schank called this knowledge a **script.** This concept is the core of his Script Applier Mechanism, **SAM.**

A much simplified account of a stereotypical trip to a restaurant is shown as Script 1 here :

Script 1: A Restaurant Script

event 1. Actor goes to Restaurant
event 2. Actor goes from Door to a Seat
event 3. Actor tells the Waiter the Order
event 4. Actor eats Food from a Plate
event 5. Actor gives Money to the Waiter
event 6. Actor leaves Restaurant

This sequence of general events is represented in memory and when a specific story is to be understood the script is activated and used to guide the understanding of the story. Consider our example story above:

Story 1

event A. Zoe walked to Pizza Hut.
event B. She had a deep pan vegetarian.
event C. Then went to the cinema.

The first problem is to 'trigger' the correct script in memory. In principle there could be many different scripts for many different stereotyped events - like going to the shops, going to work etc. The simple solution to the trigger problem adopted by SAM is to just look for special words in the story. So the program looks to see if any of the words used is stored as a "trigger" for any of the known scripts, in our case we might store "Pizza Hut" as a good restaurant trigger. Once we had decided which script to use then all that remains is to **match** events A-C in the story with events 1-6 in the script. In the above example we would have a match with A=1, B=4 and C=6. One obvious benefit from so good a match is that we can say that the intervening events such as 5 - paying for the meal - which were not explicitly mentioned, very probably occurred in this story as they do typically occur in these situations. Notice that there is much that we could do to usefully extend this simple script. For example we have clearly omitted an important act between events 3 & 4 ie. Waiter brings the Food from the Kitchen.

The stages in a session involving SAM can be summarised as:

Stage 1: Input of natural language story.
Stage 2: Translation of story into conceptual dependencies
     - not all the role 'slots' will be filled for every 'event'.
Stage 3: Script Triggering
     ie. one of the filled slots in the input story should trigger an "empty script".
Stage 4: Script Application
     - use of the script context to fill the empty slots in the input story
     & elaboration of the story to include the other events included within the script.
Stage 5: Natural language output
     eg Translation back into English of a 'disambiguated' story
          with a more general understanding of the other likely events.

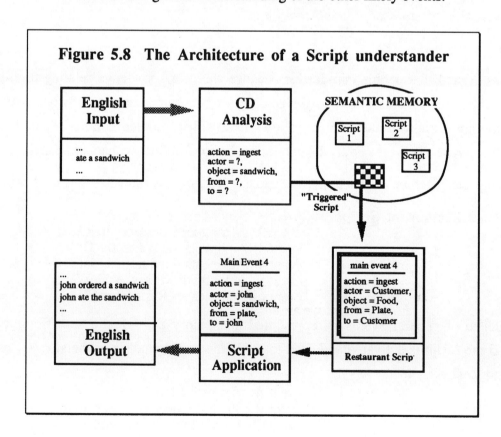

Figure 5.8   The Architecture of a Script understander

Other stages could certainly be added to this - for example a stage 6 in which another program answered questions about the story - based on SAM's understanding of it, etc. These stages are illustrated graphically in Figure 5.8. Note that this is not an accurate reflection of the original program architecture - but a simplified view which we use to illustrate our approach to this project.

5.3 Implementing the SAM Project

In implementing a simplified version of SAM by far the hardest stage for us is the first one - translating natural language into CDs. We will finesse this problem by doing the parse 'by hand' and by restricting ourselves to very simple sentences and a simplified conceptual dependency. We could represent a number of complex features explicitly in our acts including tense, amounts, the gender of human entries and so on, as does Schank. However, to make things easier for this project we will be using a very simplified version of the CD representation - with very few features and no extra instrumental acts. As it happens, actions 1 to 5 in the table of 11 acts shown in Figure 5.4 all follow a similar format with 4 essential role 'slots' so we shall adopt this format for the project. Each action must have an agent, an object, a from-direction and a to-direction. The user must imagine themselves in the role of the parser - locating the main act-verb and then assigning the surrounding noun phrases to the correct slots. Figure 5.9 illustrates a number of examples to give you the general idea.

Figure 5.9 Table of CD role slots

action	agent	object	from	to	English
atrans	john	book	john	mary	john gave the book to mary
ptrans	john	john	pub	home	john walked home from the pub
mtrans	john	information	book	john	john read the book
ingest	john	beer	glass	john	john forced down a swift beer
propel	john	ball	penalty spot	goal	john struck home the penalty

Clearly we have oversimplified the parsing problem in the above examples. Much of the richness of the natural language sentences appears to have been lost in the conversion to primitives. For example: "John staggered home from the pub" and "John strolled home from the pub" are both clearly forms of PTRANS with the same filled roles, however each carries different implications. Much of the syntactic richness is relatively easily captured by adding a variety of qualifiers to the CDs as indicated in the diagrams - but here we are after simplicity. The parsing of English into Conceptual Dependencies is actually not at all easy and itself requires the application of quite a bit of knowledge. Consider for example the understanding of a sentence containing a highly flexible verb such as "to take". Eg. "Mary **took** the train to the next town." Here the main action is a PTRANS of Mary where 'the train' is the thing that is actually doing the "taking" rather than 'Mary' as the syntax could imply. Compare this with the sentence "John **took** some aspirin" where the main action is an INGEST. Or the sentence "John **took** offence at the remark" where the action is probably some sort of MBUILD and where we are referring to some feeling or thought that John makes about some MTRANS (remark). Here the trouble for the parser arises from the many different roles that "took" can **take**.

A glance at the table of the 11 primitive actions and the CD diagrams indicates how much knowledge would have to be represented explicitly to be able to parse such sentences as "John struck home the penalty". On the other hand the final stage 5 isn't too bad - it's quite easy to translate CDs back into a rather crude English! The specification therefore will be that our project SAM takes input in the form of CDs and then complete stages 2 to 5.

5.3.1 The knowledge representation

(i) CD form for a single 'act' (ie. one CD)

We have to represent the CDs in Prolog. Since the **action** is the focus of the CD representation for an event, we adopt the notation act(Number, CD, ListOfSlots) thus, given that all our CDs have 4 fixed role slots, we have :

```
act(N,  CD,  [Agent,  Object,  From,  To])
```

for each event.

For instance, the event *"John gave the book to Mary"* would become:

```
             CD          Agent Obj    From   To
   act(N, atrans, [john, book, john, mary]).
```

This code states that there was some act N that consisted of an abstract transfer. The roles related to the ATRANS are filled by a list of four elements stating that 'John' was the agent of the act and 'book' was the object; also that the direction of the act was from 'John' to 'Mary'.

Slots may be **filled** (as above) or **unfilled** (ie. the filler is not known).
Eg. *"John went to the cinema"* would be represented as:

```
   act(N, ptrans, [john, john, X, cinema])
```

Note that the filler X for the empty slot (where John went from) is represented as an uninstantiated variable. So, whilst we know that the PTRANS act involved 'John' taking himself to the 'cinema', we do not know from where the act began.

The idea is that by accessing the stereotyped knowledge of the relevant script it may be possible to instantiate such variables - give them a value - as is discussed below.

(ii) CD form for a story

We represent a story as a 2-argument predicate story(N, S). Where N is the name of this story eg. test1 and S is a **list of events** [event1, event2, event3 ...], where each event is a predicate coded as above. So, for example the English Story *"John went to Pizza Hut, ate a pizza and left"* could be represented as the list of three events, A, B & C.

```
Story 2: story( test1,
                [    act(A, ptrans, [john, john, _, pizza_hut]),
                     act(B, ingest, [_, pizza, _, _]),
                     act(C, ptrans, [_, _, _, _])
                ] ).
```

The role of the parser - that we are fulfilling by hand ourselves here - is to detect the acts; classify them as some CD primitive and fill the appropriate slots. So we can say that the first act mentioned A, is a form of PTRANS that 'John' must have been both the agent and object of and that this act was **to** 'pizza_hut' (although where **from** is unstated in the story). The second act is an INGEST, but we can only say it involves a 'pizza' as its **object**. For the final act we can only say that 'left' is from the verb "to leave" and is therefore a PTRANS sort of act where all the possible roles are unknown from the given syntax. So the story actually reads like this

> "John physically transferred John from somewhere to Pizza Hut; someone ingested a pizza; and finally someone physically transferred something from somewhere to somewhere else".

It is important to note that at this stage the CD representation **cannot** infer that it is 'John' who ate the pizza, since this is not made **explicit** in the text. Clearly a 'pizza' is ingested, as the sentence does say "ate a pizza" which means that a pizza must have been eaten by someone - but to say *who* we would have to bring in *extra knowledge that is not given explicitly*. It is arguable that we could use knowledge about the verb "to leave" to say that it always involves a person moving themselves and thereby instantiate the first two roles of the last act C to the same variable name. This very much depends on just how much knowledge we are to attribute to our parsing module. However, it is clear that the parser would have to be *very* much smarter to know that it was 'John' rather than just the same unknown in both roles.

A note on the use of the **anonymous variable** in our CD representation.

It is worth pointing out the significance of the underscore in story2. You will recall that as a word on its own the underscore is treated as a special form of variable which saves you thinking up different variable names for entities which are **unknown** and all (possibly) **different**. We normally give names to variables so that when they are bound to something in one place we can use that value in another place. We cannot use the values of the slots in the lists above because - for all we know - they could all have different values. Of course we could give them names, for example the first underscore could be called *Fromsomewhere* as it is the *from* slot in a 'ptrans'. BUT the *from* slot in the 'ptrans' of act C must be called something else. If we used the same variable name - Prolog would insist that they meant the same place. This may well be true - but we cannot know this from just the syntactic parse of the input story! The underscore variable is handy here because it is the equivalent of "**I don't care** what its name is - it's just some anonymous unknown". So, if we did feel that the parser would know that the verb "to leave" always involved a PTRANS where the agent and object were always the same thing we could give both roles the same variable name

eg. `act(C, ptrans, [X, X, _, _])`

in the story above. The great danger in forcing the parsing module to do too much here is that you can **leave** it unable to cope with some perfectly legitimate constructions. Eg the use of 'leave' in the last sentence or "he left the pencil on the table". Neither of these uses of the verb "to leave" involves the agent acting on themselves.

(iii)   Script representation

We'll build this up in stages. The script for a particular sequence of events may be represented as a fact: `script(Name, [Event1, Event2, ... , FinalEvent ])`

This indicates that the script of some Name consists of a list of CD-based actions, with one CD-act per 'event line' of the script. A restaurant script in Prolog would consist of the following sequence as above:

  1 Actor goes to Restaurant
  2 Actor goes from Door to a Seat
  3 Actor tells the Waiter the Order
  4 Actor eats Food from a Plate
  5 Actor gives Money to the Waiter
  6 Actor leaves Restaurant

```
% ACT      CD         Agent   Object  From      To

script(restaurant,
  [
  act(1, ptrans, [Actor, Actor,  PlaceX,   Restrnt]),
  act(2, ptrans, [Actor, Actor,  Door,     Seat]),
  act(3, mtrans, [Actor, Order,  Actor,    Waiter] ),
  act(4, ingest, [Actor, Food,   Plate,    Actor]),
  act(5, atrans, [Actor, Money,  Actor,    Waiter]),
  act(6, ptrans, [Actor, Actor,  Restrnt,  PlaceY])
  ]).
```

This script definition is a fact in Prolog, (a single unconditional clause), and so any variables in it which share the same name must represent the same thing! So when a named variable in this clause is bound to some constant all subsequent references to that variable name **in this clause** will automatically share that value. This means that by making the variable `Actor` the **agent** in all the acts we are saying that as soon as we know who is the **agent** of any act - we also are saying that the same individual is the agent of them all! Also we can assume that the value of the *to* slot of the first ptrans (called `Restrnt`) will be the value of the *from* slot of the last, ie you go to a restaurant - when you leave, you leave from the same place.

(iv)   Script Triggering

The first stage after CD analysis is finding an appropriate script. This must be done by one of the concepts in the story 'triggering' one of the many possible scripts. For each script in memory we must specify a trigger word or words. This is a word which when found as the 'filler' of any slot in the story will cause us to use some particular script to understand that story. In the following we are saying that 'pizza_hut' and 'waiter' will cause us to think of restaurants.

% trigger(F, SNa) means that the filler F triggers the named script SNa

```
trigger(pizza_hut, restaurant).
trigger(waiter, restaurant).
```

Exercises 5.1 : Conceptual Dependency

We will be 'hand-coding' English input into CDs for SAM to understand. It is very important to bear in mind the limitations of the parsing process, and not do too much work as a parser. So whilst we - as people - may 'know' a great deal about what something means, it is important to ask yourself if we - as 'dumb' parsers (guided only by a limited knowledge of syntax), would also know this! As a human CD parser we should recognise the verbs and find the correct conceptual dependency to use and also be able to "look around" the verb to fill the roles of Agent/Object/From/To if (and only if) they are explicitly given in the sentence.

E 5.1.1 Code the following individual sentences into Prolog CDs - if it is not clear what the filler for a slot should be, leave it as an anonymous variable.

a) john walked from the door to a table	hint:	ptrans
b) john walked to a table		
c) the waiter took john's coat	hint:	atrans
d) john ordered beef	hint:	mtrans
e) john left for the pub		
f) mary had a drink of beer from a mug.	hint:	ingest
g) the waiter brings food from the kitchen		

E 5.1.2 Code the following story as a list of Prolog acts.

> "Zaphod went to Milliways, the restaurant at the end of the universe. After having a steak, he tipped the waiter one Arcturan mega-dollar and teleported to Betelgeuse."

5.3.2 The main inference predicates in the SAM1 program

The very first relation to define is a high-level predicate which can conveniently be used to pass the detailed arguments on to the important inference predicates. In this way we will define **test_sam1**/1 as a predicate which runs the SAM1 program on the story that is named by its one argument.

% test_sam1(N) says pick a named story N and "SAM Understand" it.

```
test_sam1(Name):-
    story(Name, Story),
        nl,write('Input Story = '), write(Story), nl, nl,
    sam1(Story, Understood_Story),
        write('Matched Story = '), write(Story), nl, nl,
        write('Matched Script = '), write(Understood_Story), nl.
```

Much of the above predicate is involved in input/output operations that report what is happening. Indeed only two lines are not concerned with this. The predicate is normally called with its argument Name bound to the name of a particular database story, eg. 'test1'. The first line involves looking up this story in the database - under the predicate **story**/2 and binding the variable Story to the list of

CD acts that is involved. On line three this list Story is handed on to the predicate **sam1**/2 which then returns the variable Understood_Story bound to the new story after SAM1 has matched it with a script. The definition of **story**/2 has already been discussed. Clearly the predicate which organises most of the inference work of this project is **sam1**/2. This is a complete program which takes input in the form of a CD story, finds an appropriate script, and fills in as many of the uninstantiated variables as possible - given what was made explicit in the input.

% sam1(IS, SE) this means that script events SE describes inputstory IS according to some script.

```
sam1(InputStory, ScriptEvents):-
    find(InputStory, ScriptName),
    script(ScriptName, ScriptEvents),
    match(InputStory, ScriptEvents).
```

This predicate takes the list of CD acts called InputStory and hands this on to **find**/2 which tells it the name of an appropriate script to apply. It then calls **script**/2 with the name it has found in order to get a list of ScriptEvents that describe the events that typically happen in the ScriptName situation. Finally it hands both the story and the script events on to the predicate **match**/2.

% find(InputStory, ScriptName) means trigger a ScriptName for the InputStory.

```
find(InputStory, ScriptName):-
    member(act(_, _, Slots), InputStory),
    member(Word, Slots),
    nonvar(Word),
    trigger(Word, ScriptName).
```

The predicate **find**/2 works by finding any constant in the InputStory which can perform as a trigger to a script named by ScriptName. It uses the standard predicate **member**/2 to generate in turn each member of the roles slots of each act of the input story. This gets the specific words used in each slot and tests to see if any word is registered in the database as a **trigger**/2 - and if so of which script. The first use of member generates each act that is a member of the story. For instance, for the story `test1` the first act to match would be act A, and `slots` would be instantiated to `[john, john, _, pizza_hut]`. The second use generates the member of each role of that act, so for `test1` the fillers `john`, `john`, `_`, & then `pizza_hut` would be generated in order. The use of the Prolog primitive **nonvar**/1 is to filter out the role slot members that are variables (such as the underscore variable in act A of the test1 story) - by insisting that it must be a specific word. Then the final line calls **trigger**/2 to see if the word is a trigger for any script. Hence for `test1` the slot filler `pizza_hut` would be the first (and only) trigger, triggering the script 'restaurant'.

The final predicate missing is the core working predicate that "matches" the input story with the triggered script. This predicate is called **match**/2 and it is a very simple recursive list-processing predicate that relies for its success on exploiting the features of the logical variable in Prolog. In essence it could alternatively be described as an 'ordered subset' or something of the sort.

% match(InputStory, ScriptEvents) means that InputStory is a sub-sequence of Script.

```
(i)      match([], _).
(ii)     match([Ln | RStory], [Ln | RScript]) :- match(RStory, RScript).
(iii)    match(Story, [_ | RScript]):- match(Story, RScript).
```

This says that a match of a script with a story is true given that each 'line' of InputStory can be matched with a 'line' of the ScriptEvents. The first clause is the "stopping check" which states that a match is complete if the story list is empty. The script can have anything still in it at the end as is indicated by the anonymous variable. This means that a story that only mentioned John going in to the restaurant and eating - and which neglected to include his leaving would still be understandable. The second and third clauses of the definition guillotine the first event off the script and recurse on the remainder of the script. Clause (ii) succeeds if the script event can match the current first line of the story (enforced by the use of the same variable name Ln for both). If they can match then the whole match is true if the remainder of the script RScript and the remainder of the story RStory can be matched recursively. The final clause simply throws away the current script event thus adding the ability to omit script events not mentioned in the story. This means that a story need not explicitly mention the paying for the meal etc so long as it matches the rest of the script.

```
              {Story}                  {Script}
(?i)     match([a, b, d, g],  [a, b, c, d, e, f, g]).    YES
(?ii)    match([a, b, z, d],  [a, b, c, d, e, f, g]).    NO
(?iii)   match([a, b, d, c],  [a, b, c, d, e, f, g]).    NO
```

Consider these direct queries of the above definition. If the script is seen as the larger list of ordered letters then the story may be seen as the shorter list of letters. In (?i) the definition states that this would be true because the letters in the story list are in the correct order. Although 'c', 'e' & 'f' are missing this is allowed in clause (ii) of the definition. However, neither (?ii) nor (?iii) are true according to the definition. In the first case there is an extra story member 'z' that is not in the "script" list - meaning that extra events in say a restaurant story - like a mention of "John going to the moon" - could not be understood in the context of the given script and so the story-script match would be rejected. In the last case one of the story members is out of sequence. This is analogous to paying for the meal after leaving the restaurant - which is again not allowed here.

It should be noted that much of the real work of the **match**/2 predicate is going on covertly in the matching of the Ln from the story with the Ln from the script in the second clause of its definition. What is happening is that:

```
     act(A, ptrans, [john, john,  _,  pizza_hut])
```

              matches with

```
     act(1, ptrans, [Actor, Actor,  PlaceX,  Restrnt])
```

from the restaurant story and script given above. So the variable bindings from this will be as follows:

```
A = 1
Actor = john
PlaceX = _      (ie still unbound),
Restrnt = pizza_hut
```

However, as the script in which the variables A, Actor, Restrnt & PlaceX appear is a single clause, then the binding of these variables to a specific value will automatically mean that any occurrence of these variables elsewhere in the script also shares this same value. This means for example that all appearances of the variable Actor derived from this script clause in the current call to it will now be bound to 'John'. From this simple effect we find that having bound the Actor of the first act - given the meaning of the restaurant script - we have determined the actor of them all!

Figure 5.10 Output from SAM1

"John went to Pizza Hut, ate a pizza and left".

Input story	SAM1 understanding
john went to pizza_hut	john went to pizza_hut
	(john went from somewhere to somewhere)
	(john told somebody something)
(someone) ate a pizza	john ate a pizza
	(john gave somebody something)
(someone) left (somewhere)	john left pizza_hut

Exercises 5.2 : SAM1

Before moving on to the rather more sophisticated SAM2 program have a go at these exercises which are based on the simple SAM1 version documented in Code Appendix 5.1 and discussed in the text above.

E 5.2.1 Run `sam1` using the `test_sam1` predicate to save you typing. Work your way through the printout checking that you understand roughly what is going on.

E 5.2.2 Make up your own input restaurant story and see whether SAM1 understands it. Add it in as a new fact under the existing definition for 'story' in the story window. Call the new story 'test2'.

E 5.2.3. Augment this script to include obvious missing events such as the waiter bringing the food. Test it out.

E 5.2.4 Add your own script for a simple shopping trip. If you really need any hints - the simplest one would do a ptrans to some shop, the shopkeeper gives you something, you give the shopkeeper something, you leave.

E 5.2.5 Test your script with this story. NB : don't forget a suitable trigger.

Story 3:   *"Suzie went to the bakers, the baker gave her some bread and she came home"*.

E 5.2.6 Look at the definition of `test_sam1` - note that it prints out the value of the variable `Story` twice. Can you see why the output is different - given that variables with the same name should have exactly the same value! Can you explain this and what the predicate does?

Note how SAM1 has identified some of the unknowns in the input story, but there are still quite a few unresolved unknowns. This brings us to the next augmentation - **sam2** includes both defaults and pretty-printing of output. It will provide an English paraphrase for its understanding of the input story.

5.3.3 The full prototype : SAM 2

This is a much fuller version and includes: two quite complex scripts (one for a restaurant and one for fast food); defaults; output of CDs in English sentence format; and a modification of the trigger mechanism to allow triggers to be strong, medium or weak in strength. This is important if you wish to access the most suitable script. Most of these additions are relatively trivial and you can easily work out their function from the code in Code Appendix 5.2. One useful addition shows you one way of adding extra constraints on the contents of slots. Rather than just variables that will match with single words we have added simple clauses which further constrain the contents of the slot. So in act 6 of the new fast_food script we have said that the object of the ingest must be food(Food) and that its destination is mouth(Actor). This mechanism is used to help out the paraphrasing production mechanism later on but is also useful to insist that only the right sort of ingest, of some X that is food(X) rather than say drink(X) or air(X), happens here. All that happens is that the input story should have slot fillers which are of this format. The defaults mechanism is slightly more interesting and difficult.

Consider this more sophisticated script for a fast food scenario.

```
script(fast_food,
[    act(1,   ptrans,  [Actor, Actor, EarlierPlace, Restaurant]),
     act(2,   ptrans,  [Actor, Actor, Door, Table]),
     act(3,   atrans,  [Hostess, Menu, Hostess, Actor]),
     act(4,   mtrans,  [Actor, Order, Actor, Hostess]),
     act(5,   ptrans,  [Hostess, Food, Kitchen, Table]),
     act(6,   ingest,  [Actor, food(Food), Plate, mouth(Actor)]),
     act(7,   ptrans,  [Actor, Actor, Table, Checkout]),
     act(8,   atrans,  [Hostess, Bill, Hostess, Actor]),
     act(9,   atrans,  [Actor, Money, Actor, Hostess]),
     act(10, ptrans,  [Actor, Actor, Restaurant, NextPlace])
     ],
[    [Actor, customer],
     [Door, door],
     [Table, table],
     [Menu, menu],
     [Hostess, hostess],
     [Order, order],
     [Food, meal],
     [Kitchen, kitchen],
     [Checkout, checkout],
     [Plate, plate],
     [Bill, bill],
     [Money, money],
     [NextPlace, place2]
]).
```

The third argument to the script is new. It is a list that contains a number of sublists that are default-value pairs. In each of these pairs, the first part of the pair is a variable - with a name corresponding to a "slot" in the main script events. The second part of the pair is an atom corresponding to the default value for this role. So for example, if we do not know who the Actor in the script actually is then assume that they are a 'customer'; similarly if we do not know the details about how the meal was paid for then just call it 'money' etc. Obviously, if we do now that the Actor was 'Bill' and he paid with a 'credit_card' then these values should be discovered from the story. But if the story has been understood in the usual way and any of these variables in this list are still unbound then these atoms are what they should be bound to. So the program required is obvious, is it not?! After **match**/2 has had a chance to fill in all these roles from the story itself a call to **name_defaults**/1 will take this list of default-value pairs from the script and check to see if any of the slots in the list still have unbound variables. If they are unbound then they should be bound to the default value given.

```
(i)      name_defaults([]).
(ii)     name_defaults([[(N),  (N)] | L]) :- name_defaults(L).
(iii)    name_defaults([[ N1,  N2] | L]) :- N1 \= N2, name_defaults(L).
```

This says that (i) if there are no defaults to deal with then succeed trivially. Otherwise, (ii) if you can bind the slot with the value, (ie if they can both be bound to the same variable N) then this will as a side effect give the role the default value. Having done this you must recurse on any remaining pairs in the tail of the input list. If not, and both entries of the pair cannot be bound together (iii) then ignore them because the role must already be bound to something and recurse on the remaining pairs.

If you compare the output of SAM2 given in Figure 5.11 with the earlier output from sam1 you will see how much extra the defaults mechanism can buy you. Have a play with it - the code is fully documented. Note how the Appendix definition D 5.2.9 : **paraphrase_cd**/2 works. A full sample printout is reproduced as Figure 5.12 - do you notice any problems with the paraphrased output? The output "the john" is surely not right?

Ideas for Advanced Projects

(i) As noted in the stages involved in SAM above, one final stage to the system would be a question-and-answer program that could be interrogated to examine the understanding of the story. One possible project would be to try to produce the program that could answer questions about the stories – perhaps using an ELIZA-like keyword matching to 'cheat'!

(ii) All the input to this prototype script applier have had to be 'hand-coded' because a parser for conceptual dependencies is not trivial. So why not try to write one and integrate it with the program. Possibly you might choose to base it on the DCG's of the last chapter, or you may choose some other special purpose parser. One of the key issues here is how to design the **lexicon**. Consider the figures given in our introductory discussion, 5.5; 5.6 & 5.7 to help you in the early design considerations.

(iii) Schank & Reisbeck (1981) discuss the implementation of a number of the programs which arose from the work of the Yale team. They show how miniature versions of these may be implemented in LISP. It would be a challenge to convert these programs into Prolog or to implement some of their more recent work. The main advantage of the Prolog form of this work is that we have to do very little to provide a matching algorithm, because Prolog is itself based around a powerful pattern matcher. Also the Prolog version can look more elegant and should avoid the pushes; pops and variable assignments of the original LISP.

(iv) Although Schank and his colleagues have always argued that their parsers are semantically driven, in fact SAM actually is better described as driven by the **pragmatics** of a situation — that is, it captures the real world knowledge about events that are likely to take place or to have taken place in a particular context. Whatever approach is taken to parsing, syntactic, semantic or mixed initiative, a useful parser must also have a means of applying pragmatic knowledge. One particularly interesting challenge would be to attempt to relate SAM-like semantic processing to a syntactic front end like that described in the previous chapter. Alternatively, you might consider comparing a "minimal-syntax" parser that goes directly to the primitives and slots with the more traditional parsers that we have examined. An examination of the virtues and vices of both extremes linguistically, psychologically and practically could keep you busy for a while.

Figure 5.11   Output from SAM2

"John went to Pizza Hut, ate a pizza and left".

Input story	SAM2 understanding
john went to pizza_hut	john went to pizza_hut
	(john went from somewhere to the table)
	(john told the waiter the order))
(someone) ate a pizza	john ate a pizza
	(john gave the waiter the money)
(someone) left (somewhere)	john left pizza_hut

Figure 5.12   Sample SAM2 output

```
?- test_sam2(test1).

input story named test1 was:
ptrans([agent(john), object(john), from(_16496), to(mcdonalds)])
ingest([agent(_16514), object(food(hamburger)), from(_16530), to(_16536)])
ptrans([agent(_16554), object(_16554), from(_16560), to(_16566)])

script triggered was: fast_food

SAMs cds are
ptrans([agent(john), object(john), from(place1), to(mcdonalds)])
ptrans([agent(john), object(john), from(door), to(table)])
atrans([agent(hostess), object(menu), from(hostess), to(john)])
mtrans([agent(john), object(order), from(john), to(hostess)])
ptrans([agent(hostess), object(hamburger), from(kitchen), to(table)])
ingest([agent(john), object(food(hamburger)), from(plate), to(mouth(john))])
ptrans([agent(john), object(john), from(table), to(checkout)])
atrans([agent(hostess), object(bill), from(hostess), to(john)])
atrans([agent(john), object(money), from(john), to(hostess)])
ptrans([agent(john), object(john), from(mcdonalds), to(place2)])

****************
SAMs understanding is

john went from place1 to mcdonalds
john went from door to table
hostess gave the menu to the john
john told the hostess the order
hostess brought the hamburger from the kitchen to the table
john ate the hamburger
john went from table to checkout
hostess gave the bill to the john
john gave the money to the hostess
john went from mcdonalds to place2
```

5.4 Later work

All natural language understanding projects must address both issues of syntax and semantics. Typically researchers will place more stress on one at the expense of the other in their work. Schank and his co-workers have highlighted the role of semantics and have shown how much can be done without being too concerned with syntax. In more recent work (eg. Schank, 1982 a & b) Schank decided that several scripts (such as a visit to a dentist and a visit to a doctor) had so much in common that it would be more adaptive to store sub-scripts (which he called Memory Organisation Packets — MOPs) to capture common elements such as being shown to a waiting room. A SAM-style script for say a visit to a doctor would be constructed from the appropriate MOPs as and when they were needed during the understanding process. Most recently he has been concerned with the relationships within these memory structures - how they may call each other in "reminding" and be used creatively in patterns of "explanations".

In general this approach is certainly open to criticism. It can be criticised as a rather ad hoc mechanistic model of understanding with a very limited theoretical basis for the selection of the conceptual primitives used. Also it appears to have avoided many of the issues that language researchers have struggled with for a long time - avoiding noticing things like the "little words" of English such as "and, but, then, that" etc. Indeed Schank enthusiastically side-steps the complexities of Natural Language Processing that still hold back research progress. Avoiding these issues means that "minimal syntax" parsing is restricted to the more simple linguistic phenomena and would, for example, have a great deal of difficulty with many of the sentences used in this chapter (like this one, which is turning out to involve more and more complex language and yet which the reader can probably follow!) Indeed, a large range of linguistic phenomena like the "transformational" phenomena of 'gaps', 'relative clauses' and so on turns out to be very hard to incorporate into this semantics-first model in any principled way, (Marcus, 1984).

As regards its strengths, it clearly does perform (in constrained domains) and it does offer an interesting level of generalisation. It provides us with a way to think about : units of meaning & memory; the role of expectation in understanding; and a top-down semantics in which the semantic parser is actually only looking for things it expects to see. SAM and its derivatives provide one of the few well-integrated, working treatments of pragmatic & memory issues within the NLP field. In fact, one of the only commercially available pragmatically-driven NLP systems has been written by a graduate of the Yale school, Schwartz (1987). The Schankian approach is by no means a complete, psychologically plausible model of human language understanding but it has brought the relationship between memory and language sharply into focus.

5.5   Further reading

The readings we have suggested are a small collection of the material available on the Schankian approach to language understanding. All general texts on AI will have a section on the work of the his team, but the two which we have noted here are Boden (1987) and Greene (1986). The best detailed description of the SAM program proper is provided by Cullingford (1981). This is part of a selection presented by Schank and Riesbeck (1981) which also contains working examples (miniatures) of the LISP versions of a number of the Yale systems. Following the evolution of the Yale work leads through the range of Schankian books and articles suggested. If pressed to recommend just one, then "Scripts, Plans, Goals and Understanding" (Schank and Abelson, 1977) is probably still the 'classic' title.

Acknowledgements

This chapter was inspired by the simple SAM given in the excellent Prolog textbook by Sterling and Shapiro (1986).

Chapter 6 : A production-system project

Modelling the development of a Piagetian Seriation Task

Production Systems are simple collections of IF-THEN rules. They have been one of the major techniques for modelling both declarative and procedural knowledge in cognitive simulations over the past 15 years. The two major complete models of cognition - J R Anderson's ACT* model (1983) and Newell et al's SOAR model (1986) are both based on a production system architecture. Both SOAR and ACT* are complete models of cognition in that they specify learning mechanisms by which productions are created and refined, and this is probably their major advantage over other types of knowledge representation. In this project we demonstrate that Prolog permits the natural modelling of a production system by creating a Prolog version of Richard Young's (1976) production system simulation of the development of children's seriation skills.

6.1   Background - Production Systems

The concept of a Production Rule (PR) was introduced by Newell and Simon (1972) to describe a simple condition—action pair of the form IF {conditions} THEN {execute actions}. That is, if the conditions specified for a particular PR are satisfied, then that PR may 'fire' ie. execute its actions. A Production System (PS) is simply an unstructured collection of independent PRs subject to 'conflict resolution' principles which specify which PR to select if several PRs could fire simultaneously. Early PSs adopted a particularly simple architecture (referred to by Anderson, 1983, as 'neoclassical'). In the neoclassical system all changing information was represented in a store labelled 'Working Memory' (WM) by analogy with models of human information processing then current. The PR memory was static and corresponded to human long term memory. Once a set of facts in WM matched all the conditions of a PR, that PR would fire, typically depositing further items in WM, thus creating the conditions for a different PR to fire, and so on, with the PS wandering off on an unpredictable, data-driven course thought to be similar to human cognition. The basic PS cycle is shown below:

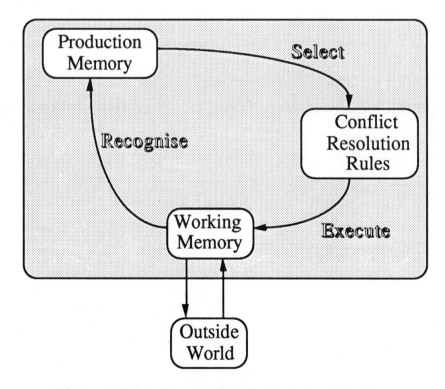

Figure 6.1   A Production System Architecture

PSs have a number of desirable features for simulation of cognitive processes — they are data-driven, they capture sequential processing well (and thus are good for modelling processes under attentional control); they are modular (ie. individual PRs may be added, deleted or modified independently of the rest of the system); they provide an explicit method of modelling Working Memory; and though a very general technique, they are constrained in principled ways. Owing to the persuasive advocacy of Newell and other leading cognitive scientists, PSs captured the high ground of theoretical cognitive science, serving as the major representational device for implementing models of human cognition. So great was the influence of PS implementations that major programming environments such as OPS5 were created to support PS modelling; most early expert systems were implemented as PSs (though the trend is now towards less constrained representations); and as noted above, the two major computational theories of cognition (SOAR and ACT*) are implemented within a PS architecture.

It is somewhat perverse to attempt to simulate PSs using Prolog, and we would strongly recommend anyone wishing to write a serious PS to use an appropriate PS environment such as OPS5. Nonetheless, it is straightforward to capture the essence of PSs in Prolog, and the completed system gives a good feel for the way a true PS works.

6.2   The project - a Production System for Seriation

Richard Young's (1976, 1978) study was one of the classic demonstrations of the applicability of AI and cognitive science techniques to the work of developmental psychology. By careful observation of an individual child's performance on the standard Piagetian seriation task, he was able to characterise the performance in terms of a small set of strategies, which in turn could be described in terms of production rules. He then built a production system which incorporated those rules, and was able to compare directly the performance of the system with the performance of the individual child. Interestingly, it turned out that, as children developed, it was possible to model their improvement on the seriation task in terms of new production systems which grew in a systematic manner out of the original one. Large changes in performance could often be attributed to the acquisition of a new (or better) production rule. Young provided analyses of seriation learning in terms of changing productions and demonstrated that his model captured the essential aspects of the development of performance on the seriation task.

6.2.1 The task

Object seriation is one of a range of experimental tasks used by Piaget (1952) to examine children's cognitive development. The essential idea is that a child is asked by the experimenter to order a pile of blocks by size. The blocks begin in a random heap and the child is asked to order them in a line on the table. Piaget noticed that performance on the task progressed through three distinct stages that appeared to correspond with the ages of the children concerned, ie four year olds were typically at stage I, five year olds at stage II and finally six year olds were typically at stage III.

> Stage I : Child fails to seriate blocks. They remain in an arbitrary sequence.
>
> Stage II : Child can seriate the blocks, but only after repeated trial and error
>   exchanges of the sequence.
>
> Stage III : Child can seriate easily. Blocks are chosen in order, one at a time.

Young (1976) performed a detailed videotaped analysis of four to six year old children doing this task to compare their individual performance strategies. He then modelled the stages and strategies employed in a production system. He showed that it was possible to represent the development of the seriation skill through the changes to the set of rules that are the core of the system.

Figure 6.2 Young's Production System architecture

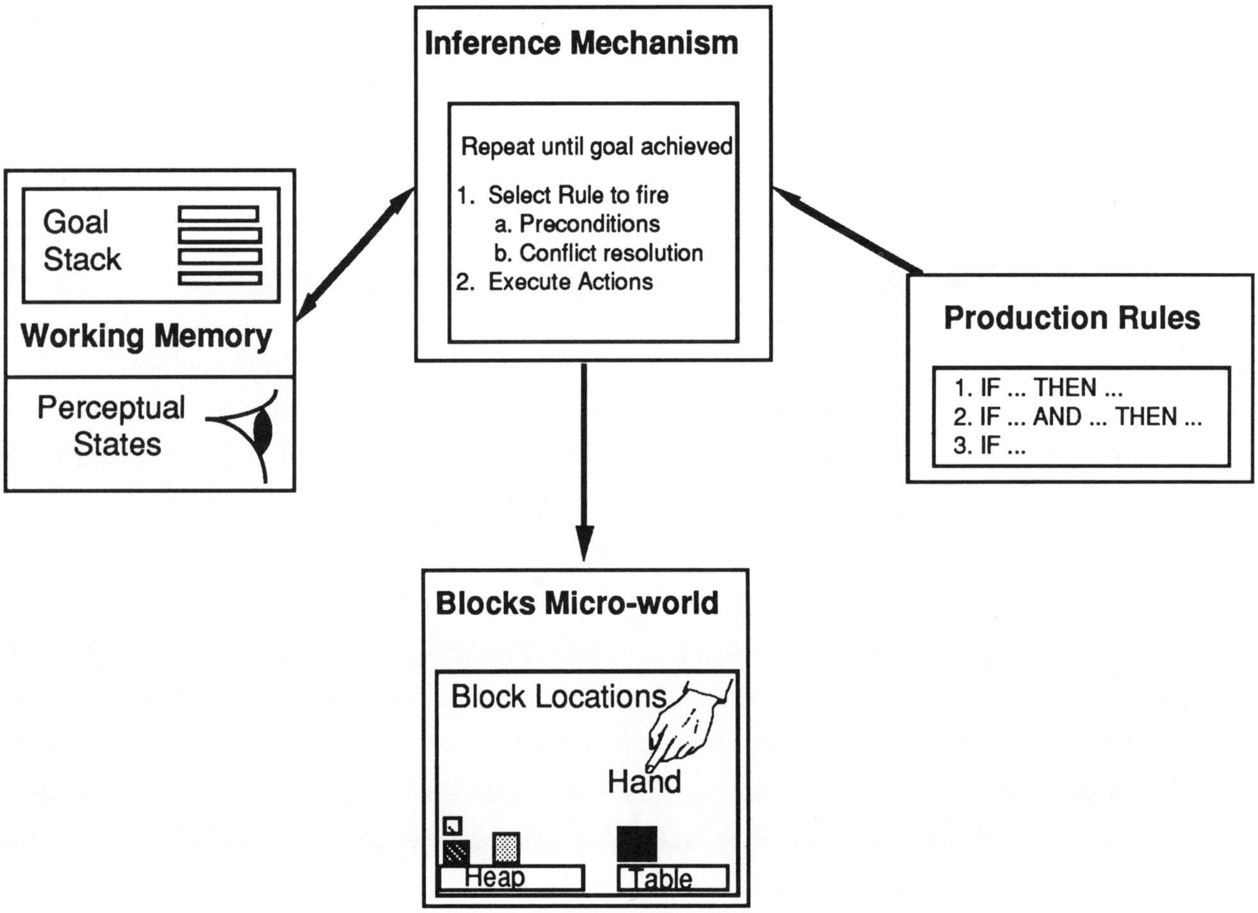

Young used a hybrid PS involving two modifications to the neoclassical model, introducing a 'goal stack' to help direct the problem solving behaviour and 'perceptual tests' to augment the material in WM. Both these enhancements reduce the simplicity of the architecture, though the need for goal-directed PS architectures is now well-established (see eg. Anderson, 1983). In illustrating the seriation system architecture used by Young we have augmented the general architecture shown in Figure 6.1 by making explicit the need for an inference mechanism to carry out the match and execute parts of the cycle. The micro-world which the productions act upon in this case is a blocks-world scene. The blocks are initially in a jumbled heap and the seriation task which the system is to attempt involves taking blocks off the heap and moving them around until they are arranged in an ordered line on the table, with the biggest block to the left, the next biggest to its right, and so on. The system can affect the world though a simulated hand which may pick up blocks from the heap and put them into some position on the table. The system has a limited number of indicators of the current 'state' of the world - Young describes them as 'perceptual tests', but in production system terminology it would be more normal to include these sorts of test as part of the description of Working Memory.

The initial set of design decisions to be faced in attempting to implement this system revolve around a choice of representation in Prolog for each of the elements of this figure. We have decided to represent the micro-world as a set of database facts for the contents of the `hand`, `heap` and `table`. The progress of the child seriator is modelled by a set of programs which will assert and retract new values for each of these definitions according to the dictates of the production rules.

6.3 A Seriation Production System in Prolog

In Figure 6.4 below we provide a simplified example of each of the important parts of the Prolog implementation of this project. The predicates associated with each part in the figure will be discussed separately and the the exercises will provide a detailed example of their use.

Figure 6.3 The Seriation Project Production system architecture

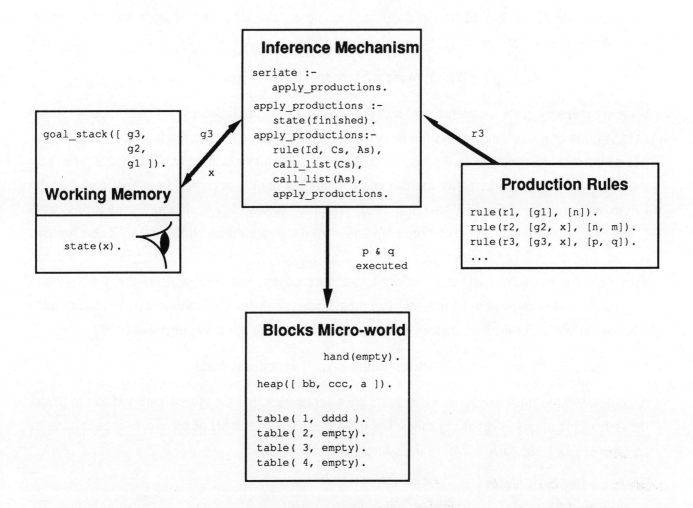

The project on Young's seriation simulation consists of five main parts. The basic assumptions behind each is summarised here, and the Prolog detail is discussed in the following sections.

(1) The micro-world.

There are four blocks which are labelled a, bb, ccc, dddd in terms of increasing size. Atomic constants have been used whose physical size corresponds to the size of the blocks they represent. So a is the smallest and dddd the biggest.

All the blocks start off on the 'heap' and may be transferred by 'hand' to a line on a table (with places 1, 2, 3, 4 available), where 1 is to the far left and 4 is to the far right. Information on the current location of the blocks is kept in three different definitions. There is a predicate hand/1 whose argument records the contents (which may be either a block or the word empty) of the simulator's hand. The predicate heap/1 has a single argument which is a list of all the blocks currently in the heap. The definitions of the hand and heap only ever have one clause. The predicate table/2 has two arguments and as many clauses as there are positions on the table. The first argument of each clause in the definition is the position on the table (1-4) and the second argument is either the name of a block in that position or the word free. So, as the simulation progresses, the heap list gets shorter, the hand holds a single block temporarily, and the table positions get filled. Success is achieved in the simulation if all four blocks end up in the line on the table in the appropriate order, ie { dddd >> ccc >> bb >> a }.

(2) Working Memory: Goal Stack

Working memory goals are represented as a **goal stack**, in the predicate goal_stack(List). where List is a list of goal elements. As the rules act upon the world to change the location of the blocks this goal list is changed to help the system to work out what it needs to do next. It is described as a stack because it may contain any number of elements but is only accessed from the front - so the system can only "see" the first goal in the list. The predicate which is able to examine this list is called top_goal(Goal) and it will only bind Goal to the first element in the stack. There are two operations that change the goal_stack list, called pop_goal_stack and push(Goal). The odd names derive from the early days of computer technology, but their actions are very simple: pop_goal_stack removes the top goal from the stack and throws it away, and push(Goal) adds Goal to the stack. So the idea is that you can **push** goals on to a stack and **pop** them off.

(3) Working Memory: Perceptual tests

A complement to the working memory goals are a set of tests that the system can perform to assess the state of the micro-world at any time. The most important of this set of predicates is state/1. Its argument records the basic 'state' of the system & micro-world.

There are five basic **states** :

just_started	- the first block not yet placed
new_arrangement	- there is a new arrangement of blocks but these have not been checked
checked(ok)	- the blocks are in the right order
checked(wrong)	- the blocks are in the wrong order
finished	- all the blocks are on the table and in the right order

However in the first seriation set of rules for a very young seriator there are only three because the middle three states are replaced by the single overall state of 'adding_blocks'. These are considered to be an easy way of characterising simple 'perceptual tests' which can be performed to "perceive" some state change in the micro-world. In practice this 'state' device represents rather indirect 'tests' in that it is only affected by the rules after a change to the microworld. So it is actually more of a special purpose flag with a similar status to the working memory goals. There is only ever one state and any new state produced by a rule supersedes and deletes any previous state. In addition to these there are a few predicates which represent more direct tests that can be used to assess the micro-world's state.

(4) The production rules

The production rules are represented in Prolog as the definition of the predicate rule/3, where

```
rule(Id, Preconditions , Actions)
```

means that a rule has the identifier Id and a list of conditions Preconditions and actions list Actions. Here we have chosen to make these rules sets of Prolog facts so that Prolog itself does no inferential work to 'prove' them true and we have provided a set of separate predicates to use these rule facts and do all the appropriate inferencing.

(5) The inference mechanism

The overall control predicate is seriate/0 which sets the simulation going. This contains the first call to the predicate which manages the use of the rules called apply_productions/0. It selects an appropriate rule and 'fires' it, recursively doing so until its stopping check is true. A rule is appropriate where its 'preconditions' are true and a rule is 'fired' by executing its 'actions'. The preconditions are typically working memory goals or perceptual tests. There is no sophisticated conflict resolution implemented, ie no way of coping with the situation where a number of rules' preconditions may true at the same time. The system simply fires the first rule it comes across with true preconditions. The 'actions' that are executed by the rule firings are themselves implemented as simple Prolog programs that change the micro-world, generally affecting block locations. As will be seen they are written using the Prolog built-in predicates assert/1 and retract/1. The assert/1 predicate adds new clauses for a definition into the database whilst the retract/1 predicate deletes clauses from the database.

6.3.1 The Seriation simulation Production Rules

In Figure 6.3 we present an English rendering of a set of production rules for a seriation task. These rules are the subject of the first set of exercises and so will not be explained in detail just now. However they are based upon a detailed description of Young's seriation production system given in Bundy and Luger (1978). It would be easy to write production rules such as those of Figure 6.3 directly into Prolog, because the format

"IF conditions THEN actions"

is very close to the standard Prolog form for rules

```
actions :- conditions.
```

You should note how this appears back to front because of the way Prolog is written! The former reads: if some conditions can be proved to be true then some actions are applicable; whilst the Prolog form would be written: some actions are applicable if some conditions can be proved. This interpretation of the production rules as Prolog rules would certainly work, but it relies on the meaning that Prolog rule interpreter gives to its own definition of **IF** (ie :-). So if you want more control over how Prolog deals with production rules then it is easier to define your own 'meta-interpreter' for these rules. ('Meta' because it is a level above that of the Prolog interpreter). To do this we have chosen to represent production rules as Prolog **facts** - with a clear declarative meaning - and we will write some meta-interpreter predicates that use these facts to actually work.

In Figure 6.4 the rules are labelled as follows: rules f1, f2, f3 are the first rules to be applied from the initial state; rule s1 is the success rule; rules a1, a2, a3 are the add-block rules; and rule p1 is the place block rule.

Figure 6.4   Example Production System rules for a naive seriator

rule : f1   **IF**   the top goal is to 'seriate' **and** the current state is 'just started'
THEN   push the goal 'add the first block' **and**
the new state is 'adding blocks'

rule : f2   **IF**   the top goal is to 'add the first block' **and** am holding a Block
THEN   put the block at the far left of a line **and** pop the goal stack

rule : f3,   **IF**   the top goal is to 'add the first block' **and** the heap is not empty
THEN   pick up the nearest block from the heap

rule : s1   **IF**   the top goal is to 'seriate' **and** the hand is empty and the heap is empty
THEN   pop the goal stack **and** the make the new state 'finished'

rule : a1   **IF**   the top goal is to 'seriate' **and** the current state is am 'adding blocks'
THEN   push the goal to 'add another block'

rule : a2   **IF**   the top goal is to 'add another block' **and** am holding a Block
THEN   pop the goal stack **and** push the goal to 'place a Block'

rule : a3   **IF**   the top goal is to 'add another block' **and** the heap is not empty
THEN   pick up the nearest block from the heap

rule : p1   **IF**   the top goal is to 'place a Block' **and** am holding a Block
THEN   put the block at the right of the current block line on the table
and pop the goal stack

In Prolog, we define the predicate `rule` with three arguments, where

```
rule(Id, Preconditions, Actions)
```

which means that a rule has the identifier `Id` and a list of conditions `Preconditions` and actions list `Actions`. The lists that make up the second and third arguments must consist of elements that are executable Prolog queries. The two examples below are taken from the rules given for the naive seriator given above in Figure 6.4. Rule (a3) has been simplified slightly.

(a) A simple production rule

rule a3:   **IF** the top goal is add_another_block   **THEN**   pick_up_nearest_block

The corresponding Prolog representation is:

```
rule(a3, [top_goal(add_another_block)], [pick_up_nearest_block]).
```

This may be read in two parts:

   (i) Match: rule a3 is applicable **IF** the condition '`top_goal(add_another_block)`' is true

   (ii) Execute: to apply rule a3 **THEN** carry out the action '`pick_up_nearest_block`'

(b) A more complex production rule

rule f2:   **IF** the top goal is 'add first block' **AND** you are holding a block
THEN   put that block at the far left of a line
AND   pop the goal stack.

Our corresponding Prolog form is:

```
rule(f2, [ top_goal(add_first_block), holding(Block) ],
                [    put_block_at_far_left(Block),
                     pop_goal_stack              ]).
```

Example (b) may similarly be read in two parts:

> (i) Match: rule f2 is applicable if the precondition 'top_goal(add_first_block)' is true

> > and the perceptual test to check that 'holding(Block)' is also true

> (ii) Execute: then to apply rule f2 carry out the action 'put_block_at_far_left(Block)'

> > and the call pop_goal_stack causes the goal stack to be 'popped'.

It should be noted that these rules do not actually "do" anything on their own - they are written here as a (relatively) declarative chunk of knowledge stating which actions are appropriate according to which preconditions. You should be able to note the analogy here between this and the ELIZA patterns used in Chapter 3 - if one argument is shown to be true then the other may be considered to be appropriate. Only this time instead of lists containing sequences of words, these lists are themselves Prolog predicates. That is to say that each of the elements of these lists has a Prolog definition somewhere. In general, the Preconditions list contains predicates which simply perform tests on the state of working memory, whilst the Actions list contains predicates which have definitions that change the state of working memory. Clearly how they are used to solve a problem will depend upon the inference mechanism that picks them up and applies them.

6.3.2 The Inference Mechanism

As one might expect by now, it is possible to capture the fundamental production system architecture in Prolog with some elegance. The productions are started by the query seriate, and you should be able to identify the sequence of three predicate calls - initialise, then apply_productions then the write command - which constitute the first clause of seriate. The second seriate clause is for completeness - indicating when the first clause fails. The call initialise is one which we have defined to simply prepare the working memory for a new run of the productions.

```
(i)        seriate:-
                    initialise,
                    apply_productions,
                    write('Finished'), nl.
(ii)       seriate:-
                    write('Failed!'), nl, fail.
```

The call to the definition **seriate/0** is true if (i) you first initialise the simulation, tidying up working memory and resetting all features of the micro-world to their starting values etc; and then apply_productions; and then write 'Finished'. **OR** it is true if (ii) you write 'Failed' (implicitly : after apply_productions has failed).

All the work is really done by the recursive predicate apply_productions/0. This is the production rule meta-interpreter which picks up the rule/3 facts and does what is to be done with each part.

You should by now be able to spot the standard recursive pair of stopping condition and recursive definition. The `apply_productions/0` predicate continues to recurse until either the stopping condition is achieved (success) or until no production can be found which satisfies the required conditions (failure).

```
(i)      apply_productions :-                        % stopping check
              state(finished).                       % success state true
(ii)     apply_productions :-
              rule(Id, PreList, ActnList),           % find a rule
              call_list(PreList),                    % check preconditions
              call_list(ActnList),                   % perform actions
              apply_productions.                     % recurse
```

As described here the first clause is a simple stopping check which states that **apply_productions** is true if the state is `finished`. Otherwise, says the second clause, it is necessary to do some work and recurse. The work which is to be done in clause (ii) is to find a `rule/3` with a true set of preconditions and then execute its actions. In fact, the predicate that you will be able to find in the Prolog program given in the Appendix (D 6.3.2) is a little more complex than this in that we have added some clauses and arguments to it to provide some screen output to tell you what it is doing and when.

So the predicates which do the real work are `rule/3` and two calls to `call_list/1`.

The call `rule(Identifier, PreList, ActnList)` in clause (ii) of this definition finds the (first) `rule/3` in the database. Each of the variables in this call to `rule` will be bound to the arguments of this (first) production-rule fact. (If any of the subsequent calls fail - then **rule** will generate the second production rule in the database - and so on). The next line gives the rule preconditions `PreList` as an argument to the predicate `call_list/1`. As we have already noted the elements of the lists in the definition of `rule` are executable Prolog predicates themselves and the `call_list/1` predicate is defined to execute each member of the list in turn. As the `PreList` is usually a sequence of tests this means that `call_list` will succeed if, and only if, all the tests in the list succeed. The success of `call_list(PreList)` will mean that the next call in this definition, will give `call_list/1` the rule actions `ActnList` to execute.

```
(i)      call_list([]).
(ii)     call_list([Goal | Remains] ) :-
              call(Goal),
              call_list(Remains).
```

The definition of `call_list/1` is included here for completeness. Again the elegant recursive definition should be immediately plain. The predicate `call/1` invoked in clause (ii) is a built-in primitive that simply executes its argument as if the user had run a query on it. So call_list(Gs) is true if all the elements in the list Gs may be executed as Prolog queries

So if you consider the following query to this sample definition:

```
        (?)   call_list([write(hi), nl, write(there),nl]).
```

hi

there

YES

will succeed by 'call'-ing each of the items in the list in turn. If any one of these items was not true then the call to `call_list` would fail. For example:

```
        (?)   call_list([write(hi), nl, integer(fred), write(there), nl]).
```

hi

NO.

So in the above query, the first item in the list succeeds with the side effect of writing 'hi' to the screen; the second item is called with the side effect of sending a new-line to the screen; but in the third call the type checking primitive `integer/1` is not given an integer number as an argument and so will fail, causing the whole call to `call_list/1` to fail.

6.4   Interacting with the Micro-world

6.4.1 Setting up the Micro-world

As already discussed in the `seriate/0` call the very first thing to do is to set up the simulation's micro-world. As the simulation progresses it continually changes its record of this world and so this needs to be reset to the initial state before any new run of the simulation begins. The call to `initialise/0` does this resetting of the basic world to its start state.

```
initialise :-
     retractall( goal_stack(_) ),
     retractall( state(_)      ),
     retractall( hand(_)       ),
     retractall( heap(_)       ),
     retractall( table(_, _)   ),
     assert( goal_stack([seriate])    ),
     assert( state(just_started)      ),
     assert( hand(empty)              ),
     assert( heap([ccc, a, dddd, bb]) ),
     assertz( table(1, free) ),
     assertz( table(2, free) ),
     assertz( table(3, free) ),
     assertz( table(4, free) ),
     write_list(['initial arrangement on heap:  ', [ccc, a, dddd, bb], nl]), !.
```

The first five calls inside this definition of `initialise/0` use the built-in primitive `retractall/1` and there are also a number of calls to the built-in primitives `assert/1` and `assertz/1`. The `retractall/1` primitive deletes a complete database definition and is fairly standard in Edinburgh Prolog implementations. These three calls then are used here to delete the complete definitions for `goal_stack/1`, `state/1`, `hand/1`, `heap/1` and `table/2`. The assert primitives are here to replace these deleted database definitions with new clauses that represent their 'start' values. The first two calls to `assert/1` simply add the single clause definitions for the memory predicates `goal_stack([seriate])` and `state(just_started)` into the database. This is so that there is an appropriate start state and a goal stack with the 'basic' goal only in it at the start of the simulation. The remainder of the asserting is for micro-world definitions. The hand starts off empty. The heap starts off with the four blocks given in a 'random' order.

The predicate `assertz` is a special call to `assert` that adds clauses into the database after any existing clauses for that definition, so the four clauses for the `table/2` definition will appear in the database in the same order as they are given in this initialise definition. (NB if assert had been used it would be in reverse order - because assert adds a clause in before any that are already there). The final call in this definition simply prints out a message to the screen informing the user of the current state of the heap.

So as a result of the work of the main part of the `initialise/0` predicate the memory and micro-world definitions will look like this at the start of the simulation run of the seriator.

```
goal_stack([seriate]).

state(just_started).

hand(empty).

heap([ccc, a, dddd, bb]).

table(1, free).
table(2, free).
table(3, free).
table(4, free).
```

The four blocks are currently in the 'heap' whilst the four table locations 1-4 are currently 'free' and the simulators 'hand' is 'empty'. It is these table locations that are filled as blocks are placed in a line on the table.

6.4.2 Working memory and perceptual state predicates

These predicates all affect working memory elements - to test or change working memory.

There are three main predicates for goal stack manipulation — `top_goal/1`, `push_goal/1` and `pop_goal_stack/0`. We have already noted the historical origin of these terms in old computer terminology. However the idea of a stack is still a very useful one which is often used despite the fact that it is no longer imposed by the hardware technology of today. Stacks contain things that will be needed in a strict sequence and their structure ensures that the sequence is maintained. In terms of the goals of the production system, each goal may generate a number of new goals to be achieved first. The new goals are placed on the stack above the current goal and as each is achieved it is removed (popped off) revealing the original goal below. This mechanism may be considered to be like an old fashioned plate stack in a restaurant. As a customer takes the top plate off the stack the one below pops up to take its place. The waiter adds new plates to the top, pushing down the plates below. In Prolog we have implemented the stack as a list called `goal_stack/1`, where only the first element is ever directly accessible.

The test `top_goal/1` states that the top goal is simply the head of the `goal_stack` list. This is its one argument. The action `push_goal(X)` adds the goal X at the top of the `goal_stack` (ie. a new first element of the goal stack list). The action `pop_goal_stack/0` works by retracting the old goal stack and asserting a new one without whatever was at the head of the old `goal_stack` list.

```
top_goal(X):- goal_stack([X|_]).

push_goal(X) :-
                retract(goal_stack(Stack)),
                assert(goal_stack([X | Stack])), !.

pop_goal_stack :-
                retract(goal_stack([_|T])),
                assert(goal_stack(T)), !.
```

So if the database goal stack was this:

```
goal_stack([go_shopping]).
```

Then the query `(?) top_goal(X).` would report YES X = go_shopping

Now if some production rules suggested that `buy_vegetables` was a goal that needed to be achieved before `go_shopping` could be achieved it would be possible to add this to the stack using:

`(?) push_goal(buy_vegetables).`

which would result in a new database definition for `goal_stack/1`.

```
goal_stack([buy_vegetables, go_shopping]).
```

This would obviously result in a new top_goal which would be responsible for driving further problem-solving by the system. Say that the next goal to be pushed was (being driven by `buy_vegetables`) this:

`(?) push_goal(buy_potatoes).` Then the new goal stack would look like this:

```
goal_stack([buy_potatoes, buy_vegetables, go_shopping]).
```

And the query `(?) top_goal(X).` would reply YES X = buy_potatoes. Now let us assume that one of the actions that we can execute permits us to actually buy the potatoes, thus achieving the top goal. Having achieved the goal, it is now possible to remove it and get back to where we were before it arose. This is done by the query

`(?) pop_goal_stack.    YES.`

This will result in a new goal stack.

```
goal_stack([buy_vegetables, go_shopping]).
```

Event	Effect	Goal stack
initial goal stack		go_shopping
after push_goal(buy_vegetables)	*puts the new goal on top of the stack*	buy_vegetables go_shopping
after push_goal(buy_potatoes)	*puts the new goal on top of the stack*	buy_potatoes buy_vegetables go_shopping
top_goal(X). X= buy_potatoes	*returns the current top of the goal stack*	
after pop_goal_stack	*throws away top goal from stack*	buy_vegetables go_shopping

From here the system is clearly back to buying vegetables and will go on to buy more (by pushing more goals to be achieved) or it will consider that it has bought what it wanted and pop this goal to get back to the original go_shopping goal. When the goal stack was empty all the systems goals had been achieved and it could stop.

The production system 'states' are similar to the goal stack except that they do not keep a record of any previous states. The state/1 is just a flag helping the system to note the current state of the micro-world.

The action newstate(S) says remove any old state (not caring what it was) and assert that the new state is now S.

```
new_state(State) :-
            retract(state(_)),
            asserta(state(State)).
```

There are three sundry other 'perceptual' predicates. They are actually very simple paraphrases of the existing micro-world predicates. So hand_empty is just another way of saying that the argument to hand/1 is empty; heap_empty is another way of saying that the heap list is [ ]; and holding/1 says that there is a block in the system's hand, ie some B that is not the word 'empty'.

```
holding(B)  :- hand(B), not(B = empty).

heap_empty :- heap([]).

hand_empty :- hand(empty).
```

6.4.3 Changing the micro-world

There are essentially five main action predicates that change the micro-world at this stage in this simulation. Three are involved with picking up blocks from the heap and two with putting down blocks on the table. The action `pick_up_block/1` is a general predicate that can pick up a named block (its one argument) from the heap. So `pick_up_block(B)` states that one may pick up a block B given that one is not holding anything else and the block B is a member of the heap list H. Given that both of these conditions hold then this action will change the location stored in the database for B by retracting the old values for the heap and hand and asserting new values for them. Before it asserts the new value for the heap it must delete the block that it has picked up from H leaving a new value NewH. This NewH is the value that is to be asserted as the new heap. The `del/3` predicate is a general utility (given in the Appendix as D 6.4.12) which simply deletes an element from one list to give another list.

```
pick_up_block(B)  :-
            hand(empty),
            heap(H),
            member(B, H),
            retract(heap(H)),
            retract(hand(empty)),
            del(B, H, NewH),
            assert(heap(NewH)),
            assert(hand(B)).
```

The next two predicates are simply two more specific versions of pick_up_block. They give `pick_up_block/1` its argument as a specific block to pick up. The first picks up the nearest block, the second picks up the biggest.

The predicate `pick_up_nearest_block/0` calls `heap/1` using a guillotine to bind Block to some specific block which will be the 'nearest' block to the seriator. The name of this block is passed on to `pick_up_block/1` to be picked up.

```
pick_up_nearest_block :-
            heap([ Block | _ ]),
            pick_up_block(Block).
```

The predicate `pick_up_biggest_block/0` picks up the biggest block from the heap in a more sophisticated way. It uses the utility predicate `bsort/2` which sorts the list given as its first argument into an ordered list which is returned as its second argument. A definition for this utility is given the Appendix as Defn 6.4.10. It has been written so that it orders a list with the biggest element first (usually a 'sort' is the other way around).

```
pick_up_biggest_block :-
            heap(H),
            bsort(H, [ BigBlock | _ ]),
            pick_up_block(BigBlock).
```

If you consider this call to bsort/2 :

(?) bsort([a, b, n, m, z], S) YES where S = [z, n, m, b, a]

As it is the biggest block that we want pick_up_block/1 to pick up the second argument of sort is called with a guillotine that will bind the first element of the sorted list to the variable BigBlock and ignore the rest of the sorted list.

There are only two predicates that put blocks down on the table, as our seriator can only put blocks down in the line on the table at the first available position in the line working from the left. So the basic action is to put_block_at_right/0.

```
put_block_at_right :-
            holding(Block),
            retract(hand(Block)),
            retract(table(N, free)),
            assert(hand(empty)),
            assertz(table(N, Block)).


put_block_at_far_left :-
            table(1, free),
            put_block_at_right.
```

It states that if it is holding a Block then retract it from the hand and assert that the hand is now empty, also retract that the table position is free and assert that it now contains the previously held Block. It should be noted that this requires that the table/2 definition has the positions 1-4 in the correct order so that the first free one it comes across in the database definition is also the leftmost position. It assertz's the new clause for the table definition, after the remaining parts of the definition, for tidiness sake. The predicate put_block_at_far_left/0 is a special case of this for the first block which it will put down on the table in the far left slot if it is free.

6.5   The development of seriation skills

Figure 6.5 shows the Prolog implementation of the rules for a naive or very young child doing the seriation task. An English interpretation of these rules was given as Figure 6.3. This set of rules models a child at stage I of the Piagetian task where they fail to seriate the blocks, typically at around four years of age. These rules can be made to reflect the developmental sequence in that they can be changed in a number of different ways to model the changes that appear in childrens performance over time. No automatic mechanism is proposed in this simulation to implement these developmental changes - the rules are simply changed by hand-coding and re-run. So this study is a descriptive one - it does not explain why these changes happen or how. It just explores what changes would be needed to exhibit the behaviour.

Figure 6.5   Production Rule Model for a very young child seriator

```
% rules f1, f2, f3 are the first rules to be applied from the initial state
% rule s1 is the success rule
% rules a1, a2, a3 are the add-block rules
% rule p1 is the place block rule

rule(f1, [top_goal(seriate), state(just_started)],
              [push_goal(add_first_block), new_state(adding_blocks)]).
rule(f2, [top_goal(add_first_block), holding(Block)],
              [put_block_at_far_left, pop_goal_stack]).
rule(f3, [top_goal(add_first_block), not(heap_empty)],
              [pick_up_nearest_block]).

rule(s1, [top_goal(seriate), hand_empty, heap_empty],
              [pop_goal_stack, new_state(finished)]).

rule(a1, [top_goal(seriate), state(adding_blocks)],
              [push_goal(add_another_block)]).
rule(a2, [top_goal(add_another_block), holding(Block)],
              [pop_goal_stack, push_goal(place_block(Block))]).
rule(a3, [top_goal(add_another_block), not(heap_empty)],
              [pick_up_nearest_block]).

rule(p1, [top_goal(place_block(Block)), holding(Block)],
              [put_block_at_right, pop_goal_stack]).
```

In the above Figure 6.5 all of the rules are shown as Prolog facts with three arguments: a rule name; the rule's IF part; and the rule's THEN part. The IF parts all contain a reference to the current top goal in the goal stack and typically another perceptual test or 'state' test. The THEN parts all contain actions to be carried out on the IF part being true. An English transcription of these rules would read as follows. The first three rules f1-3 relate to the initial state of the production system - getting started. The first rule f1 says that if the top goal of the system is called 'seriate' and the state is called 'just started' then change the state to 'adding blocks' and push a new goal 'add first block' on to the top of the goal stack (ie above the current 'seriate' goal). This new goal is referred to by the next two rules. Rule f2 says that if the top goal is to add the first block and the system is currently holding any block (called Block) then put it at the far left of the line on the table and pop the current goal off the goal stack (because it has achieved it). Alternatively, rule f3 says that if the top goal is 'add first block' and there is a block on the heap then pick the one up that is nearest.

Moving on to the rules s1-3 you will note that these are quite similar to rules f1-3. Indeed rules f1-3 are separate only so that we can examine the behaviour surrounding the first block picked up and placed independently from all other blocks picked up and placed. So the rule a1 uses the goal 'add another block' to 'trigger' the firing of rules a2 & a3 which are responsible for changing the goal into placing a block (if it is holding one) or picking one up (if there is at least one left). The actual placing of the block onto the line on the table is handled by a separate rule p1 which waits for a goal telling it to place a specific block before putting it on the right of the line that is being built on the table.

Here we can note that the rule ordering of Prolog clauses, where clauses are tried in order in the definition, ensures that there is *implicit* conflict resolution. So placing rules f1-3 before the others ensures that these are tried first, before a1-3 for example. Now as it happens these rules will never conflict anyway because of the 'states' that are included in the definitions. Rule f1 cannot fire again after having done so once because it changes a state called 'just started' into 'adding blocks' and this remains the state until the final rule s1 changes the state to 'finished'. Indeed rule s1 not only changes the state to 'finished' but it also empties the goal stack entirely by popping the 'start' goal "seriate" (if this is the top goal and both the heap and its hand contains no more blocks).

Exercises 6.1 Modelling a very young seriator

Load the **Seriation 1** program. This consists of the naive seriator rules given in Appendix 6.1 and all of the various seriation definitions given in Appendix 6.3. In addition the rule tracing facilities and general utilities of Appendix 6.4 are also required.

E 6.1.1. Run the production rules with the query **(?) seriate**. This should produce a trace of the seriator's performance very much like that given in Figure 6.6. What is happening?

E 6.1.2. Change the **start state** of the production system run by changing the definition of the predicate **heap/1** which is asserted in the **initialise/0** definition to assert:

heap([dddd, ccc, bb, a]). What differences does it make?

Now try this :

heap([a, bb, ccc, dddd]). What differences does this make?

E 6.1.3. In a set of videotaped studies of children performing this task Young noted that one common behaviour of a slightly more sophisticated child seriator was to start off the line with the largest available block from the heap but then to default to the 'nearest' (random) placement strategy. Try to augment the rules of Figure 6.4 so that the child modelled starts off with the biggest block.

HINT : there is a Prolog definition for pick_up_biggest_block which could be used in production **f3** instead of 'nearest'.

E 6.1.4. Find the definition of the predicate **flag/1**. This tells the predicate that prints out messages to you describing what is happening how much detail to go into. If you change its argument to 'complex_output' and query **seriate/0** again you will see much more of what is happening.

Figure 6.6   Simple trace of production firings for the 'very young child' model

This trace was produced by the rules given in Figure 6.5.

(?) seriate

initial arrangement on heap: [ccc, a, dddd, bb]

1 From Rule f1 : push_goal(add_first_block) &
        new_state(adding_blocks)
: Table : { free >> free >> free >> free }
: Hand : empty
: Heap : [ccc, a, dddd, bb]

2 From Rule f3 : pick_up_nearest_block
: Table : { free >> free >> free >> free }
: Hand : ccc
: Heap : [a, dddd, bb]

3 From Rule f2 : put_block_at_far_left & pop_goal_stack
: Table : { ccc >> free >> free >> free }
: Hand : empty
: Heap : [a, dddd, bb]

4 From Rule a1 : push_goal(add_another_block)
: Table : { ccc >> free >> free >> free }
: Hand : empty
: Heap : [a, dddd, bb]

5 From Rule a3 : pick_up_nearest_block
: Table : { ccc >> free >> free >> free }
: Hand : a
: Heap : [dddd, bb]

6 From Rule a2 : pop_goal_stack &
        push_goal(place_block(a))
: Table : { ccc >> free >> free >> free }
: Hand : a
: Heap : [dddd, bb]

7 From Rule p1 : put_block_at_right & pop_goal_stack
: Table : { ccc >> a >> free >> free }
: Hand : empty
: Heap : [dddd, bb]

8 From Rule a1 : push_goal(add_another_block)
: Table : { ccc >> a >> free >> free }
: Hand : empty
: Heap : [dddd, bb]

9 From Rule a3 : pick_up_nearest_block
: Table : { ccc >> a >> free >> free }
: Hand : dddd
: Heap : [bb]

10 From Rule a2 : pop_goal_stack &
        push_goal(place_block(dddd))
: Table : { ccc >> a >> free >> free }
: Hand : dddd
: Heap : [bb]

11 From Rule p1 : put_block_at_right & pop_goal_stack
: Table : { ccc >> a >> dddd >> free }
: Hand : empty
: Heap : [bb]

12 From Rule a1 : push_goal(add_another_block)
: Table : { ccc >> a >> dddd >> free }
: Hand : empty
: Heap : [bb]

13 From Rule a3 : pick_up_nearest_block
: Table : { ccc >> a >> dddd >> free }
: Hand : bb
: Heap : [ ]

14 From Rule a2 : pop_goal_stack &
push_goal(place_block(bb))
: Table : { ccc >> a >> dddd >> free }
: Hand : bb
: Heap : [ ]

15 From Rule p1 : put_block_at_right & pop_goal_stack
: Table : { ccc >> a >> dddd >> bb }
: Hand : empty
: Heap : [ ]

16 From Rule s1 : pop_goal_stack & new_state(finished)
: Table : { ccc >> a >> dddd >> bb }
: Hand : empty
: Heap : [ ]

Finished

Yes

Figure 6.7   Rules for a competent seriator

```
rule(f1, [top_goal(seriate), state(just_started)],
         [push_goal(add_first_block)]).
rule(f2, [top_goal(add_first_block), holding(Block)],
         [put_block_at_far_left, new_state(new_arrangement),
             pop_goal_stack]).
rule(f3, [top_goal(add_first_block), not(heap_empty)],
         [pick_up_biggest_block]).

rule(s1, [top_goal(seriate), hand_empty, heap_empty],
         [pop_goal_stack, new_state(finished)]).

rule(a1, [top_goal(seriate)],
         [push_goal(add_another_block)]).
rule(a2, [top_goal(add_another_block), holding(Block)],
         [pop_goal_stack, push_goal(place_block(Block))]).
rule(a3, [top_goal(add_another_block), not(heap_empty)],
         [pick_up_nearest_block]).

rule(p1, [top_goal(place_block(Block)), holding(Block)],
         [put_block_at_right, new_state(new_arrangement)]).

rule(e1, [top_goal(place_block(Block)), state(new_arrangement)],
         [examine(Block, Result), new_state(checked(Result))] ).
rule(e2, [top_goal(place_block(Block)), state(checked(ok))],
         [pop_goal_stack]).
rule(e3, [top_goal(place_block(Block)), state(checked(wrong))],
         [switch_blocks(Block, Left), new_state(new_arrangement)]).
```

6.6   Modelling a competent seriator

A new set of rules for a more competent seriator is given as Figure 6.7 and a sample simulation run using these rules is given as Figure 6.8. The competent seriator can succeed at this task because it can look at the blocks on the table and shuffle them into order. To do this it has some more production rules, e1-3, that expand the state 'adding_blocks' into three more useful states which help it work out if a block is in an 'ok' position on the table. The seriator knows that there is a 'new_arrangement' of blocks on the table once a new one has been added to the line because the production rules that add block also add this as the new state. Before continuing, the blocks must be checked and changed around if necessary. Production rule e1 does the checking using the predicate examine/2 which returns its second argument Result bound to either 'ok' or 'wrong'. This then becomes the new state as checked(ok) or checked(wrong). If the state is checked(ok) then rule e2 will simply confirm that the goal of placing the block is now done by popping the goal off the goal stack. Otherwise rule e3 will note that the Block it is trying to place must be switched with the block to its immediate left and a new_arrangement of blocks pertains. It should be noted that in this set of rules the goal `place_block(Block)` remains in force not only until the block is placed on the table but until it is placed in an 'ok' position with regard to the other blocks in the line.

The new predicates that do the examining and switching are as follows.

```
(i)        examine(Block, ok) :-
                table(1, Block), !.
(ii)       examine(Block, IsOk) :-
                table(N, Block),
                N1 is N - 1,
                table(N1, Block1),
                bigger_than(Block1, Block, IsOk).
```

The `examine/2` predicate is actually begging for improvement, but it is capable of being faulty like the child it is simulating. It is a limited test for comparing the size of blocks in a line on the table. It is called from production rules just after a block has been placed on the table to check that it is ok in this position. It relies on the fact that this seriator only ever places blocks on the table from the left hand side. This is why clause (i) can get away with assuming that a block is automatically ok if it is in position 1 (ie the leftmost slot in the line) because it must be the first block to have been placed! Clause (ii) only actually checks that any block not in table position 1 is smaller than the block to its immediate left! It does this by doing a little arithmetic – making N1 a number which is 1 smaller than itself and getting the name of the block in that location. It hands this `Block` and the one to the left, `Block1`, on to a predicate which checks that `Block1` is `bigger_than` `Block`. The `bigger_than/3` predicate will return a value via its last argument. Either 'ok' or 'wrong' depending on whether the block to the left is bigger or not. This value can then be used by `examine/2` as the `IsOk` result.

```
(i)        bigger_than(A, B, ok):- A > B.
(ii)       bigger_than(A, B, wrong):- A < B.
```

In `bigger_than/3` the names of the blocks are compared directly using the arithmetic operators (greater-than and less-than). In most versions of Prolog this will work fine because dddd > c > b > a. In some Prologs you may need to use the "sorting" operators @> and @< instead. This is a convenience that we have just exploited directly here.

```
(i)        switch_blocks(Block, _) :-
                table(1, Block), !.
(ii)       switch_blocks(Block, Left) :-
                table(N, Block),
                N1 is N - 1,
                table(N1, Left),
                retract(table(N, Block)),
                asserta(table(N1, Block)),
                retract(table(N1, Left)),
                asserta(table(N, Left)), !.
```

The `switch_blocks/2` predicate looks a little similar to the `examine` predicate. It takes two arguments: a block to be switched and the block immediately to its left which it is to be switched with. Clause (i) says that a Block need not be switched with anything if it is already in position 1 on the table (at the far left). Otherwise find the block in the position to the immediate left of this current block (it will be this block's position - 1) and assert and retract the appropriate `table/2` statements about the new positions.

You will see why the examining and switching, as defined here, works if you examine the trace for the competent seriator given in Figure 6.8 (eg see 19-25). If a block is placed that is "bigger" than two blocks already on the table then `examine/2` is called to check it and by returning 'wrong' will force the block and its left-most partner to be switched. The switch will not have been assumed to fix matters because this block will be examine-d again. If the block to its left is still smaller it will be switched again, and so on. For example:

```
{ ccc >> a >> dddd >> free }          examine(dddd, X) where X = wrong
                                      so switch(dddd, a) to give

{ ccc >> dddd >> a >> free }          examine(dddd, X) where X = wrong
                                      so switch(dddd, ccc) to give

{ dddd >> ccc >> a >> free }          examine(dddd, X) where X = ok
```

Clearly this only works because each block is checked and switched to its correct ordering as it is put down. If any block was placed but not checked immediately then it will never get into the right position.

Exercises 6.2 A Competent Seriator

E 6.2.1. Load the **Seriation 2** program which consists of the seriation rules of Appendix 6.2 and all the various seriation definitions of Appendix 6.3, plus the utilities etc of Appendix 6.4.

Run the productions using the seriate query. Examine the printout produced - can you see what is happening and why?

E 6.2.2. Omit rule **e3** by commenting it out (/* immediately in front; */ immediately after the clause). What effect will this have? Check your hypothesis by running the usual query - it should now fail. Scrutinise the productions log - where did it go wrong? You can also check the state of the databases by examining the Working Memory definitions and the micro-world definitions.

E 6.2.3. Brown & Burton (1978) in a very influential paper in *Cognitive Science* demonstrated that many errors in children's arithmetic could be attributed to consistent **mal-rules**. The concept of correct rules, mal-rules and missing rules has been the underpin to attempts to model the student-user in most 'Intelligent Tutoring Systems'.

So, now introduce a mal-rule (**bug**) by de-commenting rule 'e3' (which you did in 2 above) and then change it so that its second action is to create the state `checked(ok)` rather than `new_arrangement`. Try to work out in which circumstances this would matter, and check your hypothesis by selecting an appropriate starting arrangement of blocks.

Figure 6.8   Complex trace of production firings for a competent seriator

: seriate

initial arrangement on heap: [ccc, a, dddd, bb]

1   By rule f1
IF   top_goal(seriate) & state(just_started)
THEN   push_goal(add_first_block)
: Table : { free >> free >> free >> free }
: Hand : empty
: Heap : [ccc, a, dddd, bb]
: Goal Stack : [add_first_block, seriate]
: State : just_started

2   By rule f3
IF   top_goal(add_first_block) & not heap_empty
THEN   pick_up_biggest_block
: Table : { free >> free >> free >> free }
: Hand : dddd
: Heap : [ccc, a, bb]
: Goal Stack : [add_first_block, seriate]
: State : just_started

3   By rule f2
IF   top_goal(add_first_block) & holding(dddd)
THEN   put_block_at_far_left &
        new_state(new_arrangement) & pop_goal_stack
: Table : { dddd >> free >> free >> free }
: Hand : empty
: Heap : [ccc, a, bb]
: Goal Stack : [seriate]
: State : new_arrangement

4   By rule a1
IF   top_goal(seriate)
THEN   push_goal(add_another_block)
: Table : { dddd >> free >> free >> free }
: Hand : empty
: Heap : [ccc, a, bb]
: Goal Stack : [add_another_block, seriate]
: State : new_arrangement

5   By rule a3
IF   top_goal(add_another_block) & not heap_empty
THEN   pick_up_nearest_block
: Table : { dddd >> free >> free >> free }
: Hand : ccc
: Heap : [a, bb]
: Goal Stack : [add_another_block, seriate]
: State : new_arrangement

6   By rule a2
IF   top_goal(add_another_block) & holding(ccc)
THEN   pop_goal_stack & push_goal(place_block(ccc))
: Table : { dddd >> free >> free >> free }
: Hand : ccc
: Heap : [a, bb]
: Goal Stack : [place_block(ccc), seriate]
: State : new_arrangement

7   By rule p1
IF   top_goal(place_block(ccc)) & holding(ccc)
THEN   put_block_at_right &
new_state(new_arrangement)
: Table : { dddd >> ccc >> free >> free }
: Hand : empty
: Heap : [a, bb]
: Goal Stack : [place_block(ccc), seriate]
: State : new_arrangement

8   By rule e1
IF   top_goal(place_block(ccc)) &
        state(new_arrangement)
THEN   examine(ccc, ok) & new_state(checked(ok))
: Table : { dddd >> ccc >> free >> free }
: Hand : empty
: Heap : [a, bb]
: Goal Stack : [place_block(ccc), seriate]
: State : checked(ok)

9   By rule e2
IF   top_goal(place_block(ccc)) & state(checked(ok))
THEN   pop_goal_stack
: Table : { dddd >> ccc >> free >> free }
: Hand : empty
: Heap : [a, bb]
: Goal Stack : [seriate]
: State : checked(ok)

10   By rule a1
IF   top_goal(seriate)
THEN   push_goal(add_another_block)
: Table : { dddd >> ccc >> free >> free }
: Hand : empty
: Heap : [a, bb]
: Goal Stack : [add_another_block, seriate]
: State : checked(ok)

11   By rule a3
IF   top_goal(add_another_block) & not heap_empty
THEN   pick_up_nearest_block
: Table : { dddd >> ccc >> free >> free }
: Hand : a
: Heap : [bb]
: Goal Stack : [add_another_block, seriate]
: State : checked(ok)

12   By rule a2
IF   top_goal(add_another_block) & holding(a)
THEN   pop_goal_stack & push_goal(place_block(a))
: Table : { dddd >> ccc >> free >> free }
: Hand : a
:   Heap : [bb]
: Goal Stack : [place_block(a), seriate]
: State : checked(ok)

13   By rule p1
IF   top_goal(place_block(a)) & holding(a)
THEN   put_block_at_right &
        new_state(new_arrangement)
: Table : { dddd >> ccc >> a >> free }
: Hand : empty
:   Heap : [bb]
: Goal Stack : [place_block(a), seriate]
: State : new_arrangement

14   By rule e1
IF   top_goal(place_block(a)) & state(new_arrangement)
THEN   examine(a, ok) & new_state(checked(ok))
: Table : { dddd >> ccc >> a >> free }
: Hand : empty
:   Heap : [bb]
: Goal Stack : [place_block(a), seriate]
: State : checked(ok)

15   By rule e2
IF   top_goal(place_block(a)) & state(checked(ok))
THEN   pop_goal_stack
: Table : { dddd >> ccc >> a >> free }
: Hand : empty
:   Heap : [bb]
: Goal Stack : [seriate]
: State : checked(ok)

16   By rule a1
IF   top_goal(seriate)
THEN   push_goal(add_another_block)
: Table : { dddd >> ccc >> a >> free }
: Hand : empty
:   Heap : [bb]
: Goal Stack : [add_another_block, seriate]
: State : checked(ok)

17   By rule a3
IF   top_goal(add_another_block) & not heap_empty
THEN   pick_up_nearest_block
: Table : { dddd >> ccc >> a >> free }
: Hand : bb
:   Heap : [ ]
: Goal Stack : [add_another_block, seriate]
: State : checked(ok)

18   By rule a2
IF   top_goal(add_another_block) & holding(bb)
THEN   pop_goal_stack & push_goal(place_block(bb))
: Table : { dddd >> ccc >> a >> free }
: Hand : bb
:   Heap : [ ]
: Goal Stack : [place_block(bb), seriate]
: State : checked(ok)

19   By rule p1
IF   top_goal(place_block(bb)) & holding(bb)
THEN   put_block_at_right &
new_state(new_arrangement)
: Table : { dddd >> ccc >> a >> bb }
: Hand : empty
:   Heap : [ ]
: Goal Stack : [place_block(bb), seriate]
: State : new_arrangement

20   By rule e1
IF   top_goal(place_block(bb)) &
        state(new_arrangement)
THEN   examine(bb, wrong) & new_state(checked(wrong))
: Table : { dddd >> ccc >> a >> bb }
: Hand : empty
:   Heap : [ ]
: Goal Stack : [place_block(bb), seriate]
: State : checked(wrong)

21   By rule e3
IF   top_goal(place_block(bb)) &
state(checked(wrong))
THEN   switch_blocks(bb, a) &
        new_state(new_arrangement)
: Table : { dddd >> ccc >> bb >> a }
: Hand : empty
:   Heap : [ ]
: Goal Stack : [place_block(bb), seriate]
: State : new_arrangement

22   By rule e1
IF   top_goal(place_block(bb)) &
        state(new_arrangement)
THEN   examine(bb, ok) & new_state(checked(ok))
: Table : { dddd >> ccc >> bb >> a }
: Hand : empty
:   Heap : [ ]
: Goal Stack : [place_block(bb), seriate]
: State : checked(ok)

23   By rule e2
IF   top_goal(place_block(bb)) & state(checked(ok))
THEN   pop_goal_stack
: Table : { dddd >> ccc >> bb >> a }
: Hand : empty
:   Heap : [ ]
: Goal Stack : [seriate]
: State : checked(ok)

24   By rule s1
IF   top_goal(seriate) & hand_empty & heap_empty
THEN   pop_goal_stack & new_state(finished)
: Table : { dddd >> ccc >> bb >> a }
: Hand : empty
:   Heap : [ ]
: Goal Stack : [ ]
: State : finished

Finished
Yes

6.7   Learning with Production Rules

J R Anderson (eg. 1983) has taken the analysis of cognition in terms of productions very much further in his ACT* theory, and claims that productions underlie the whole of human cognition. He has a model of the acquisition of expertise in procedural skills which involves three stages:

declarative encoding	creating the productions
knowledge compilation:	
production composition	combining several productions into 1
proceduralisation	cutting out the working memory load
Production tuning:	
generalisation	making more general
discrimination	making more specific
strengthening	making stronger

Exercises 6.2 provided good examples of **declarative encoding** of new productions (eg. the invention of the 'examination' productions e1, e2, e3) to help the naive seriator become competent and also of the tuning of productions by **discrimination**. However, neither strengthening nor proceduralisation is practical with the current simulation. **Strengthening** a production would mean adding weight to a 'good' production so that it fired more frequently than a competing production, but in our current system we have carefully avoided competition. **Proceduralisation** means turning a declarative rule into a procedure that would be more efficient. If you consider the predicate `examine/2` (Code Appendix D 6.3.17) this could clearly be re-written so that it was itself a set of production rules using working memory and so on, but in the project it is written directly as a Prolog procedure to examine the blocks. Proceduralisation would mean re-writing the rules given as these (more efficient and direct) procedures.

We have no examples of **generalisation** in the current project, but language acquisition shows some clear generalisation effects, such as the combination of a series of specific productions like:

IF	want plural of horse	THEN	say horses
IF	want plural of cow	THEN	say cows
IF	want plural of dog	THEN	say dogs

combine into a more general production using variables:

IF	want plural of Word	THEN	join Word with 's' making Word1 & say Word1

Exercises 6.3. Learning

E 6.3.1. Reload the original Competent Seriation program afresh - without any of the changes you may have made to it in the last few exercises.

There is a good example of **production composition** in the seriation tasks. Have a look through the production logs you have produced. (If you cannot see them on your computer you can simply examine the printout shown as Figure 6.7). Can you find a set of three productions that appear together in the same sequence repeatedly?

E 6.3.2. Try to write a new production which achieves the effect of all three.

Tiny Hint: Start off with the 3 productions a1, a3 & a2 which always appear in the same order. Try to write a production ('a0' say) which has the conditions of a1 (which comes first), the effects on working memory (actions) of a2 (which comes last) and collects together any other important actions en route. Type it in to the seriation rules window **above** a1, so that Prolog will test it before the other (a) rules. It should work in 20 or so productions for the [ccc, a, dddd, bb] start.

Giveaway Hint for the Terminally Stuck:

You won't need 'add_another_block' to be a goal at all as this is entirely internal to the set of 3 rules, but you will need to push_goal(place_block(Block)) at some point as this is needed for the examination (e) rules to 'fire'. Don't forget that the variable Block will need to have a value before it is pushed as the next goal - how about looking to see what you are holding, before adding it.

E 6.3.3. Now try modifying a0 so that it absorbs production p1 to give a production 'm1'. This ends up with a single rule that should reduce the productions to 16 or so.

E 6.3.4. Add another block 'eeeee' into the simulation - this will clearly take more productions.

E 6.3.5. As a final try at efficiency, how about going for the shortest possible number of productions, by always selecting the biggest block and cutting down the examination to a minimum.

6.8   Further work on the simulation

As noted earlier, conflict resolution is needed whenever two or more rules could 'fire' at the same time in that both their sets of conditions are satisfied. The conflict resolution principles common in the OPS system (McDermott, 1981) include a combination of refractoriness, recency, specificity and production ordering, in decreasing order of priority. **Refractoriness** is included primarily to avoid infinite loops and prevents a production firing if it matches the same data structure (in WM) again. **Recency** is especially important for PSs with unlimited WM and selects the production which matches the most recent data in WM (on the grounds that in a sequence of operations the elements most recently added will be most relevant). If two productions match exactly on recency, the **specificity** criterion is invoked. This selects the production with more conditions.

For instance, given

> P1: IF the plural of a noun is required THEN add 's'
> P2: IF the plural of a noun is required AND the noun is bus THEN add 'es'

The specificity principle correctly selects P2 in the appropriate circumstances.

If all else fails to resolve a conflict between two productions, then OPS falls back on the default **rule ordering** principle that we are using here.

In fact, Young appears to have designed his system so that conflicts will not normally occur. Nonetheless, he defines a specificity mechanism in which more specific rules have higher priority. This can be achieved easily in Prolog by merely rearranging the rules so that those with the most conditions precede those with less conditions - because Prolog tries out each rule in turn, starting at the top until one succeeds.

A more complex resolution mechanism would require a slightly more sophisticated approach. It would be natural to implement 'recency' for example, by using the inbuilt ordering on the non-goal WM and checking each element of WM in order to see which, if any, of the production rules it matches. If none matched then the second element of WM would be checked and so on, whereas if one did match, the remainder of its conditions would be checked. In fact one major feature of the goal stack structure is to ensure that the PS remains on course towards the overall objective, and the top stack may be thought of a one element embodiment of the recency principle — productions which do not match the current goal are, by definition, not selected.

Possible Advanced Projects

Project 1. (Easy). Modify the seriation PS so that it embodies the recency principle and has no goal stack.

Project 2. (Hard). Implement a Production system for Addition.

One of the classic cognitive science papers was the demonstration by Brown and Burton (1978) that many 'bugs' in children's arithmetic were systematic misunderstandings of the procedural rules involved. Soon afterwards Young and O'Shea (1981) showed that representing the arithmetic procedures within a production rule format allowed one to identify the 'buggy rules' as missing individual productions. The technique of modelling both correct procedural knowledge and potential bugs all within a production rule format has become an established technique for creating 'Intelligent Tutoring Systems' (ITS). These are computer programs that 'understand' a domain and are therefore able to give intelligent advice on how to proceed and to diagnose the causes of any errors. See Sleeman and Brown (1982) for a collection of classics and Anderson et al (1990) for a recent review of a common methodology. Building an ITS would be a very advanced project indeed, but it is possible to get a feel for the technique by creating a production system for doing two column addition.

The simplest two column addition involves adding the contents of a column together and entering their combined value beneath the column. This is made more complicated by numbers which when combined are greater than 9 and require the use of a carry. In Figure 6.9 below, the sum 67 + 58 requires two carry operations.

Figure 6.9 A traditional approach to 2 column addition

Stage 1	Stage 2	Stage 3	Stage 4	Stage 5
6 7	6 7	6 7	6 7	6 7
5 8 +	5 8 +	5 8 +	5 8 +	5 8 +
?	5	? 5	? 2 5	1 2 5
?	1	1	1	1

(i) Try writing a production rule system to implement this. In Figure 6.10 we have made some suggestions for what your rules might look like. These rules are not definitive - just view them as hints to get you started. Short of implementing it all for you we can only suggest that most of the operations required are relatively straightforward. Your first problem is to consider how to represent the sum itself - in its columns - plus the answer and possible carry columns also. To get you started here is a suggestion for one of the trickier operations:

```
%  decompose(TU,Tens,Units) means
%   decomposes the 2 digit number TU into its constituent Tens and Units
```

```
decompose(TU,T,U):-
        member(T,[0,1,2,3,4,5,6,7,8,9]),
        member(U,[0,1,2,3,4,5,6,7,8,9]),
        TU is (10*T)+U.
```

A query to `(?) decompose(85, 8, 5).` Should say YES. Whilst the more normal query would be `(?) decompose(85, X, Y).` Which should say : YES. Where $X = 8$ and $Y = 5$. Like many more Prolog definitions this is not particularly efficient but it is quite powerful.

Figure 6.10   Suggested Production System Rules for Addition

rule :   s1   **IF**   the top goal is to 'do addition' **and** the current state is 'just started'
THEN   push the goal 'add units column' **and**
the new state is 'adding units'

rule :   u1   **IF**   the top goal is to 'add units column' **and** the current state is 'adding units'
and top_unit(U1) **and** bottom_unit(U2)

THEN   set_wm(U1) **and** add_to_wm(U2)

and the new state is 'column added'

rule :   u2, **IF**   the top goal is to 'add units column' **and** the state is 'column added'
and wm(Sum)

THEN   decompose(Sum, Tens, Units) **and** enter(Units)

and set_wm(Tens) **and** the new state is 'entering carry'

rule :   u3, **IF**   the top goal is to 'add units column' **and** the state is 'entering carry'
and wm(0)

THEN   pop the goal stack **and** push the goal 'add tens column'

and the new state is 'adding tens'

rule :   u4, **IF**   the top goal is to 'add units column' **and** the state is 'entering carry'
and wm(Carry)

THEN   enter(Carry) **and** pop the goal stack

and push the goal 'add tens column'

and the new state is 'adding tens'

rule :   t1   **IF**   the top goal is to 'add tens column' **and** the current state is 'adding tens'
and top_tens(T1) **and** bottom_tens(T2)

THEN   add_to_wm(T1) **and** add_to_wm(T2)

and the new state is 'column added'

rule :   t2, **IF**   the top goal is to 'add tens column' **and** the state is 'column added'
and wm(Sum)

THEN   decompose(Sum, Tens, Units) **and** enter(Units)

and set_wm(Tens) **and** the new state is 'entering carry'

rule :   t3, **IF**   the top goal is to 'add tens column' **and** the state is 'entering carry'
and wm(0)

THEN   pop the goal stack **and** new state 'finished'

rule :   t4, **IF**   the top goal is to 'add tens column' **and** the state is 'entering carry'
and wm(Carry)

THEN   enter(Carry) **and** pop the goal stack **and** new state 'finished'

(ii) Create a 'buggy rule' which forgets to add in the carry. Add a few more mal-rules — maybe one that adds the tens column before the units, another that when adding a 0 always gives the sum as 0, another which forgets to enter the carry in the final column, and so on. You might want to refer to Young and O'Shea (1981) to give you some ideas about how to make this model a more accurate reflection of children's performance.

(iii) A very advanced project would be to amend your version to try to **diagnose** errors. That is, the answer is stored alongside the sum, and the system has to try to find a buggy rule which generates the incorrect answer. So the tutoring part of the system has a "correct" set of production rules - that calculates what each answer entered by the student should be. Whenever the student's input does not match the "correct" one the system should look at a 'library' of buggy rules to see what each would produce at this point. If there is one buggy rule that generates the same error as the student then the system might suggest that this is the problem. It might, for example, print out a piece of advice that could be stored with each rule eg. "You are forgetting to add in the carry in the last column." One possible further complexity is to deal with a situation where there may be a number of buggy rules that would account for the same error. A very sophisticated tutor should be able to generate new problem sums for the student to try that help to distinguish between the competing hypotheses of the student's problem.

6.9   Further Reading

The "traditional" approach to cognitive modelling in Cognitive Science is based upon the premise that researchers should describe events with the language of abstract symbol manipulation (Newell & Simon, 1972). The two major symbolic architectures are ACT* / PUPS (Anderson, 1983; 1989) and SOAR (Laird, Newell & Rosenbloom, 1986; Newell, Rosenbloom and Laird, 1990). Both are expressed in terms of production systems related to the one developed in this project. By far the biggest issue raised by the project simulation is that it is descriptive - it does not explain why the production rule developmental changes happen or how. It is simply an experiment to examine the changes which would be needed to exhibit the observed behaviour. These workers have gone much further than this analysis.

An excellent contrast with this work is the recent research that has been directed towards modelling cognition at a sub-symbolic level - in terms of neural networks (eg. Rumelhart et al, 1986). Neural net or "connectionist" models distribute knowledge amongst a set of nodes and the links between them. The links between the inputs to the system and its outputs are established through a lengthy "training" process. In this, the net learns to associate some input values with some other output values. So, neural nets do not manipulate explicit symbols as in the rules of the production system, instead the knowledge of the system is implicit in its behaviour. The net "learns" to perform in a way that is rule governed (consistently associating inputs and outputs), but without the explicit rules.

Acknowledgements

As has already been noted the form of the production rules used in the sections above is based upon a presentation of Young's system by Luger (1978) in an excellent Open University workbook.

Chapter 7 : Planning and Problem Solving

Adaptive problem solving lies at the heart of intelligent behaviour — even encyclopaedic knowledge would be of limited value to a person without the ability to apply the right pieces of that knowledge to the right situations. One of the major goals of early AI research was to attempt to build artificial problem solvers capable of intelligent behaviour in a range of situations. In this chapter we shall investigate some classical general problem solving methods which make the assumption that many problem domains may be characterised as a finite 'state space' in which the problem solver may 'operate' by moving from one state to another - making a legal (allowed) move. The three techniques we shall investigate are 'depth-first search' (an example of exhaustive search techniques); 'heuristic search'; and 'Means-Ends Analysis'. The first two approaches will be applied to a simple 'blocks world' domain while the third will be set in the much more interesting 'robot world' domain invented by Fikes and Nilsson (1971) for their STRIPS problem solver.

7.1 Background - State Space Search

The first thing to consider in modelling any cognitive mechanism is how to *represent* the important aspects of it, and the second thing to consider is how to navigate through this representation to use it to solve some problem. Using a representation involves *search*. In the project on semantic memory the representation was a semantic network of facts about the properties of living things and the search was how this network was traversed to answer questions about the living things. In the previous project on a production system the representation was production rules and the search was the mechanism used to fire the rules to seriate the blocks. Search implies choice. Given a set of things that can be done at any one time to help solve a problem, which of these things do you do and in which order? The search problem is most apparent in the area of **planning**.

7.1.1 Representing a problem domain

The key to a representation is what information it makes explicit. Alan Newell and his colleagues have argued over a period of decades (eg. Newell, Shaw & Simon 1958, Newell & Simon 1972, Laird et al 1986) that representing a domain as a 'state space' is a powerful representational device well suited to modelling 'weak' (domain independent) problem solving. The main features of a state space analysis are:

(i) A problem domain (henceforth the 'micro-world') is partitioned into a finite set of 'states'. These states represent the space of all the possible arrangements of all the elements in the microworld. Chess is a common micro-world – whose state space consists of all the possible board configurations of chess pieces.

(ii) The state space is structured in that one state may be related to another state by virtue of a simple change in the world. The micro-world changes state due to the action of an 'operator' which has a determinate action. A chess operator might be 'move Queen'. This operator joins two states where the only difference is that the Queen piece was in one position or another

(iii) Following from this it is clear that the state space can be quite constrained in that not all operator actions are permissible from a given state. This means that the operator connections between states are limited to the set of 'legal moves' which are possible. In chess the concept of legal moves is all pervasive. From a given state the operator 'move Queen' may not be possible (legal), and even if it is there will only be so many places that the piece may move to – each one representing a new state.

(iv) There are normally two special states in the state space: a 'start' or 'initial state' and a 'goal state'. In chess the start state is that single state with the pieces lined up in opposition, while the goal state is any state where the king is threatened by an enemy piece – 'check' – and cannot get out of check. The problem for any planning system is to work out how to transform the start state into the goal state. A solution to the problem – a plan – would normally comprise a set of operations which perform this transformation. Much problem solving involves the discovery of a 'good' solution, (usually the shortest plan), though for some problems any solution will be satisfactory.

7.1.2 State Space Search

Having decided how to represent the important aspects of a domain, the second thing to consider in modelling some cognitive mechanism is how to navigate through this representation to use it to solve some problem. Terminology in problem solving reflects historical developments rather than an orderly analysis and so it can be rather confusing. In computer science it has been the custom to use the analogy for the state space of a spatial layout rather like a maze, in which each state is represented by a single point (or 'node'), with each node linked to other nodes if there is a legal move between them. Using this spatial representation makes it natural to equate finding a solution with discovering a route or *path* through the 'maze' from the start state to the goal state, that is, 'searching' through the network of possible states starting from the start state until the goal state is reached. The search metaphor seems natural for problems such as the 'travelling salesman' problem, the 'hobbits and orcs' problem and even for adversarial games such as chess. It becomes strained for problems, such as, say, making a cup of coffee, in domains which have a richer structure, and in such cases it is more normal to refer to the problem solving as 'planning' or even 'control'. We shall use the generic term problem solving throughout this chapter.

7.2 State Space Search in a Blocks World

Consider a simple micro-world of blocks like the one used in the seriation project. Only this time all the blocks are the same size and placed upon a table. The planner must 'stack' these blocks to make a specific block-tower. Planning is required because there are a large number of ways in which this can be done - and we want it done in the most efficient way possible - employing the least number of operator 'moves'.

Figure 7.1 illustrates an example of a partial state space search diagram for a simple 'blocks world'. In this world the blocks are in one set of positions in the initial or current state and this state can be changed to eventually achieve a specific target or 'goal state'. The diagram shows only a selection of the many possible states that could be involved in the state space for this problem.

In Figure 7.1 the block states are outlined connected by an operator which can move one block at a time to a new position. The start state of the world is that block **a** is upon block **b**, whilst block **c** is on its own to the right. From this state there are four possible new states that could be produced by applying our 'move-one-block' operator. Either blocks **a** or **c** can be moved (**b** cannot be moved because it has a block on top of it) and there are two possible places that each block could be placed. From each of these new possible states the operator may be applied again to produce a further set of new possible states[1]. The problem solver can keep generating new possible blocks-world states until it produces one which matches the goal state - in this case the goal is to have **a** upon **b** upon **c** at the right of the world state. The challenge to the problem solver is to navigate through the many possible states that could be generated from the initial one to find the shortest possible path to the goal state.

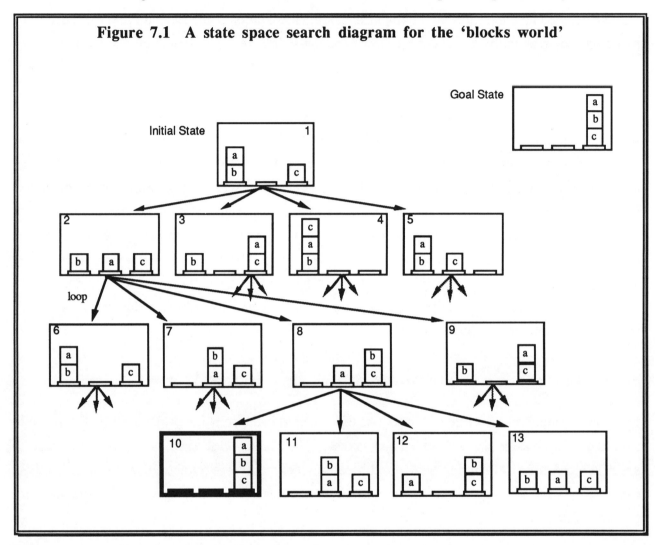

Figure 7.1 A state space search diagram for the 'blocks world'

This is not a trivial problem because there may be very many alternative possible states that need to be considered - this figure shows only a few of the states for clarity. Also our example has only three blocks and positions, but the problem becomes exponentially more complex with each block or position added! In the current figure the most efficient set of moves leads from state 1 to 2 to 8 and then to 10, but if the problem solver just made a random move it might take a very long time to find this goal state, if it could find it at all.

---

[1]It is important to note that, although the search space is represented as a hierarchical tree, it is better seen as a richly interconnected network. For instance, note that states 1 and 6 are in fact identical, and therefore the tree leading from 6 is identical to that leading from 1 ... There is clearly a danger of infinite loops in such a representation!

Exercises 7.1   Representing States and legal moves in the blocks world

Representing a state. In our Prolog implementation of this problem we represent each possible arrangement of blocks by a state. Assume there are 3 blocks: a, b and c, and there are 3 piles: pile1, pile2 and pile3. A state may be represented as a list of three 'upon' relations which specify the arrangement of blocks **a, b** and **c** respectively. For instance, state 1 in Figure 7.1 could be represented as the list   [upon(a, b), upon(b, pile1), upon(c, pile3)].

Representing a move. A move is a relation like **move(a, c, pile1)** which means 'move block a from on c to on pile1'. A move is only 'legal' in a given state if the block to be moved is clear (ie has no block on top of it) and its destination (whether block or pile) is also clear.

Implement the program **Blocks World**. It is given at the start of Appendix 7.1, and defines the representation for states, moves and legal actions in the blocks world.

E 7.1.1 Using pencil and paper work out all the legal moves from this state

        [upon(a, c), upon(b, pile2), upon(c, pile3)].

E 7.1.2 Check your answer via 'All solutions' to the following query:

        (?)   legal_action(Act, [upon (a,c), upon (b,pile2), upon (c,pile3)]).

E 7.1.3 Find the definition for legal_action/2. Look through it carefully to check how it works. What is the purpose of the restriction: Block \= Destination ? If you're not sure comment it out (remember to adjust the commas and full-stop) and re-run the query in E7.1.2 above with this definition. NB: Re-insert the proper definition immediately afterwards!

E 7.1.4 It is hard to see at a glance what the state is from the upon(a, c) etc format, so to help you visualise the state we have introduced the predicate piles(State, Piles). Using specially constructed queries work out what it does.

    Hint. Try (?)   piles([upon (a,c), upon (b,pile2), upon(c, pile3)], Ps).

7.3   Exhaustive Search Methods

Exhaustive search methods are sometimes called 'brute force searches' because they don't use any 'intelligence' but rely upon the efficiency of the computer in doing many calculations very quickly. If implemented properly they can 'guarantee' that a solution is found. The two simplest brute force methods are depth-first and breadth-first search. Figure 7.2 shows the 'patterns' of each type of search as they might be overlaid on the search space of Figure 7.1.

Breadth-first search looks at each layer of the tree in turn for the goal state. So for the space of Figure 7.1 it considers each of the moves from state 1 in turn: checking 2, 3, 4, and then 5. As none is the goal state it must go down one level and then do the same again from there: checking 6, 7, 8 and 9 from state 2; then all from state 3; then all from state 4, etc.

Depth-first search is typically implemented in conjunction with left-first search and backtracking. This means that they will try alternatives left-to-right, and if they get stuck for some reason they can 'go back' to a previous state to try again. Depth-first search means taking the left-most alternative operator 'move' to a new state and following it through by taking the next left-most alternative – checking for the 'goal' state as it goes down. It does not bother to look at the other alternatives on each level until it is forced to backtrack. So in Figure 7.1 the left-most alternative is to move block a off block b to produce state 2. The next left-most move is to move block a again, this time onto block b in state 6. This illustrates why 'backtracking' is essential for depth-first search because state 6 is identical to state 1 where we came from originally! If the problem solver continued with this left-most move it may well loop around the same set of states indefinitely. However, if it is able to detect this loop as being a 'dead-end' it must **backtrack** from 6 to 2 and try the **next** left-most move to 7 and so on.

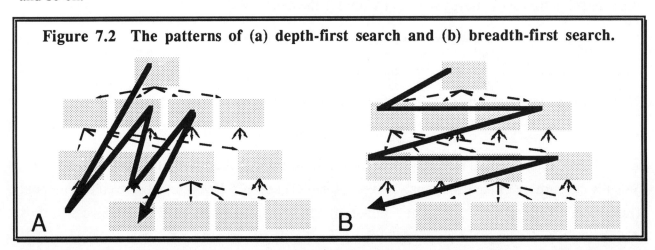

Figure 7.2   The patterns of (a) depth-first search and (b) breadth-first search.

Both of these forms of search may traverse the whole tree of possible states until the goal state is found. The main difference is in the search pattern produced through the state space - as implied by their names. As shown in Figure 7.2 depth-first (a) will go downwards first whilst breadth-first (b) will search along before going down. Both can be implemented in Prolog, but depth-first is more natural to Prolog's own style of problem-solving and so we have chosen to illustrate only depth-first search in our exercises here.

7.3.1 The df0 depth-first search predicate

This is the simplest version of depth-first search you could implement. It doesn't work properly but forms the basis for viable methods such as df1 and df2. We have had to complicate the Appendix definition somewhat to give an informative printout, but the core of the definition is shown below:

```
df0(State, State):-                             % stopping condition
    write('** success **').
df0(State, GoalState) :-
    legal_action(Action, State),                %  generate an Action to try
    update_state(Action, State, NewState),      %  find the NewState
    df0(NewState, GoalState).                    %  recurse
```

The call to this definition df0(S, G) means that the depth first search is working on current state S and hoping to find the goal state G. The first clause is (of course) the stopping check and states that if the current state is exactly the same as the goal state then succeed trivially, just printing out '** success **'. Otherwise the call legal_action(Action, State) generates a legal action Action that is true in the current State. This action is used to update the state to a new state with update_state/3. This new state and the same goal state is passed on to a recursive call. The definition for legal_action/2 was the subject of an exercise above, and the definition for update_state/3 is documented in the Appendix as Defn 7.1.9.

It's actually rather like a drunkard wandering aimlessly round a maze, not noticing where he's going, but hoping eventually to stumble across the way out!

Exercises 7.2 df0

We have constructed the query test_df0(test1) to help you test the search methods easily. Specific start and goal states are stored under the label 'test1' in initial_state and goal_state. So, a query of test_df0(test1) essentially passes these state lists on to df0 as the values for the Start and Goal states. Try the query. Interrupt it after 6 or so recursions.

E 7.2.1 Examine the printout produced. What is going wrong?

E 7.2.2. Try test2. Is it any better?

E 7.2.3. Why do you think it always chooses the action move(a, b, c) or failing that move(a, c, b) ?

Hint : Check the legal moves for the initial state for test1 as in 1(ii) above. Which one came first? Why do you think Prolog generated the block a to move first, rather than b or c?

7.3.2 The df1 depth-first search predicate

The df1/3 predicate is an improvement on df0 which will always find a solution (if one exists) in a finite search space. The crucial difference is that it keeps track of where it has been, and never explores the same state twice, thus avoiding endless loops. The basic code is shown below:

```
df1(State, State, Visited):-                        % stopping condition
    write('** success **').
df1(State, GoalState, Visited) :-
    legal_action(Action, State),                     % generate an Action to try
    update_state(Action, State, NewState),           % find the NewState
    not(member(NewState, Visited)),                  % prevent infinite loop
    df1(NewState, GoalState, [NewState|Visited] ).    % recurse
```

Note how df1 takes 3 arguments - in addition to the current state and goal state it has a list Visited of states it has already explored. Notice how we make use of the list guillotine constructively to add the NewState on to the Visited list for the recursive call (line 5 of second clause). This is a very common technique in Prolog.

Exercises 7.3 df1

E 7.3.1 Run the queries `test_df1(test1)`, `test_df1(test2)` and `test_df1(test3)`. Examine the printouts. Why was `test3` harder to achieve? Hint: look at the goal states.

A note on Backtracking. Notice that there is a message "backtracking" in `test3`. This indicates that there were no unexplored routes from that state, and so it was necessary to retrace the previous action and try again. You might like to check explicitly that this was correct by working out the possible states and checking whether they had been visited.

E 7.3.2 Modify **df1** so that, when it succeeds, it prints out the list of states visited. Hint: modify the message given in the first clause of df1.

7.4   Heuristic Search

The definition `df1/3` was ok in that it guaranteed a solution, but it can be very inefficient. As discussed above, the search process is blind, and takes no account of what the goal state is (until it happens to blunder across it). It would be much better if we could somehow guide the choice of legal action made at each point by means of some heuristic which improved the chances of reaching the target goal.

7.4.1 The df2 depth first heuristic search predicate

This is done in `df2/3` by means of the `suggest/3` predicate. The basic code is as follows:

```
df2(State, State, Visited) :-              % stopping condition
    write('** success **').
df2(State, GoalState, Visited) :-
    suggest(GoalState, State, Action),     % generate a sensible move
    update_state(Action, State, NewState), % find the NewState
    not(member(NewState, Visited)),        % prevent infinite loop
    df2(NewState, GoalState, [NewState|Visited] ).  % recurse
```

The first clause of this new definition is identical to that for `df1/3`. The difference is that instead of `legal_action/2` just generating a legal move the predicate `suggest/3` is used to generate a 'good' action. Just how good the suggested action is depends on the simple 'heuristics' that the new predicate is using - ours is very simple indeed.

Exercises 7.4   df2

E 7.4.1 Look at the code for `suggest/3` below. Can you see what it does? When will it be useful?

```
suggest(TargetState, CurrentState, move(Block, _, Place)) :-
    upon(Block, Place, TargetState),
    place(Place),
    legal_action(move(Block, _, Place), CurrentState).
suggest(_, CurrentState, Move) :-
    legal_action(Move, CurrentState).
```

E 7.4.2 Run the `test1`, `test2` and `test3` queries as before. Compare the printouts with those for `df1`. Look very carefully at the printout for `test3`. Can you see why it is so much shorter than `df1`'s attempt at `test3`?

Exercises 7.5   Prolog Clause order effects

The fact that Prolog will always attempt to prove the first (top) clause of a predicate definition first often has major effects on the efficiency of a program. This is certainly true for df1 where the depth first problem solving is by no means 'blind' but actually follows an implicit heuristic of its own.

E 7.5.1 Look at the `is_clear` predicate (Appendix Defn 7.1.4). This comprises two clauses, one relating to blocks and the other to piles. Change round their order. Rerun the query (?) `test_df1(test1)`. What has happened? Why has it happened? *Hint: look at the very first move - what is the difference? How can it be related to the change in the isclear ordering?*

E 7.5.2 Try to predict the effect of changing the order of the clauses which make up the block definition to

```
block(b)  .
block(c)  .
block(a)  .
```

Check your predictions.

E 7.5.3 Introduce a fourth block `d`. You will need to add new start and goal states for four blocks. Try this one:

```
test_states(test4,
     [ upon(a,b),  upon(b,pile1),  upon(c,pile3),  upon(d, pile2) ],
     [ upon(a,b),  upon(b,c),      upon(c,d)  ,     upon(d, pile3) ] ).
```

Predict what effect `d` will have on the search time. Try it and see?

E 7.5.4 Implement the **towers of hanoi** game. This uses four discs of different sizes, which can only be piled so that smaller blocks go on top of larger ones. Assuming a<b<c<d (ie a is smallest etc) modify the definition of `legal_action` so that the hanoi rule applies.

For most implementations of Prolog you only need change the last line of the second clause of the `legal_action` program, ie change the = to < in that line. Predict what effect this restriction will have on the solution time. Try it and see.

Advanced Search Exercise – Best-First search

In fact, the suggest predicate is an extreme example of a common technique in heuristic search, that of providing an evaluation function. This attempts to quantify how 'good' the outcome of each possible move is with the intention of selecting the move that has the best outcome. This strategy is often known as 'best-first search'. An example of this, based on the depth-first predicates already explored is shown as bf/3 here.

```
bf(State, State, Visited) :- write('Success!').      % stopping condition
bf(State, GoalState, Visited) :-
    setof((E, A),
          (legal_action(Action, State), eval(A, GoalState, E)),
          [(Eval, Action) | Rest]
        ),
                                              % best evaluation function
    update_state(Action, State, NewState),    % find the NewState
    not(member(NewState, Visited)),           % prevent infinite loop
    bf(NewState, GoalState, [NewState|Visited] ).    % recurse
```

Evaluation functions must be chosen with great care. For instance, the obvious evaluation function for the blocks world domain is to give one point for each block which is the required pile (in the goal state). The evaluation function would therefore range between 0 and 3.

Write a few evaluation functions. Compare performance on the various tests.

Another advanced exercise would be to implement a breadth-first search — see Bratko (1986) for some hints.

7.5   Means-Ends Analysis

Having spent some time developing the concepts of exhaustive search and heuristic search, it is fair to say that derivatives of heuristic search techniques have been applied reasonably successfully in a number of domains, such as computer chess, with potentially very large search spaces. It is important to stress, however, that the technique becomes much less attractive as the number of alternatives at each state increase. Consider a real life problem such as deciding how to get to work from your home. There are innumerable possible actions you could do at home — make coffee, read a book, pick up car keys, scratch head, play chess etc and only a few of these actions could be useful for getting to work. The fundamental problem is that a simple state space search has no knowledge about the use of appropriate means of achieving the desired ends. The search space of all possible actions in all possible combinations is inconceivable. It would be much more sensible to have each possible action explicitly marked as suitable for one thing or another. The problem-solver could then consult this explicit representation and only bother to search with those that were marked as appropriate for the desired end. A strategy based upon representing symbolic knowledge about the search problem was proposed in seminal research by Newell, Shaw and Simon (1958) in their GPS (General Problem Solver) program. GPS was a *tour de force* in that, not only did it solve a wide range of problems but it also did it in psychologically plausible way. GPS is probably best seen as a planner, producing a top down plan to achieve the goal state rather than searching blindly through the state space. The key concepts introduced in GPS included:

(i) states and **state space** (as we have seen these concepts have more general applicability)

(ii) **operators** (again a familiar concept now — an operator is a means of transforming one state into another)

(iii) **means - ends analysis**. This gave GPS its distinctive and intuitively plausible approach. Newell and his colleagues argued that much human problem solving involved an analysis of what the desired ends were (transforming the initial state into the goal state: eg. getting from home to work) and what the available means were (eg. making coffee, walking, getting a taxi, driving etc.) and then using one's knowledge of the applicability of the different operators to construct a plan.

(iv) Key concepts within means-ends analysis were **preconditions** (conditions that had to be achieved before an operator became available — eg. having the car keys for driving a car); **problem decomposition** (splitting the main problem into a set of subproblems — eg. get in car, drive to station, get train, get taxi etc.).

(v) The major heuristic for problem solving was **difference reduction**. This was much more powerful than having a global and blind evaluation function such as distance from goal, for GPS problem solving proceeded by trying to eliminate differences between the goal state and the target state. In effect, this meant trying to satisfy the preconditions for each of the operators required. For instance, one precondition for 'fly by plane' is say 'me at airport'. Therefore, in order to minimise the difference between the current state and the goal state, it is first necessary to minimise the difference between 'me at home' and 'me at airport' ie. to achieve the precondition. In this way a series of subproblems is set up recursively, and (all being well) the sequence of sub-problem solutions will provide a plan for the whole problem.

Unfortunately, one problem left implicit in GPS is how to order the possible operators so that an appropriate one will be selected. Clearly this requires domain knowledge. The approach used by GPS was the difference-procedure table (see Figure 7.3). It may be seen that a great deal of work is required to set up this domain knowledge, and a critic might argue that most of the intelligence of a GPS application resides in the difference-procedure table rather than the general problem solving procedures.

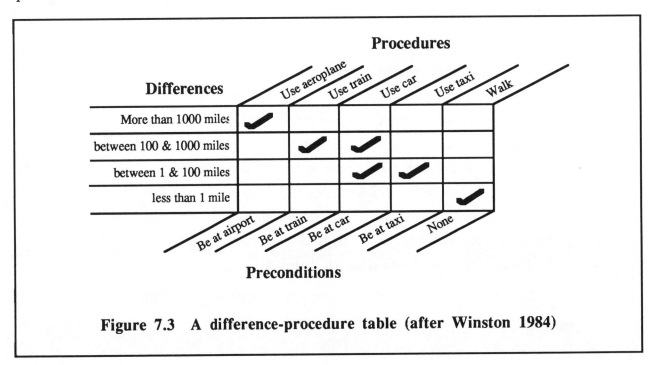

Figure 7.3   A difference-procedure table (after Winston 1984)

In view of these difficulties, research on problem solving split into two strands. One approach was to abandon weak problem-solving methods altogether, and to concentrate on domain-specific problem solvers. This branch has seen by far the most success and resulted in production system methodologies, expert systems research and frame-based knowledge representations. The other branch, and the one we explore in the following project, attempted to systematise the representation of domain knowledge so that general problem solving could still take place.

7.6   The STRIPS problem solver

The STRIPS problem solver (STanford Research Institute Problem Solver) was a direct descendant of GPS. Like GPS, STRIPS uses an initial state, a goal state, a set of operators that can change the state, and it uses means-ends analysis. STRIPS differs from GPS in that a standardised method was introduced for describing an operator, in terms of its **preconditions**, its **add-list** (the new state characteristics which obtain after its operation) and its **delete-list** (the state characteristics which no longer obtain after its operation) attached to each operator in order to update the state. By combining this operator representation with explicit backward chaining from the goal, Fikes and Nilsson (1971) were able to avoid the need for explicit difference-reduction tables.

7.6.1 The Robot Micro-World

STRIPS was a planner attached to SHAKEY, a mobile robot who inhabited the micro-world illustrated in the two Figures 7.4 and 7.5. The first shows the overview of the set of rooms involved and all the 'unchanging' features of this world. The second shows the things in the robot world that can be changed by the actions of the planner. These things are all conveniently situated in room 1 of this world.

As can be seen from Figure 7.4 the four side rooms 1-4 are joined by one long corridor room 5. All the rooms open out (via doors - numbered as per side room) onto the corridor room. In a more realistic room layout the positions within each room would be represented as a set of coordinates. However, to simplify the project we have followed Fikes and Nilsson and have marked 6 specific points within the world where things can stand. By point 4 in room 1 there is a light switch upon the wall. The world is populated with a robot and some boxes.

The basic layout of the rooms in the robot world is always the same. There is nothing that the robot can do to move the doors or walls, so these things in the world are represented as a list of relations in the definition always/1. There are a large number of relations that describe the robot world and these are all collected together in one enormous list. As you may note from this, the robot's world is much richer than the simple blocks world. Nevertheless this list could clearly have been very much larger - we have been very selective in listing relations describing the world which are going to be 'useful' to the problem-solver.

The first three lines state that there are three pushable boxes 1, 2 & 3. More about them later. The remainder of the entries in this list refer in one way or another to the locations of unchangeable things. Lines 4-9 use the relation location/2 to indicate the location of 6 individual points on the floor of a variety of rooms. Line 10 uses the relation at/2 to connect the one light switch in the environment with a specific floor point. Lines 11-19 use the relation connects/3 to say how each door connects each room. There are two entries for each door because it can be approached both ways. Similarly there are two entries for each door in the in_room/2 predicates used in lines 20-23.

Figure 7.4 The STRIPS robot world - Always True

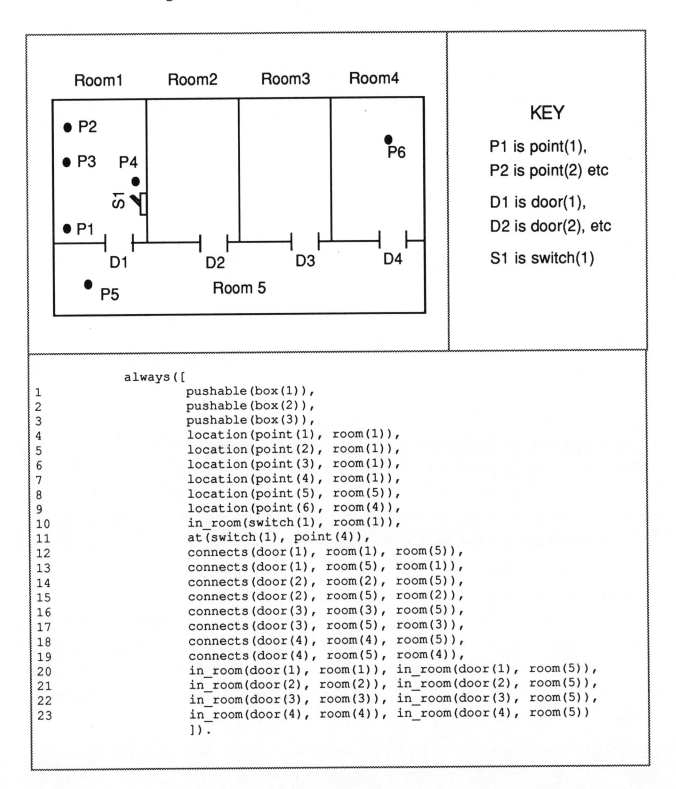

These place the doors in specific rooms. So for example door(1) not only connects rooms 1 and 5 (and vice-versa) but it is also explicitly stated as physically being in both rooms 1 and 5.

The states which are not always the same are given in a separate definition called start_state/1. A definition for this predicate is included beside Figure 7.5. It contains the initial state of the changeable relations in the robot world and is one that you can change to make the robot start off with an easier or more complex world. There are currently three boxes in the current robot world - we have already noted that each is explicitly described as 'pushable' in the always/1 definition. The first three entries in the start_state/1 list give a position for each of these boxes. The fourth item gives an initial position for the robot itself. The next four relations explicitly note which rooms the boxes and the robot currently inhabit (although this could obviously be inferred from the floor position). The final two items note that the light switch has the status off and that the robot is currently on_floor (ie on the floor - not on a box).

Figure 7.5 The STRIPS robot world - State dependent

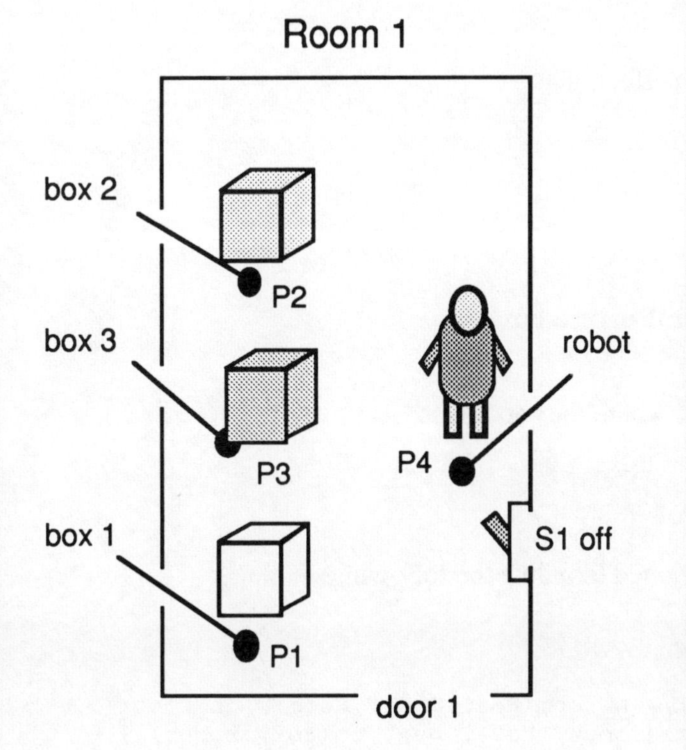

```
start_state(
    [
    at( box(1), point(1) ),
    at( box(2), point(2) ),
    at( box(3), point(3) ),
    at( robot,  point(4) ),
    in_room( box(1), room(1) ),
    in_room( box(2), room(1) ),
    in_room( box(3), room(1) ),
    in_room( robot,  room(1) ),
    status( switch(1), off ),
    on_floor
    ]).
```

7.6.2 The Operators

The operators are the actions that the robot can perform to change the state of the world. All the operators are represented in the definition can/4. The first argument of can/4 is the name of the operator. The names of operators are themselves standard Prolog relation names, ie they can take arguments - to indicate that they act upon specific things. There are three basic robot world operators which get the robot around: walk_to, walk_next_to & walk_through. So walk_to(P, Rm) is used to say that the robot can walk to a specific point P in a room Rm; walk_next_to(T, Rm) says that the robot can walk next to a thing T (either a door or a box) in some room Rm; and walk_through(Dr, Rm1, Rm2) says that the robot can walk through a door Dr from room Rm1 to room Rm2. The second argument of the can/4 definition is the list of operator preconditions. These dictate the conditions that need to be true before the operator can be used. The remaining two arguments to the can/4 definition dictate the effects of the operator on the world. As the world consists of a set of relations the operator works by deleting some 'old' relations and adding some new ones to the world state list. So the definition consists of a set of facts where the call can(Action, Preconds, Del, Add) means that the Action is possible only if the Preconds are true. The result of applying Action to the world would be to delete the contents of the list Del from current state and add to it the contents of the list Add. Consider this example operator - we have put comments by each argument list to make it easier to read:

```
              can( walk_to(Place, Room),

/* if  */         [ location(Place, Room), in_room(robot, Room), on_floor  ],
/* del */         [ at(robot, _), next_to(robot, Box), next_to(Box, robot) ],
/* add */         [ at(robot, Place) ]
                 ).
```

The operator walk_to(Place, Room) says, in effect, that:

The robot **can**

>   **walk_to** a Place in a Room

>   **if**   Place is in the Room

>>   & the robot is in the same Room

>>   & the robot is on_floor (rather than on a box)

>   and the **effect** of walking will be

>>   to **delete** any information about where the robot was

>>>   & whatever the robot was next_to

>>   and to **add** that the robot is now at Place.

The other two robot-movement operators mentioned look like the following:

```
              can( walk_next_to(BoxOrDoor, Room),

/* if  */         [ in_room(robot, Room), in_room(BoxOrDoor, Room), on_floor ],
/* del */         [ at(robot, _), next_to(robot, Box), next_to(Box, robot) ],
/* add */         [ next_to(robot, BoxOrDoor) ]
                 ).

              can( walk_through(Door, Room1, Room2),

/* if  */         [ in_room(robot, Room1), connects(Door, Room1, Room2),
                    next_to(robot, Door), on_floor],
/* del */         [ next_to(robot, box(Box)), next_to(box(Box), robot),
                    at(robot, _), in_room(robot, Room1) ],
/* add */         [ in_room(robot, Room2) ]
                 ).
```

The **walk_next_to(BoxOrDoor, Room)** operator says that a robot can walk next to something ie a BoxOrDoor in some Room. Before a 'walk_next_to' can happen we must insist (the 'if' list) that both the robot and the BoxOrDoor are physically located in the same room and that the robot is on the floor. The result of the action happening is to adjust the positions that are noted for these things in the predicates **at/2** and **next_to/2**. As we will see in a later exercise, implementing the action in this way has some undesirable side-effects which we will pass over for the time being.

The **walk_through(Door, Room1, Room2)** operator definition of **can**/4 states that a robot can walk through a Door if the robot is in Room1 and there is a connecting door with Room2 and the robot is actually next to this door and is standing on the floor. If these are true then the result of applying the action would be to delete that the robot was next to any box in the old room (if appropriate) and that the robot was in the old room, and to add that the robot was now in the new room Room2.

In the exercises there are a number of other operators introduced so that the robot can plan to push boxes about in the world and climb on and off them.

7.6.3 Means-Ends Analysis

The above operators could obviously be applied to the robot world using brute-force search methods. However STRIPS used a much more powerful technique that made use of the way that knowledge was represented in these operators. This arises from the fact that the operators are all rather different and do different things (cf only one operator for moving blocks above). So if the robot were to plan to go to some point in a room, then it makes sense to look first at those operators which are responsible for adding that fact to the world state. In the case of moving to some point in a room there is actually only one robot operator that can achieve this **walk_to(Point, Room)** so this is the action that is required. However, it may not be possible to apply this straight away as its preconditions may not be true. For example the operator requires that the robot be on the floor in the room which contains the point it wants to walk to. If the robot is in another room then it will need to plan to achieve these preconditions before it can use the operator. If it is in another room then clearly it should examine operators that move it to a new room. Again there is only one operator which does this in its add list **walk_through(Door, Room1, Room2)**. But before this operator can be used its preconditions must be made true, and so on.

In this way the planner works backwards through the problem from where it wants to be to where it currently is! One helpful way of picturing this search is a large **triangle-table** of operators and goals. The triangle table idea was used by Fikes, Hart & Nilsson (1972) as a method of learning and generalising the plans produced by STRIPS. Here we just use a simplified version of it to help explain the problem solver.

In reading the partial table shown in Figure 7.6 (for the example we were just discussing) column 0 contains relations that are initially already true in the robot world The subsequent columns 1-3 headed by an operator indicate the effects which that operator has upon the world. The rows ending in an operator b-d indicate the relations that must be true for the operator to be applied. A full triangle table includes the details of the current state at each stage of the plan. For example the columns beneath an operator typically contain the relations that remain true given the effects of each of the operators in the rows. However this can get complicated and is rather hard to read, so our use of the table here is very much simplified. The triangle table is traversed from the bottom right to the top left to solve the problem, and the plan is read off in the opposite direction. Consider the example shown in Figure 7.6. The entry point of the triangle is at level (a) on the bottom right (column 3) with the initial goal **at(robot, point(5))**. If the robot is already at point(5) then this is true and we don't need any plan of actions. If not then means-ends analysis instructs us to find an operator which can help by adding this goal as one of its effects. The only appropriate 'means' available is to use the walk_to operator. It is "appropriate" because it is the only available operator that 'adds' that the robot is at some point. The preconditions of this operator are shown in the table to its immediate left on level (b). These become the new goals to achieve. In Figure 7.5 we have included the goals as they appear in the operators "if" list, but we have separated them out into those which are initially true, (shown in column 0) and those which need to be achieved (replaced by an arrow pointing to the column shift). All of the preconditions of this action are already true in the initial state of the world except for one: the robot must in the same Room as point(5) in order to walk_to it.

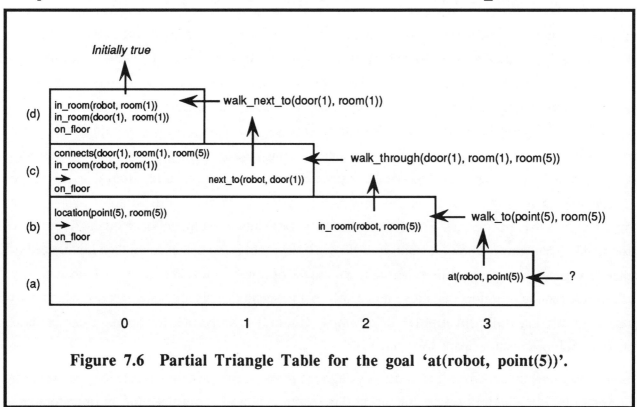

Figure 7.6   Partial Triangle Table for the goal 'at(robot, point(5))'.

Assuming that the robot is actually in room(1) in the initial world then we need an operator that adds the required in_room relation. Moving up a row to level (c) we see that there is an operator walk_through which does this add (and its preconditions are again to the left). We need to walk through a connecting door from a room in which the robot is and the robot must be next to the door. As before, the preconditions of this operator are all initially true anyway apart from one: next_to(robot, door(1)).

The operator which adds this relation is shown above it in the table: walk_next_to the door. Finally we have found an operator on level (d) whose preconditions are all already true in the current state of the micro-world. To walk_next_to a door the robot must simply be in the same room as the connecting door (room(1)) and on the floor. Having reasoned back to the current state we can now read off the plan from this table.

In order to be `at(robot, point(5))` the robot needs to :

(1)   `walk_next_to(door(1), room(1))`

(2)   `walk_through(door(1), room(1), room(5))`

(3)   `walk_to(point(5), room(5)).`

7.6.4 The Planner

This start state is used in the highest level call to the planner `test/1`. The test definition consists of a number of pre-packaged problems for the planner to solve, each numbered for convenience. Eg problem 1 is as follows:

```
test(1)  :-
        start_state(StartState),
        strips(StartState,  [at(robot, point(1))] ).
```

A call to this definition `(?) test(1).` would first pick up the initial state of the changeable relations in the world from start_state/1 and then hand this onto the predicate `strips/2`. The second argument to the `strips/2` call in this definition is a list of goals that the robot is requested to plan to achieve. In this case STRIPS is asked to achieve the goal `at(robot, point(1))` from the `StartState`. The number of other calls to `test/1` vary the target goals which must be achieved. So if we consider the definition of `strips/2` itself we can see that it is simply used here to hand on the start and goal states it is given to the `plan/3` definition - printing out some information to the screen before it starts.

```
strips(StartState, GoalState):-
        write('** Goals: '), nl,
        write_list(GoalState), nl,
        plan(1, GoalState,StartState).
```

The predicate `plan/3` is a standard recursive meta-program which tries to achieve a list of goals by passing them one at a time to `solve/3`. The query **plan(GList, CurrS, GoalS)** plans to achieve a list of goals GList. As you can see from the definition (i) if GList is empty (no more goals to plan for) then it should be the case that both the current state and the goal state are the same (will both bind with the same variable State). Otherwise (ii) says that plan should take the first goal in the GList and hand it on to `solve/3` along with the current state of the 'changeable' world. The solve definition should plan to achieve this goal and return a new state - with some things changed. This new state should be handed to the recursion (with any remaining tail goals Gs) as the new current state.

```
(i)         plan([], State, State).              %  stopping condition.
(ii)        plan([Goal | Gs], CurrS, GoalS):-
                solve(Goal, CurrS, NewS),        %  solve the first goal
                plan(Gs, NewS, GoalS).           %  then recurse on the rest
```

The `solve/3` definition deals with one goal at a time. The call **solve(Goal, CurrS, NewS)** tries to achieve a single `Goal` by finding an `Action` and planning to achieve its list of `Preconds`.

The means-ends analysis occurs in the third clause of solve, where an operator is selected which would, if its preconditions were satisfied, add the goal to the current state. The STRIPS mechanism then tries to plan to achieve this new precondition list, which may involve the selection of another operator, thus another set of preconditions, more planning ... until finally the preconditions are all true. The complete set of operators is then generated as the recursion 'unwinds'. Note that the program listing discussed here is significantly simpler than the actual Appendix code, which also builds up the plan as an extra argument as it goes along, but the core of the definition is the same.

```
(i)         solve(Goal, State, State):-
                member(Goal, State ).
(ii)        solve(Goal, State, State):-
                always(TrueFacts),
                member(Goal, TrueFacts).
(iii)       solve(Goal, State, NewState):-
                can(Action, Preconds, Dels, Adds),
                member(Goal, Adds),
                plan(Preconds, State, State1),
                update_state(Dels, Adds, State1, NewState).
```

In this definition clause (i) says that if the `Goal` is a member of the current state (second argument) then this is solved trivially and new state (third argument) will be identical to this current state. Similarly, clause (ii) states that if the `Goal` is a member of those facts that are always true anyway then it is trivially true and the new state will be the same as the current state. Otherwise, look for an appropriate Action which has `Goal` in its addlist, plan to achieve the `PreConds` and finally update the state to produce the `NewState`. The only remaining definition to discuss is `update_state/4` which is used to change our record of the state of the robot world relations after a planned actions execution.

```
update_state(DeleteList, AddList, State, NewState) :-
    del(DeleteList, State, State1),
    add(AddList, State1, NewState).
```

The call `update_state(Dels, Adds, State, NewState)` simply says that the list of relations `Dels` is deleted and the list of relations `Adds` is added to `State` to produce the list `NewState`. The definition given here is not really very helpful as it simply relies on two further definitions `del/3` and `add/3`. These are responsible for deleting and adding each member of the appropriate list from the state to produce a new one. Their definitions are given in the Code Appendix 7.

Exercises 7.6 Starting with STRIPS

E 7.6.1 Load the **STRIPS** program (code given in Appendix 7.2). Try the first test query `test(1)` which like the `test_df` queries has been designed to pick up appropriate states to save typing. Examine the printout. We have used >> to indicate that a new goal has been created, and << to indicate that it has been achieved. Note that when the `walk_to` operator is initially selected, there is an unbound variable in the slot for the Room. In the Complete Plan this variable has been bound (correctly) to `room(1)`. This occurs because the first of the three preconditions `location(point(1), Room)` is solved by taking `Room=room(1)`. This also satisfies the second condition - it is true in the current state that robot is in `room(1)`, and the third condition (`on_floor`) is also true.

(ii) Try `test(2)`. This involves moving from one room to another. Note that three operators are required, and they are selected backwards from the goal state, but achieved forwards from the current state. The number in the margin is to help you keep track of which goal (ie the preconditions for which operator) is being 'solved'.

The printout should look like this:

```
: test(2)
** Goals:
        at(robot, point(5))

    1: >> Trying to achieve : at(robot, point(5))
            Action : walk_to(point(5), _1161)
            Conditions :  location(point(5), _1161)
                                  & in_room(robot, _1161)
                                  & on_floor
    2: >>>> Trying to achieve : in_room(robot, room(5))
            Action : walk_through(_1713, _1714, room(5))
            Conditions : connects(_1713, _1714, room(5))
                                  & in_room(robot, _1714)
                                  & next_to(robot, _1713)
                                  & on_floor
    3: >>>>>> Trying to achieve : next_to(robot, door(1))
            Action : walk_next_to(door(1), _2318)
            Conditions : in_room(robot, _2318)
                                  & in_room(door(1), _2318)
                                  & on_floor
    3: <<<<<< Achieved Goal : next_to(robot, door(1))
    2: <<<< Achieved Goal : in_room(robot, room(5))
    1: << Achieved Goal : at(robot, point(5))

**  Complete Plan is
walk_next_to(door(1), room(1))
walk_through(door(1), room(1), room(5))
walk_to(point(5), room(5))
```

Try to check how we were able to construct the triangle table Figure 7.6 from the printout given by `test(2)`. Note, in particular how, when solving the three preconditions for the operator `walk_to(point(5), Room)`, the first condition `location(point(5), Room)` binds the variable `Room` to `room(5)`, and it is this value which is passed to the second condition `in(robot, Room)`, thus resulting in the choice of the operator `walk_through(Door, R1, room(5) )`.

Exercise 7.7 Adding box-moving operators.

We have produced an outline of the necessary preconditions, add-lists and delete-lists for three more operators:

```
push_to(Box, point(N), Room)          - push the Box to point(N) in the Room
push_next_to(Box, BoxOrDoor, Room)    - push Box next to BoxOrDoor in Room
push_through(Box, Door, Room1, Room2)  - push Box through Door from Room1 to Room2
```

Fill in all the necessary details. All that needs replacing is where we have put the word 'unknown'. Check your answer by using test queries 4, 5, 6, 7.

Exercise 7.8 Operators for the robot turning on and off the light.

Following the original article, we assume that the robot is too short to reach the switch, and must therefore climb on a box first! Consequently four operators are needed:

```
turn_on(   switch(S) )
turn_off(  switch(S) )
climb_on(  box(B)    )
climb_off( box(B)    )
```

In these you will need to fill in the 'unknown' slots as before. Check your efforts by test(8).

Exercises 7.8 Problems for STRIPS.

E 7.8.1 **Goal interaction.** Try test(9) which asks the robot to climb on a box at point(6).
```
test(9) :-
    start_state(StartState),
    strips(StartState,  [on(robot,box(1)), at(robot,point(6))] ).
```

E 7.8.2 **Gross inefficiency.** Try test(10) - this is the same as test(9) but with the two goals re-ordered. Try it. What is happening?
```
test(10) :-
    start_state(StartState),
    strips(StartState,  [ at(robot,point(6)), on(robot,box(1))] ).
```

Ideas for Advanced Projects

As planning is an ongoing research theme there is a great deal that you could do to extend and improve upon this simple project. Here we suggest a couple of simple experiments.

(i) Could you adapt df2 to the robot world domain? How would one decide the legal actions in a given state? What heuristics would one try to apply? How long would it take to come to a solution?

(ii) Next, could you adapt STRIPS to the much simpler blocks world domain? In fact it's quite easy to rewrite the legal moves in terms of add-lists and delete-lists, but paradoxically the simpler domain is less well-suited to our STRIPS because it immediately falls into an infinite loop, just as df0 did. We would have to augment it to compile a list of visited states, as for df1!

7.7   Further Developments & Readings

Much has happened in planning since the classical STRIPS work and numerous alternatives to means-ends analysis have been explored. The most obvious initial development for you to consider is the WARPLAN planner of Warren (1974, 1976) which was actually a further development of a STRIPS-like system in Prolog. A few features of our representation for STRIPS, like the `always` predicate, are due to David Warren's Prolog planning work. The two references we have given for this work are both equally difficult to obtain as they are - like much work in artificial intelligence - lab memos and conference proceedings papers. If you cannot get hold of the original papers then the best discussion of the system with code that we have found is in Kluzniak & Szpakowicz (1985). WARPLAN was rather more sophisticated than STRIPS in a number of ways. For example it had a `holds` mechanism to handle some goal interactions – that is, that it was able to check that an old goal still `holds` true when an new goal is attempted.

Further developments in the area include considerations of: planning abstraction levels; opportunistic planning; detecting and correcting interactions; resource management, and interleaved planning and acting.

The concept of different levels of abstraction in search simply involves the idea that plans can be layered. That is, that one has operators to achieve high level goals such as "take taxi" that could appear as one part of a plan involving say "getting to train station". But that "take taxi" itself might involve a plan that had sub-goals within it like "phone taxi company" requiring the use of a "pick up phone" operator. Furthermore this operator might itself require a sub-plan that involved you getting to a phone etc. Rather than develop the plan as one long chain as STRIPS would, a hierarchical planner could develop separate plans in layers for each level of abstraction. Such a planner might not end up wasting time trying to work out how to get to a phone until it was confident that taxi taking was fruitful; and not spend time considering taxis until the next layer up was confirmed as useful etc. One of the earliest hierarchical planners was a direct descendant of STRIPS, called ABSTRIPS (Sacerdoti, 1974).

An opportunistic planner is simply one which tries to not make firm decisions until sufficient evidence is available. For example, MOLGEN (Stefik, 1981) was a hierarchical planner which designed experimental procedures in molecular genetics and was able to intelligently schedule its goals rather than deal with them in a fixed order. So it could make decisions about operations that it was more confident about sooner than ones that it was less confident about. Indeed having made commitments to some parts of a plan can often make other parts of the plan easier to determine. Similarly, there is no point in planning to do something that a later action may have to undo - better to suspend it and consider the later action. The fact that goals and operators may conflict with each other is considered by a number of planners. HACKER, (Sussman, 1975) was one early program that attempted to learn from its experiences of goals conflicting with each other. In a simple blocks world even when just stacking blocks it is easy to do an action that needs to be undone later before another action can be done. So to get a tower of a upon b upon c, there is no point in putting block a upon b first as you may have to take it off before you can put b upon c. HACKER has a similar solution to that of the opportunistic planners in that it can change the ordering of its goals, but it does so by examining the interactions between them.

Later work on planning has considered the more complex issues that the real world presents - such as finite resources and a changing world. Planners like SIPE (Wilkins, 1988) can keep a track of scarce resources that it might require during the execution of a plan; can monitor the effect of executing the plan; and even has some consideration of the effect of multiple actions that can happen together. If we recall a robot world example, there is no point pushing a box through three rooms to help switch on a light if there is already a suitable box in the light switch's room or en route. Neither should an intelligent planner give up on finding that a door turns out to be locked half way through executing a plan - it must monitor the execution and replan as required.

Epilogue

Throughout this book we have presented a number of projects based upon the interpretation into Prolog of some classic Cognitive Science research ideas. We have sought thereby to demonstrate some of the important problems of representation and search encountered in this relatively new discipline. We have not presented a full or formal analysis of Cognitive Science itself. Instead, we have attempted to breathe some life into the introductory study of Cognitive Science. We have indicated in our background discussion how these demonstration projects might fit in with a more formal study of each problem. Here we suggest a few ideas for where the user may look to find further project challenges.

Some Ideas for further projects

• Introductory Prolog programming texts are a very good possible source of further ideas. For example, the excellent text by Sterling and Shapiro (1986) has a number of simple definitions that could be built into more full-scale projects.

• However, the dominance of the programming language LISP means that some of the best sources of ideas can be found in LISP based guides and handbooks. If you feel up to the task of translating from the LISP code into a more declarative Prolog form then the excellent suite of programs from the Schankian school presented by Schank and Riesbeck (1981) is a good source of project material.

• The burgeoning artificial intelligence literature – especially through the journal *Artificial Intelligence* – has to be a major source of ideas for more advanced projects. Some very good collections of work – primarily from journals like *Artificial Intelligence* – present the classical papers all neatly bundled up for the reader. Particularly recommended are the series by Morgan Kaufman which includes: Nilsson and Webber (1981); Brachman and Levesque (1985); and Grosz et al (1986).

• At the start of the book in figure 1.2 we noted a few 'contextual' projects in the history of cognitive science in areas such as learning and perception that we were avoiding in this book. You may now want to turn to these (see eg Brachman and Levesque (1985)).

To conclude this book we should note the progress that we have made. On the surface level we feel confident that anyone working through the chapters will have gained worthwhile knowledge and skills — exposure to logic programming techniques, detailed discussion of some central topics in cognitive science, and hands-on experience of an interesting set of reconstructions of Cognitive Science classics written in a consistent and approachable style. Furthermore, we hope that the reader will leave the book with a sense of excitement - that here are interesting problems, some of which are worthy of more detailed investigation.

References

Aitkenhead, A. M. & Slack, J. M. eds (1985) *Issues in Cognitive Modeling.* Lawrence Erlbaum, London.

Allen, J. (1987) *Natural Language Understanding.* Benjamin/Cummings, California.

Anderson, J. R. (1983). *The Architecture of Cognition.* Cambridge MA: Harvard University Press.

Anderson, J. R. (1989) A theory of the origins of human knowlege. *Artificial Intelligence,* **40,** 313-351

Anderson, J. R. & Bower, G. H. (1973). *Human Associative Memory.* Washington DC. Winston.

Anderson, J. R., Boyle, C. F, Corbett, A. T. and Lewis, M. W. (1990). Cognitive Modeling and Intelligent Tutoring. *Artificial Intelligence,* **42,** 7-49.

Atkinson, R. C. & Shiffrin, R. M. (1968). Human memory: a proposed system and its control processes. In K.W. Spence and J.T. Spence (eds). *Advances in the Psychology of Learning and Motivation: Research and Theory, Vol. 2.* Academic Press, New York.

Baddeley, A. (1982) *Your Memory: A User's Guide.* Penguin.

Barr, A. & Feigenbaum, E. (1981) *Handbook of Artificial Intelligence.* Pitman, London.

Berry, A. (1983) *The Super Intelligent Machine.* John Cape, London, UK.

Bobrow, D. G. (1968) Natural Language Input for a Computer Problem-Solving System. In M. L. Minsky (ed) *Semantic information processing.* MIT Press.

Boden, M. (1977; 2nd ed 1987) *Artificial Intelligence & Natural Man.* Open University Press.

Boden, M. (1988) *Computer Models of Mind.* Cambridge University Press.

Born, R. (1987) *Artificial Intelligence - The Case Against.* Croom Helm, London.

Brachman, R. J. & Levesque, H. J. eds. (1985) *Readings in Knowledge Representation.* Morgan Kaufman, Los Altos, California.

Bratko, I. (1986) *Prolog programming for artificial intelligence.* Addison-Wesley.

Broadbent, D. E. (1958). *Perception and Communication.* Pergamon Press, London.

Brown, J. S. and Burton, R. R. (1978). Diagnostic models for procedural bugs in basic mathematical skills. *Cognitive Science,* **2,** 155-192.

Chomsky, N. (1957) *Syntactic Structures.* Mouton, The Hague.

Chomsky, N. (1965) *Aspects of the Theory of Syntax.* MIT Press, Cambridge Mass.

Clocksin, W. F. & Mellish, C. S. (1981; 2nd ed 1986) *Programming in Prolog.* Springer-Verlag, Berlin Germany.

Colby, K. M. (1973) Simulations of Belief Systems. In R. C. Schank & K. M. Colby, *Computer Models of Thought and Language.* Freeman, San Francisco.

Colby, K. M., Webber, S. & Hilf, F. D. (1971) Artificial Paranoia. *Artificial Intelligence,* **2,** 1-26.

Collins, A. M. & Loftus, E. (1975). A spreading activation model of semantic processing. *Psychological Review,* **82,** 407-428.

Collins, A. M. & Quillian, M. R. (1969) Retrieval time from semantic memory. *Journal of Verbal Learning and Verbal Behaviour,* **8,** 240-247.

Collins, A. M. & Quillian, M. R. (1972) Experiments on semantic memory and language comprehension. In L.W. Gregg (ed), *Cognition in Learning and Memory.* Wiley, New York.

Conrad, C. (1972) Cognitive economy in semantic memory. *Journal of Experimental Psychology,* **92**, 149-154.

Cullingford, R. (1981) SAM. In Schank, R. C. & Reisbeck, C. K. eds. *Inside Computer Understanding*. Lawrence Erlbaum. Also In Grosz, B. J., Sparck-Jones, K. S. & Webber, B. L. eds. *Readings in Natural Language Processing*. Morgan Kaufman. 1986

Dreyfus, H. L. (1972, 2nd ed 1979) *What computers can't do*. Harper and Row, New York.

Dreyfus, H. L. (1981) From micro-worlds to knowledge representation: AI at an impasse. In Haugeland, J. (ed) *Mind Design*, MIT Press.

Fikes, R. E., Hart, P. E. & Nilsson, N. J. (1972) Learning and Executing Generalised Robot Plans. *Artificial Intelligence*, **3**, 251-288.

Fikes, R. E. & Nilsson, N. J. (1971) STRIPS: A new approach to the application of theorem proving to problem solving. *Artificial Intelligence*, **2**, 189-208.

Gardner, H. (1985) *The mind's new science: A history of the cognitive revolution*. Basic Books, New York.

Gazdar, G. & Mellish, C. (1989) *Natural Language Processing in Prolog*. Addison Wesley.

Green, B. F., Wolf, A. K, Chomsky, C. & Laughery, K. (1963) Baseball: an automatic question answerer. In E. A. Feigenbaum and J. Feldman (eds) *Computers and Thought*, McGraw-Hill.

Greene, J. (1986) *Language Understanding - A cognitive approach*. Open University Press.

Grosz, B. J., Sparck Jones, K. & Webber, B. L. eds. (1986) *Readings in Natural Language Processing*. Morgan Kaufman, Los Altos, California.

Haugeland, J. ed (1981) *Mind Design: Philosophy, Psychology, Artificial Intelligence*. Cambridge Mass, MIT Press.

Hofstadter, D. R. (1979) *Godel, Escher, Bach: An Eternal Golden Braid*. Basic Books.

Hogger, C. J. (1984) *Introduction to Logic Programming*. Academic Press, London.

Hollan, J.D. (1975). Features and semantic memory: Set -theoretic or network model? *Psychological Review*, **82**, 154-155.

Hubel, D. H. and Wiesel, T. N. (1959) Receptive Fields of Single Neurones in the Cat's Striate Cortex. *Journal of Physiology*, **148**, 579-591.

Kluzniak, F. & Szpakowicz, S. (1985) *Prolog for Programmers*, Academic Press.

Laird, J. E., Newell, A. & Rosenbloom, P. S. (1986). Soar: an architecture for general intelligence. *Artificial Intelligence*, **33**, 1-64.

Lehnert, W. G. & Ringle, M. H. eds (1982) *Strategies for Natural Language Processing*. Hillsdale, NJ. Lawrence Erlbaum Associates.

Lighthill, J. (1973) Artificial Intelligence: A general survey. In *Artificial Intelligence: A Paper Symposium*. Science Research Council, London.

Luger, G. (1978) Unit 28: Formal Analyses of Problem Solving Behaviour. In A. Bundy and G. Luger *Cognitive Psychology: Learning and Problem Solving (part 3)*. Block 4 of the Open University D303 course. Milton Keynes, Open University Press.

Marcus, M. P. (1984) Some inadequate theories of human language processing. In Bever, T. G., Carroll, J. M. & Miller, L. A. *Talking minds: The study of Language in Cognitive Science*. MIT Press, Cambridge Mass.

Marr, D. (1977) Aritificial Intelligence: A Personal View. *Artificial Intelligence*, **9**, 37-48.

Marr, D. (1982) *Vision*. W. H. Freeman & Co.

Mayhew, J. E. W. & Frisby, J. P. (1984) Computer Vision. In O'Shea, T. & Eisenstadt, M. (eds) *Artificial Intelligence: Tools, Techniques and Applications*. London, Harper & Row.

McCorduck, P. (1979) *Machines who think*. Freeman, San Fransisco.

McDermott, J. (1981). R1: the formative years. *AI magazine,* **2**, 21-29.

Minsky, M. L. (1975). A framework for representing knowledge. In P. Winston (ed). *The Psychology of Computer Vision.* McGraw-Hill, New York.

Newell, A., Rosenbloom, P. S., & Laird, J. E. (1990). Symbolic architectures for cognition. *In* M I Posner *(ed) Foundations of Cognitive Science (op cit).*

Newell, A. & Simon, H. A. (1963) GPS, a program that simulates human thought. In Feigenbaum, E. A. & Feldman, J. (eds) *Computers and Thought,* McGraw Hill, NY.

Newell, A. & Simon, H. A. (1972). *Human Problem Solving.* Englewood Cliffs, NJ: Prentice Hall.

Newell, A. (1973). You can't play 20 questions with Nature and win. In W. Chase (ed). *Visual Information Processing.* London: Academic Press.

Newell, A., Shaw, J. C. & Simon, H. A. (1958) Elements of a theory of human problem solving. *Psychological Review,* **65**, 151-66.

Nilsson, N, J. & Webber, B, L. eds. (1981) *Readings in Artificial Intelligence.* Morgan Kaufman, Los Altos, California.

Norman D.A, Rumelhart D.E. (1975). *Explorations in Cognition.* Freeman, San Francisco.

Parkinson, R. C., Colby, K. M. & Faught, W. S. (1977) Conversational Language Comprehension Using Integrated Pattern-Matching and Parsing. *Artificial Intelligence,* **9**, 111-134

Pereira, F. C. N. & Sheiber, S. M. (1987) *Prolog and Natural Language Analysis.* CLSI, Stanford.

Piaget J. (1952) *The origins of intelligence in children.* NY: International Universities Press.

Posner M.I. ed. (1990) *Foundations of Cognitive Science.* MIT Press, Cambridge, Mass.

Rosch, E. (1975). Cognitive representations of semantic categories. *Journal of Experimental Psychology: General,* **104**, 192-233.

Rumelhart, D. E., McClelland, J. L. & the PDP Research Group. (1986) *Parallel Distributed Processing: Explorations in the Microstructure of Cognition I: Foundations.* Cambridge MA: MIT Press.

Ryle, G. (1949) The concept of mind. Hutchinson, London. (Reprinted 1963, Harmondsworth).

Sacerdoti, E. D. (1974) Planning in a Hierarchy of Abstraction Spaces. *Artificial Intelligence,* **5**, 115-135.

Sachs, J. S. (1967) Recognition memory for syntactic and semantic aspects of connected discourse. *Perception and Psychophysics,* **2**, 437-442.

Schank, R. C. (1973) Identification of Conceptualizations Underlying Natural Language. In Schank, R. C. & Colby, K. M. (eds) *Computer Models of Thought and Language.* Freeman.

Schank, R. C. (1982a) *Dynamic Memory.* Cambridge University Press, Cambridge, Mass.

Schank, R. C. (1982b) Reminding & Language Organisation. In : Lehnert, W. G. & Ringle, M. H. (eds) *Strategies for Natural Language Processing.* Hillsdale, NJ. Lawrence Erlbaum Associates. Also reprinted in : Aitkenhead, A. M. & Slack, J. M. (1985) (eds) *Issues in Cognitive Modeling.* Lawrence Erlbaum, London.

Schank, R. C. & Abelson, R. P. (1977) *Scripts, Plans, Goals and Understanding: an enquiry into human knowledge structures.* Erlbaum, Hillsdale, NJ.

Schank, R. C. & Colby, K. M. (1973) *Computer models of thought and language.* Freeman Pub Co, San Fransisco

Schank, R. C. & Riesbeck, C. K. (1981) *Inside Computer Understanding: Five programs plus miniatures.* Erlbaum, Hillsdale, NJ.

Schwartz, S. P. (1987) *Applied Natural Language Processing.* Petrocelli Books, Princeton, NJ.

Searle, J. R. (1980) Minds, Brains & Programs. *Behavioural and Brain Sciences*, **3**, 417-24.

Skinner, B. F. (1957) *Verbal Behaviour*. Appleton Century Crofts.

Sleeman, D. & Brown, J. S. eds. (1982) *Intelligent Tutoring Systems*. Academic Press, London.

Smith, N. & Wilson, D. (1979) *Modern Linguistics*. Penguin.

Smith, E. E., Shoben, E. J. & Rips, L. J. (1974) Structure and process in semantic memory: a featural model for semantic decisions. *Psychological Review*, **81**, 214-241.

Stefik, M. (1981) Planning and Meta Planning: Molgen Part 2. *Artificial Intelligence*, **16**, 141-169.

Sterling, L. & Shapiro, E. (1986) *The Art of Prolog*. MIT Press.

Stillings, N. A., Feinstein, M. H., Garfield, J. L., Rissland, E. L., Rosenbaum, D. A., Weisler, S. E. & Baker-Ward, L. (1987) *Cognitive Science: An Introduction*. MIT Press.

Sussman, G. J. (1975) *A computer model of skill acquisition*. New York: Elsevier.

Tulving, E. (1972). Episodic and semantic memory. In E. Tulving and W. Donaldson (eds), *Organization of Memory*. Academic Press, New York.

Turing, A. M. (1950) Computing Machinery and Intelligence. In Feigenbaum, E. A. & Feldman, J. (eds) *Computers and Thought*. McGraw-Hill, NY. pp 11-35

Warren, D. H. D. (1974) WARPLAN : a System for Generating Plans. Dept. of Computational Logic, *Memo 76 Artificial Intelligence*, Edinburgh University, UK.

Warren, D. H. D. (1976) Generating conditional plans and programs. *Proceedings of the AISB Summer Conference*, pp344-354, University of Edinburgh, UK.

Warren, D. H. D & Pereira, F. C. N. (1982) An efficient Easily Adaptable System for Interpreting Natural Language Queries. *American Journal of Computational Linguistics*, **8**, 3-4, 110-122.

Weizenbaum, J. (1966) ELIZA - a computer program for the study of natural language communication between man and machine. *Communications of the Association for Computing Machinery*, **9**, pp36-45

Weizenbaum, J. (1976) *Computer Power and Human Reason: From Judgement to Calculation*. San Francisco, Freeman.

Wilkins, D. E. (1988) *Practical planning: extending the classical AI planning paradigm*. San Mateo, CA: Morgan Kaufmann.

Winograd, T. (1972) *Understanding Natural Language*. Academic Press, New York.

Winston, P. H. (1974), Learning structural descriptions from examples, in Winston P.H. (ed), *The Psychology of Computer Vision*, McGraw Hill.

Winson, P. H. (1977, 2nd ed 1984) *Artificial Intelligence*. Reading, Mass. Addison Wesley.

Young, R. M. (1976) *Seriation by children : an artificial intelligence analysis of a Piagetian task*. Birkhauser, Basel.

Young, R. M. (1978) Strategies and the Structure of a Cognitive Skill. In G. Underwood (ed) *Strategies of information processing*, Academic Press, London.

Young, R. M. & O'Shea, T. (1981). Errors in children's subtraction. *Cognitive Science*, **5**, 153-177.

Tutorial Appendix 1 : A Short Prolog Tutorial

In this appendix we provide some more general background to the Prolog language using the 'Edinburgh' syntax. We indicate some of its main features and the principal techniques that are employed in its use. The collection of features discussed includes pattern matching, negation-as-failure, inference and backtracking. The techniques noted include list-processing and recursion. Familiarisation with Prolog is illustrated via a family database set of definitions. This short set of notes cannot possibly hope to replace a textbook which is wholly devoted to teaching Prolog programming. However, we include it as a necessary background tutorial for the reader who is new to Prolog and wants to get on with the projects without delay. The Prolog concepts introduced here will be covered in more detail in the context of the specific projects.

Tutorial Appendix 1.1   Introduction

The purpose of this chapter is to provide the reader who is completely new to Prolog with a rapid tour of some of the features of the language. It is intended that it should give you a feel for the flavour of working in Prolog and provide a programming context for the projects which follow. It is not a computer-scientist's guide nor a user manual for your own version of Prolog, both of which we recommend to be read in conjunction with this book.

Prolog programs reside in a database or knowledge-base as sets of definitions that you query. The query is taken up by the Prolog engine which searches through the database definitions for a solution that it can present to you. It will always result in a reply to you of "YES, your query has succeeded" or "NO, your query has failed". You can use several models to help you picture how Prolog works. The most formal is to see the Prolog engine as a theorem prover which takes your query as a theorem to be proved. A less formal model sees it as a database query language that is simply looking-up a large table of data entries (where a clause is thought of as being each row of the table) to find a match for your query pattern. Both of these views can be helpful.

Tutorial Appendix 1.2   The Syntax of Prolog

Just like English - any computer language such as Prolog has a syntax which determines what is acceptable to say and how. If you do not keep to the language's limited syntax you will get a series of error messages when you "compile" or "consult" your code.

The simplest element of Prolog is the constant. The most important element of Prolog is the constant which is called an **atom**. An atom is an individual word of Prolog which contains no special characters or spaces and starts with a lower case letter (basically a-z, 1-9, and the underscore _). It should be noted that you can include anything in an atom by enclosing it in single quotes, but it is usually simpler to stick to lower-case and underscores. The atom is often used in Prolog to refer to a single specific known thing.

The second most important element in Prolog is the **variable**, which follows the same rules as atoms, but must begin with a capital letter, (or unusually, an underscore character). So the elements: `fred`, `silly_me` and `'Bird_Brain'` are all atoms; whilst the elements: `Bird`, `X` and `_fred` are all variables. Variables are often used to refer to a specific but as yet unknown thing.

These elements are often combined to make a third element of Prolog, the **term**. Terms are made up of predicates with some optional arguments, where the predicate is an atom that may have arguments in brackets. If there is more than one argument they are separated by commas. Terms may have no arguments, eg `raining` could be a term used to mean "it is raining"; one argument, eg `female(elizabeth)` could mean that elizabeth is female; or any number of arguments. So the term: `owns(anne, prolog_book)` may be used to mean that the atom `anne` is to be described as having the relationship **owns** to the atom **prolog_book**. Indeed, predicates are sometimes called *relations* because they often represent the relations between their arguments.

Apx 1.2.1 The elements of 'Edinburgh' Prolog syntax

Comment markers **/* ... */** may contain anything. Slash-Star opens the comment and Star-Slash closes the comment. Some Prologs support an additional comment marker such as %. This is used to indicate that Prolog is to ignore the remainder of the line after the marker. We will use the Percent comment marker more than the Slash-Star & Star-Slash combination.

Anything outside of the comments is Prolog code and must obey the strict syntax of the language.

- **Constants** - (also known as **atoms**) - must start with a lower-case letter, normal words can include the underscore character, this is because the space isn't allowed. Abnormal words are ok if they are surrounded in single quotes.

    ```
    fred

    fred_is_ok

    'fred  again'  'Fred'  '&876@aaa m'
    ```

- **Variables** - meaning an unknown individual - start with an uppercase letter; can also begin with an underscore character; underscore on its own is a special variable name.

    ```
    X

    Fred

    Person1
    ```

- **Lists** - are structures which represent sets of individuals. The set is surrounded by square brackets with set members separated by commas.

`[ ]`	The empty-set list.
`[a, b, c, d]`	List with four members.
`[[bread, potatoes], [milk, sugar], salt]`	List with three members, two of them also lists.

- **Terms** - consist of a **predicate** and some bracketed **arguments**

    predicate(argument)

    ```
    person(fred)

    state_of_mind(fred, happy)

    days([mon, tues, wed, thurs, fri, sat, sun])
    ```

Apx 1.2.2 Prolog database syntax

Prolog programs consist of Prolog terms made up of the basic elements, that appear in the database as either **facts** or **rules** in a **definition**.

- **Facts** are single terms that are in the database followed by a full stop.

```
person(fred).

state_of_mind(fred, happy).

days([mon, tues, wed, thurs, fri, sat, sun]).

mammal(rat).
```

These may be read as saying that it is true that fred is a 'person'. That it is true that the 'state_of_mind' of fred is happy. That 'days' are the elements included in the list [mon ... sun]. Also that it is true that a rat is a 'mammal'.

- **Rules** are complex terms that are in the database followed by a full stop. They consist of one single term that is the head of the rule. A Prolog 'if' symbol :- and a conjuction of one or more terms in the body or tail of the rule. The comma connecting terms in the tail of a rule can be read as meaning 'and'.

```
mammal(X):- warm_blooded(X), furry(X).
```

This can be read as meaning that X is a mammal IF X is warm blooded and furry.

- **A Definition** in Prolog is a collection of facts and rules that has the same predicate and number of arguments. We call the individual fact or rule entry in the definition a **clause**. Each single clause in the definition corresponds to an alternative in that definition. Our convention for discussing specific definitions is to give its name then a slash and then the number of arguments that it has. So we would descibe the following definition as being for **bird**/1.

```
bird(heron).

bird(eagle).

bird(X):- warm_blooded(X), lays_eggs(X).
```

This defines the relation 'bird' to be any of three things: either a bird is a heron; **or** a bird is an eagle; **or** a bird is something that is warm_blooded and lays_eggs. This is the complete definition - and is ALL that is known about the predicate relation 'bird'. It is good practice to keep all clauses that refer to the same definition together - with the clauses contiguous - but some Prologs will insist upon it.

You may see the number of arguments that a predicate takes referred to as its **arity**. So for instance, in saying **bird**/1 we are saying that the predicate **bird** has arity 1. The arity that a predicate has is very important. The same predicate can have different numbers of arguments, but if it does then it is effectively a different definition - as it must have a slightly different meaning and be used differently. Prolog cares about a predicate's arity - as it always looks for a predicate with a specific number of arguments.

Given these three essential elements it is next necessary to see how they appear in Prolog programs. The Prolog **knowledge-base** consists of terms written as facts and rules.

Apx 1.2.3 Syntax for knowledge-base facts & rules

FACTS : General form: *Relation_name(Argument1, ... Argumentn).*

A fact that appears in the Prolog knowledge-base is simply a single term followed by a **full-stop**, (or period character "."). Its presence in the knowledge-base is taken to mean that this relation is true for these arguments. The following knowledge-base facts are given with some plausible English interpretation.

Eg	*Prolog*	*English*
	`male(philip).`	philip is male
	`male('Philip').`	'Philip' is male
	`father(philip, charles).`	philip is the father of charles

RULES : General form:

```
head_relation(argument1, ... argumentn) :-
    tail_relation1(argument1, ... argumentn),
    ...,
    tail_relationn(argument1, ... argumentn).
```

Rules are also terminated by a full-stop, however the distinguishing feature is the presence of the ":-" symbol which may be read as meaning "IF". So rules read as: the single head relation is true if all of the tail relations can be shown to be true. As already noted, the commas which are used between the tail relations logically mean the conjunction 'and', that is the term before the comma and the term after the comma must be true. The following knowledge-base rules are given a plausible English meaning.

Prolog :   `uncle(U, NephewOrNiece) :-`
                    `brother(U, Someone) ,`
                    `parent(Someone, NephewOrNiece).`

English :   U is the uncle of `NephewOrNiece` **if**
                the individual U is the brother of `Someone` **and**
                that same `Someone` is the parent of the `NephewOrNiece`

Note: The Semantics of Knowledge-base definitions

Even if you get the syntax correct, then knowledge-base facts and rules only "mean" what you intend them to mean. Prolog evaluates truth and falsity of queries according to the knowledge-base entries alone. So if the knowledge-base contains the fact `female('Philip')` then the semantics of this are that 'Philip' is female and it is up to you to ensure that entries are *semantically* correct! Consider why the following definition, though syntactically OK is semantically incorrect.

```
grandmother(X, Y):- mother(X, Z), mother(Y, Z).   (Wrong)
```

Apx 1.2.4 Built-in Relations

Most of the discussion about Prolog so far has been about database definitions that are entirely the responsibility of the user. Prolog must have the appropriate syntax, but the user dictates the definitions' form and meaning. The user is expected to note the built-ins used and check that their own version of Prolog has these relations. We will point out an interesting built-in when it is first introduced, but one of the most interesting features of using the Prolog language compared with the standard procedural languages is just how few built-in functions are regularly used in programming. Typically, we are not trying to instruct the computer in a language it understands using its own primitives, but rather we are building a complex representation of a problem which must be internally consistent and meaningful to us.

The simplest built-in relations are those like = (equals, ie will match), and its opposite number \= (not-equals, ie will not match). Then there are relations like `call`/1, which takes its argument and treats it as a query to the database, succeeding if it is true; `not`/1 which does the same, only succeeding if its argument is not true in the database; `fail`/0 which is automatically not true; and `true`/0 which automatically is true, and will succeed.

There are the usual range of arithmetic functions (+ - / *), but we cannot use equals = as it has a different meaning – as 'will match' – so we use the relation **is**/2. Now as we are more used to seeing arithmetic written out between its arguments most versions of Prolog will let you do this. For example, we are used to 3 + 4, rather than the more Prolog-like +(3, 4), (the former style is technically called "operator syntax"). So if you want to know the result of this sum you must force Prolog to match the product of the expression with an unbound variable. This is what **is**/2 does. So you query (?) X is 3 + 4. And Prolog will reply YES, where X = 7. Now beware if you know some procedural programming! You may well be used to adding 1 to some number to increment it for use later on by doing something like this: X is X + 1. This is clearly not going to be allowed in Prolog as it is semantically impossible - how can any number ever be equal to itself plus one?

The other important built-in relations worth mentioning at this stage are input-output predicates, like `read` and `write`, `assert` and `retract`, `get` and `put`, `consult` and `reconsult`, and quite a few more. We do not intend to replace your Prolog user-manual so, whilst we try to make a minimal use of such built-ins, when we do use them we will provide a little explanation at the time. Some are introduced below.

Tutorial Appendix 1.3   Using Prolog

Apx 1.3.1 Querying the Prolog knowledge-base

The figure below illustrates some of the elements that are involved with using Prolog. You interact with the environment by asking Prolog to solve QUERIES. A query can be a single term or a conjunction of any number of terms. The Prolog inference engine takes your query and looks in the knowledge-base for a solution, amongst the relevant facts and rules which may be there. Depending on what is in the knowledge-base, Prolog will reply to your query. In this book the convention for introducing queries is that we will precede the query with a (?) symbol.

Tutorial Appendix Figure 1.1   The Prolog Engine

For example, if the knowledge-base contains only these facts which make up the definition of the predicate `bird`:

```
bird(heron).
bird(swallow).
bird(vulture).
```

and you give Prolog the query `(?) bird(heron).` Prolog will reply 'YES' because the query term is in the knowledge-base. If you query `(?) bird(sparrow)` then Prolog will reply 'NO' because it only 'knows' about the birds above. Of course, as with other terms, queries can contain variables. So if you query `(?) bird(X).` then Prolog will look for the bird relation but with a variable argument. The first one it will find is `heron` and will tell you so:

```
X = heron
```

If you only asked for the 'first' reply then Prolog will stop looking. However, there are clearly some more potential answers and Prolog will report them to you if you ask for them.

```
X = swallow
X = vulture
   No more solutions
```

This behaviour clearly indicates one aspect of the way that the Prolog engine works. It looks through the the relations in the knowledge-base one at a time, starting with the first.

Apx 1.3.2 Inference

Inference in Prolog is represented in database rule terms. In the above example the rule for the relation son is

```
son(X, Y) :- father(Y, X).
```

This says that **X** is the son of **Y IF Y** is the father of **X**.

Declaratively this means that son(X, Y) is true if father(Y, X) is true.

Procedurally this means that you can prove that X is the son of Y if you can find a definition in the database that proves that Y is the father of X.

So consider the query **(?) son(charles, philip)**. Prolog will match this query term with the head of the rule binding X to charles and Y to philip. The Prolog theorem prover will say that the head of the rule is true if the tail is true, (ie the bit after the ':-' is provable).

Apx 1.3.3   Unification and Pattern matching

In the above, Prolog is matching the query term with the database term and reporting any variable bindings that it has had to do to make the match. **Unification** in Prolog refers to the "binding" of the variables within any expression of Prolog. The most important aspect of unification is that variables of the *same name* in the same Prolog clause all have the *same value*. ie they refer to the same individual! Outside of the Prolog clause a variable name can refer to anything else - but within the clause (up to a full-stop) it refers to the same thing. So in the son rule just given, if we ask **(?) son(charles, philip).** then these arguments will match with the rule variables such that **X is bound to charles** and **Y is bound to philip**. As soon as X and Y have a value then unification dictates that all other variables with these names will share this value, so Prolog will try to prove father(Y, X) with these bindings, ie.

```
father(philip, charles).
```

Proving things in Prolog mean that the Prolog engine takes the superficial patterns formed by the words and the brackets and compares the query with the database. Logical variables match with any one syntax element.

The **Query** matches with	the **Database** to give	the variable **Binding**
person(X)	person(fred).	X = fred
father(X, Y)	father(anne, zara).	X = anne, Y = zara
shopping(S)	shopping([lettuce, ham]).	S = [lettuce, ham]

You can use a built-in relation to force Prolog to match two term structures together. The equals relation = can be queried to ask if two terms can match each other.

So the queries:

```
fred(hello) = fred(hello)        will reply YES
fred(hello) = fred(X)            will reply YES, where X = hello
fred(hello) = X                  will reply YES, where X = fred(hello)
fred(hello) = fred(hi)           will reply NO.
```

In fact the equals relation is rarely used explicitly because Prolog automatically applies it in matching and unification with queries and database terms anyway.

Apx 1.3.4 Backtracking

Backtracking is where you assume that a solution you found is wrong and look back to see if there is another solution that you can take instead. In the bird definition above, when we ask (?) bird(X). we get the reply YES where X = heron; Or X = swallow; Or X = vulture; No More Solutions. The replies after the first one are delivered via the Prolog backtracking mechanism and require the unbinding of the variable X to heron. We are asking Prolog to return to reconsider a solution to the query we have been given. As there are alternative clauses for the same definition in the database Prolog can match these with the query pattern. You can think of the Prolog engine working its way through a definition leaving a pointer at each clause it tries. If the clause proves to be true then it reports success, but if there are any clauses below the pointer, then there are other alternatives to consider. If the user asks to see these, then Prolog simply returns and moves the pointer on to the next clause in the definition.

However, it must be noted that backtracking will often occur without the user needing to request it. It is an integral part of the work of the Prolog engine even before the user is offered the chance to force it to happen. Even in a normal search through a set of definitions the Prolog engine may end up following a rule which turns out to be a failure, and backtracking is an essential means for it to return to an alternative path that might prove more successful.

Consider this simple example, which lays down some simple rules for defining what a bird is.

```
(i)      bird(X):- lays_eggs(X), flies(X).

(ii)     bird(X):- has_feathers(X).
```

If we queried this definition with (?)   bird(penguin). then Prolog would match this term with the head of the first rule, binding X to penguin. Now the rules of inference followed by the Prolog engine dictate that this is true if lays_eggs(penguin) and flies(penguin) are both true. Assuming that there were suitable definitions for these relations somewhere in the database then Prolog might succeed in proving that a penguin could lay eggs, but fail to find proof in the database that a penguin could fly. However it is not forced to report failure to the user, because there is a second clause to try. Prolog will undo the search that lead it to try 'flies(penguin)' and backtrack to the second clause. The second clause matches in the same way as before and is true if has_feathers(penguin) is true in the database. Assuming that it is, Prolog can report success.

One special built-in predicate which we have not yet mentioned is the cut ! (the exclamation character). This is a special predicate which has no declarative reading but is connected with the backtracking mechanism. It always succeeds, but it prevents backtracking from considering the alternatives that were before it in the clause or in any subsequent clauses within the same definition.

Consider for example a complex definition of bird compiled from the ones given above with some cuts added. This now states that either a bird is a heron or a swallow or a vulture or something that lays eggs and flies, or it is something which has feathers.

```
(i)      bird(heron):- !.

(ii)     bird(swallow):- !.

(iii)    bird(vulture):- !.

(iv)     bird(X):- lays_eggs(X), flies(X).

(v)      bird(X):- has_feathers(X).
```

The function of the cuts in the first three clauses of the definition is to prevent any of the later clauses being considered if any of these match. So if we ask (?) bird(vulture). then neither of the first two clauses will match this query. However clause (iii) matches exactly and will be true if the cut ! is proved. The cut succeeds and Prolog will reply YES. However if you ask for more solutions Prolog will say NO because the cut prevents it from using the lower clauses (iv) and (v). In this way you might read the cuts in this definition as meaning that if one of these is true then you don't need to bother attempting the other definitions. (Athough we should perhaps put a cut after flies(X) in clause (iv) so that if this succeeds then you should not look at (v). Note that there is no point in putting a cut at the end of the last clause, as there are no alternatives to consider at this point anyway). It is often used for efficiency - to stop Prolog wasting time in a backtracking search that could never produce anything useful. But it is a tricky thing to use properly and can drastically alter the meaning of the definition it is in. In our bird example, the query (?) bird(X). now no longer means "what birds are there?" because of the cuts. It will match with the very first clause, binding X to heron, but will only deliver this single solution. The cut in clause (i) prevents backtracking from using any of the lower clauses to find out about more birds.

The cut will be used very sparingly in the project programs - mainly in the case when you only want one solution from a definition and you don't want backtracking to produce any more solutions from any alternatives it may try.

Apx 1.3.5 The Logical Variable

Procedural programming involves variables, as does logic programming, and it is vital to recognise the radically different nature of the two uses. In procedural programming a variable is merely a container for a value, and the procedures work by 'destructive assignment' replacing whatever was in the container with some new value (LET N=N+1, PUT 10 INTO MAX, REPEAT WITH N=1 TO MAX represent typical destructive assignments). The procedural interpreter or compiler will give an error message (one hopes) if it encounters a variable that has no value assigned. A procedural variable will do exactly that — vary — as different values are entered into it.

In logic programming the role of a variable is much more like that of the 'unknown' in elementary algebra (let x represent the required velocity ...). The 'logical variable' is almost always introduced without a corresponding value, and as a logic program executes, a 'binding' may be found for it. Although this binding may be undone by later backtracking, it does not vary in the procedural sense. The scope of the logical variable is the clause (terminated by a full-stop). This local scoping is an important concept in Prolog. It means that when some unknown in a clause gets a value - is bound to something - then every occurence of that variable in the clause has the same value, but that this variable name outside the clause is not affected by any such binding and can have any value.

So consider this part of the definition above - just on its own - where this is all that is known about:

```
bird(X):- lays_eggs(X), flies(X).
```

If we query (?) bird(B). meaning "what birds are there?" then this can match with the head of this rule. The variables B & X (in the query and matched definition respectively) are both unknown and can bind together. Prolog then treats the tail of the rule as the new query and tries to find an X that lays eggs and that flies. If the first X that is true of the lays_eggs definition is say an ostrich, then X is bound to 'ostrich' and Prolog attempts to prove the remainder of the conjunction. However, now it is attempting to prove flies(ostrich) because the X in the rule is bound to this value - as are all Xs until the full-stop. Now this binding lasts until the query is finished with this rule - or backtracking undoes it. So for example if there is no entry in the database for flying ostriches then Prolog will move back a stage, unbind the value for X and try lays_eggs(X) again for another solution. If it eventually succeeds then X and B will share their value and the query will report YES, Where B = falcon, or whatever.

You must take great care with variable names in Prolog. Usually we will use single letter variable names, but you can call variables whatever you like to help you recall what it is you intend it to be bound to in due course. But if you were to ask this about birds (?) bird(Eagle). you may get confused because Eagle starts with a capital and so is a variable which just means 'some unknown' which is the argument of the predicate bird. It does not refer to any individual eagle! So, as with the above, Prolog is going to reply YES, Where Eagle = falcon, or whatever.

Apx 1.3.6 Explicit passing of values via arguments and binding

If you are used to other computer languages you may have encountered variables that can be either *global* or *local*. In procedural languages global variables are available to all programs, whilst local variables are only used "locally" in one program and their 'name' may be used elsewhere with different values. All Prolog variables are strictly *local* to the clause in which they appear.

The only "global" values in this sense are the arguments to definitions that are in the database. These are available from anywhere by queries to the relevant definition. As Prolog definitions can be changed dynamically - from within other definitions, using the built-in's `assert` and `retract` - this is the equivalent of a "global" value.

The fact that Prolog variables are entirely local to clauses has two major implications. Firstly, the names they are given are only important within any single clause in that two or more variables which share the same name also share the same value whenever one of them is bound to a specific value in matching. The same variable name can be used again in any other clause to refer to something quite different. Secondly, the normal way to give values to programs is to provide them as explicit arguments to the database definition. This tends to mean that all the inputs and outputs to any given program are explicitly specified in the arguments to its definition.

Consider a simple mathematical example, converting centigrade into farenheit using your own definition `convert/2`. So `convert(C, F)` means that C is centigrade where F is farenheit. Now it is entirely possible that you might want to give this predicate two numbers and thereby ask if one number is the centigrade equivalent of the other. But a more usual use would be where you wanted to give it one number and have it hand back the other after having worked it out. In this case you would give one argument as a number and give the other as a variable which you wanted to be returned bound to a number. For instance.

```
(?) convert(100, X).   YES   Where X = 212.
```

This shows a typical way to write simple Prolog definitions which have an explicit input and output. Conventionally, one treats the first argument(s) as the input and the later argument(s) as the output. In this case we could define the mathematical operations required as one single line of arithmetic. For example, `F is ((C / 5) * 9) + 32`. But for expository purposes let us imagine that the definition looks as follows.

```
convert(C, F):-
        divide_by_5(C, D),
        multiply_by_9(D, E),
        add_32(E, F).
```

This shows the three mathematical operations that are required upon the input to find a value for the output as separate calls to further definitions. It is assumed that the three further definitions are available elsewhere - indeed each is very simple. So for example D is the result of dividing C by 5; E is the result of multiplying D by 9; and F is E with 32 added to it. In Figure 1.2 we have written out this definition with extra spaces in the arguments and arrows to indicate which variables will bind together. Technically, the arrows should be on both ends of each line, as these variables simply "share" values, but we have only given one arrow-head to indicate which variable from the example query (with C as 'input' and F as 'output') will bind first and thereby pass its value to the other variable of the same name.

Tutorial Appendix Figure 1.2   The binding of variables in `convert/2`

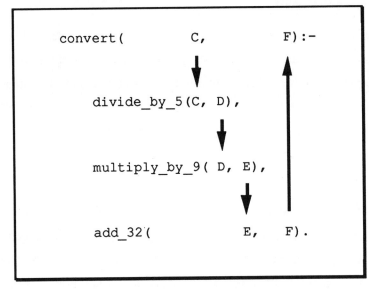

So if we follow the figure considering our sample query `(?) convert(100, X).` we can see that C will be bound to 100 and F will share its value with the X of the query. When the "if" part is proven, the C is given to `divide_by_5` as 100 and D is unbound. Presumably this call goes away and returns D now bound to 20. The conjuctive call of `multiply_by_9` is given D as 20 and E unbound. Presumably, it too will go off to be proven (matched with its definition elsewhere) returning with E bound to 180. The final conjuctive call to `add_32` is given E as 180 and presumably returns F bound to 212. Now the "if" part of the rule has succeeded and so the clause succeeds with YES. and as the F of the final call and the F of head of the rule have the same name they have the same value. Similarly, as F is "sharing" its value with the X given in the query then X too is bound to 212 which it will report.

Apx 1.3.7 Non-deterministic programming

The capability of using a logical variable to represent a currently unknown concept provides great power, supporting a unique logic programming style known as non-deterministic programming (NDP). The two most distinctive aspects of NDP are the reduced need for explicit program control structures, and the availability of multiple solutions to queries (via backtracking). A further reflection of NDP is the possibly powerful (and confusing) indifference of Prolog to mode of execution.

For instance, the predicate `add(A, B, AB)` could potentially be used (with a single appropriate definition somewhere):

to add

        (?) add(6, 5, Sum).   YES Where Sum = 11

or to subtract

        (?) add(6, X, 11).   YES Where X = 5

or even provide multiple solutions via backtracking

```
(?)  add(X, Y, 11).   YES Where
                            X = 0 AND Y = 11
                      OR  X = 1 AND Y = 10
                      OR  X = 2 AND Y = 9
                      OR  X = 3 AND Y = 8
                      ... etc
```

whereas, at least two separate operations would need to be defined for a typical procedural program.

Apx 1.3.8 Negation as Failure

Truth and falsity in Prolog do not mean quite the same as in real life.

Truth in Prolog means - "can be proved using the database definitions".

Falsity means - "cannot be proved using the database definitions".

This restriction of the logical meaning of no to 'not proven' is often referred to as the 'closed world assumption', in that it is only logically correct in a closed world where facts are always either provably true or false.

So with the definition of 'father' in the database being only:

```
father(philip, charles).
father(philip, anne).
```

Then the query (?) `father(elizabeth, philip).` will fail and report NO simply because the Prolog theorem prover cannot match the query term with any part of the definition - not for any other reason eg it does not know that elizabeth is a woman and women are never fathers - indeed it does not know ANYTHING that it has not been told explicitly via this definition about the meaning of 'father'.

So the query (?) `father(philip, andrew).` will also fail - even if true in reality - because it is not part of the Prolog definition of the predicate.

The responsibility for semantic truth and validity lies squarely with the programmer. If the fact `father(elizabeth, a_large_oak_tree)` was added to the database definition then it would be considered - for the sake of the Prolog theorem prover - logically true.

Tutorial Appendix 1.4   The Family Database

We have chosen our first database example from a small family tree. The tree we are using is shown in Figure 1.3 and represents a selection of family relations based upon some members of the British Royal Family. Our task is to represent information about individuals in the family and their relationships to one another. The set of basic facts that we will use as the basis for the family relationships consists of four simple definitions: male, female, parent and husband. The relations male and female are used to describe single individuals in the family and there is an entry in one or other definition for all the individuals known. For the names of the people concerned we will use the convention of simply giving their names as simple atoms - one word beginning with a lower case letter. So in the Prolog definition the individual Philip is represented by the word `philip`. This convention is made possible by the convenient circumstance that all individuals in our family here have unique names. Had we wished to extend the tree back to another individual called Elizabeth we would have to ensure that they were named differently so as to refer to different people, (eg. we might call one `Elizabeth I` and the other `Elizabeth II` - single quoting the names because they include 'funny' characters).

So, to state that Philip is male we have simply to give his name as an argument to the predicate `male` in the **male**/1 definition.

% male(X) states that X is a male

```
male(philip).
male(charles).
male(mark).
male(andrew).
male(andrew).
male(edward).
male(william).
male(harry).
male(peter).
```

% female(X) states that X is female

```
female(elizabeth).
female(diana).
female(anne).
female(sarah).
female(zara).
```

% parent(P, C) states that P is the parent of C

```
parent(philip, charles).        parent(elizabeth, charles).
parent(philip, anne).           parent(elizabeth, anne).
parent(philip, andrew).         parent(elizabeth, andrew).
parent(philip, edward).         parent(elizabeth, edward).
parent(charles, william).       parent(diana, william).
parent(charles, harry).         parent(diana, harry).
parent(mark, peter).            parent(anne, peter).
parent(mark, zara).             parent(anne, zara).
```

% husband(H, W) states that H is the husband of W

```
husband(philip, elizabeth).
husband(charles, diana).
husband(mark, anne).
husband(andrew, sarah).
```

The relations `parent/2` and `husband/2` have two arguments which are the individuals for whom these relations hold. By providing this set of relations as a Prolog definition we are effectively providing Prolog with a code version of the parentage and marriage links that are illustrated in Figure 1.3. Now clearly there are a vast number of other relationships that we can infer as following from the tree representation. We could explicitly include each relation as a new definition consisting of a new set of facts. So if we wanted to explicitly represent the relation 'father' we could provide a set of facts like these (as we suggested some way above).

```
father(philip, charles).
father(philip, anne).
... etc
```

However this is very inefficient. We could more effectively make use of the inference mechanism that Prolog can use to represent a simple rule for the new relations in terms of the simpler ones already known, and get Prolog to do some work as a theorem prover. So the definiton of father might look like:

```
father(X, Y):- parent(X, Y), male(X).
```

We have discussed this rule before. It simply states that someone X is a father of someone Y if X is a parent of Y and X is a male.

Tutorial Appendix Figure 1.3   A Family Tree

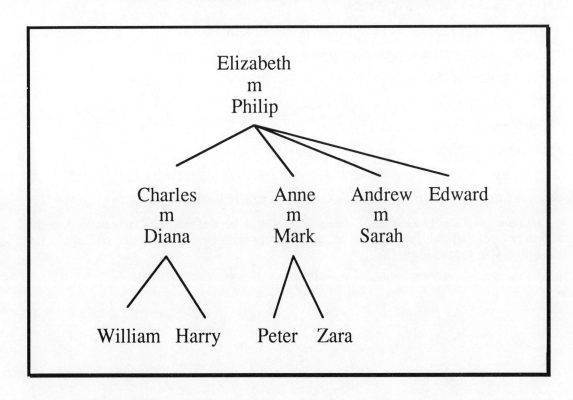

Exercises 1.1 The Royal Family Tree

E 1.1.1 Try the following queries to the family database definitions:

```
(? i)   male(philip).

(? ii)   female(philip).

(? iii)   male(rod).

(? iv)   parent(charles, philip).
```

Can you explain why Prolog gives the answers it does?

E 1.1.2 Logical variables

(a) try these queries – you are interested in 'All solutions'

```
(? i) parent(Someone,william).

(? ii) parent(X,william), female(X).

(? iii) parent(elizabeth, Person), parent(Person, Child).
```

Try to write out the declarative meaning of the queries.

NB: Remember the comma between the terms in ii & iii means "and".

(b) construct queries which have the following meaning:

(i) who are the children of charles?

(ii) who was the grandfather of zara?

(iii) who is the wife of mark?

E 1.1.3 Defining Rules

(a) Type in the declarative meaning and the Prolog code for

(i) `mother(M, C)`

(ii) `grandfather(G, C)`

(iii) `wife(Woman, Man)`

(iv) `sibling(Child1, Child2)`

(v) `cousin(Person1, Person2)` - nb. this is quite tricky!

(b) Check your program semantics by trying the following queries:

```
(? i) sibling(Person, zara).

(? ii) grandfather(philip, Grandchild).

(? iii) cousin(Person, harry).
```

Do you get **all** the right answers and **only** the right answers?

A note on Answers: it is often possible to define a rule in different ways.

For instance, `cousin(Person1, Person2)` could be defined as 'two people with the same grandparent but different parents' or as 'two people with parents who are siblings'. Both should work fine if you get the logic OK.

Tutorial Appendix 1.5   Welcome to Lists

If you want to describe something which has a lot of elements, perhaps an arbitrary number of them, such as items you need to get during a shopping expedition, you would use a list. Lists are a very powerful representational device in AI, indeed some languages such as LISP are founded on principles of **LISt** Processing.

Lists in Prolog are simply structures surrounded by square brackets, where each element of the list is separated by commas.

> `[a, b, c]` is a list of three elements: the atoms a, b and c.

> `[fish, sugar, milk, flour, corn_flakes]`   is a list with five elements

But of course, lists can contain any legal Prolog elements: atoms, variables, terms, even other lists.

> `[[spuds,carrots], [butter,milk], [oranges,lemons]]`

is a shopping list with three elements: all three are themselves lists, the first has vegetables, the second has dairy products and the third is fruit. The first sub-list has two elements and so on.

As with the family database you can try matching lists through queries. Consider a database definition which contains two shopping lists:

```
shopping_list( [carrots, potatoes, milk, eggs, butter, soap, shampoo] ).
shopping_list( [ [spuds, carrots], [butter, milk], [oranges, lemons] ] ).
```

Exercises 1.2 Elementary Lists
Exercise 1.2.1   Finding Shopping

With the two shopping list clauses in the database - try matching the shopping lists with the queries:

```
(? i)     shopping_list( X ).
(? ii)    shopping_list( [X, Y, Z] ).
(? iii)   shopping_list( [C, P, M, E, B, So, Sh] ).
```

NB: What would happen if you just used S, S instead of So, Sh for the last two elements? Why?

As you will see this is fine so long as you know how many elements there are in a list whose elements you are trying to get at. What you can't do is pick out eggs (on their own) from this list unless you know exactly where 'eggs' is in the list.

Exercise 1.2.2   Matching more words in lists

The second list exercise gropes towards the idea of sentence parsing, and involves a sentence represented as embedded lists of words. Type this definition for `sentence/1` into the Prolog database:

```
sentence([[ the, hippy ],  [[ kissed, the, debutante ], [ in, the, park ]]]).
```

Be sure to get the bracketing right and try to match it with queries

(? i)   `sentence( [NounPhrase,  VerbPhrase]).`

(? ii) `sentence([ [Det,  Noun], [VerbPhrase,PrepPhrase] ]).`

(? ii) `sentence( [ [Det1, Noun1], [ [Verb,Det2,Noun2], [Prep,Det3,Noun3] ] ] ).`

Storing and retrieving lists

After going to the trouble of typing in a complex list, it is useful to able to store it for future use. While it is possible in Prolog to type, say

```
X = [ [the,boy],  [[hit,the,dog], [with,a,stick] ]  ].
```

This is really only meaningful within a query, and since the variable X is local to that specific query if you ask a second query Prolog will no longer have X instantiated to that list but will produce a 'fresh copy' of the variable X.

The way to store a list is to give it a name, and type into a database definiton.

eg. `sentence1( [ [the, boy],  [ [hit, the, dog], [with, a, stick] ] ]  ).`

It may then be accessed when you want it by Prolog's built-in matcher eg.

(?) `sentence1(List)`

will match `List = [ [the, boy],  [[hit, the, dog], [with, a, stick] ]   ]`

which is why the 3 queries above have the effect they do: eg

(?)   `sentence1([[Det1, Noun1], [ [Verb, Det2, Noun2], [Prep, Det3, Noun3]]]).`

will return

```
Det1 = the,        Noun1 = boy,    Verb = hit,   Det2 = the,  Noun2 = dog,

Prep = with, Det3 = a, Noun3 = stick.
```

Of course we have "cheated" by giving the variables meaningful names – in fact these names are only meaningful to us – they have no meaning in Prolog. We would have had the same effect with:

```
sentence1( [ [A, B], [ [C, D, E], [F, G, H] ] ] )
```

which means exactly the same to Prolog.

These examples anticipate the DCG chapter where we start to use lists in the parsing of sentences. One of the major difficulties is to take an input sentence and find the parse tree in the first place. In the next section we introduce some relations which will enable us to process the elements of any list.

Apx 1.5.1 Processing Lists

Prolog is an extensible language - it is possible to define any relation you want in terms of more fundamental 'primitive' relations, and these new relations can be incorporated into the Prolog environment. Most often, the more primitive relations will be ones that you have defined yourself, the simplest being facts that require no further inference, but some relations are already provided by Prolog as built-in.

There are two list processing definitions which most versions of Prolog will already have as built-in. The first is member/2, the other is append/3. You can actually define these relations yourself, (think about that --- that you could write the Prolog computer language in Prolog!). But first you must explore what these relations do. If your version of Prolog does not have its own definition of member/2 or append/3 as a built-in then you will need to type them in from the general predicates in appendix 1.

The way that you go about designing a Prolog relation is first to specify what it should mean.

A specification for **member** would be :

member(Element, List) means that Element is a 'member' of the List.

So the first argument is a possible element of the second argument, which must be a list.

This is not overly helpful in this abstract form and it is as well to consider what a variety of specific queries to this relation would mean.

So for **member/2** :

```
(?) member(a, [n, m, o, a, b]).     Should reply   YES.
(?) member(d, [a, b, c]).           Should reply NO.

etc ...
```

Exercise 1.2.3   List Processing with member

What do these queries mean?

```
(? i)    member(X, [albert, mike, susan, fred]).
(? ii)   member( X, [carrots, potatoes, milk, eggs, butter, soap, shampoo]).
(? iii)  shopping_list(List), member(X,List).
```

Think up some other queries on lists of your own. Are you clear WHAT member is doing?

A specification for **append**/3:

append(A, B, AB).

means that list AB is the result of appending (sticking together) the two lists A and B.

```
eg.    append( [a, b], [c, d, e, f], [a, b, c, d, e, f]).

       will succeed.
```

Exercise 1.2.4   List Processing with append

Your exercise here is to examine the relation via some specific queries to it.

(? i) `append( [humpty, dumpty], [sat,on,a,wall], X).`

(? ii) `append( [humpty, dumpty], Y, [humpty,dumpty,sat,on,a,wall]).`

(? iii) `append( [], [fred], List).`

> Query 3 should return `List = [fred]`   Think about it!

Apx 1.5.2 Your Own List Processing

You already know about lists. And that this:

    complaint([i, hate, computers]).

in the database will match with query: (?) `complaint(X)` to reply

    X = [i, hate, computers]

Also if you know how long the list is you can obviously pick out the elements;

`complaint([i, hate, computers]).`

will match with query: (?) `complaint([X, Y, Z])` to reply

    X = i,
    Y = hate,
    Z = computers

However there is a special Prolog operator for getting at the elements of lists where you don't know (and don't care about) the list length.

The separator bar | is a list **guillotine** as it is used to separate the HEADS from lists.

Tutorial Appendix Figure 1.4
The List Guillotine

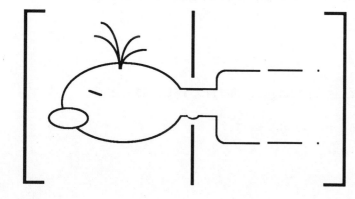

The terminology "list guillotine" is our own, but we feel that it is quite evocative of the bar's function. The vertical bar usually has a space in the middle when shown on the screen or on the keyboard. It is always used inside the square list brackets. You must know how long the Head is, but the remainder (the Tail or Body) of the list can be any length and is itself a list.

The guillotine is usually used in this form **[Head | Tail]** where Head is just one element and Tail is a list representing the original list without its Head. In a call using this format the guillotine Tail is always a Variable.

So matching the above Prolog relation:

```
complaint([i, hate, computers]).
```

with the query : `(?)  complaint([Head | Tail])`

will reply

`Head = i`, and

`Tail = [hate, computers]`.

As noted the Head need not just be one element. If you know for sure that a list has at least two elements, you could explicitly guillotine both, or however many you wished. BUT the Tail must always be just the one element (and always a list). So:

```
complaint([i, hate, computers]).
```

with the query : `(?)  complaint([First, Second | Tail])`

will reply

`First = i`, and

`Second = hate`, and

`Tail = [computers]`.

The most obvious relation we can immediately define is **first/2**, after all this is what the guillotine does anyway. We give three different definitions, in order of increasing sophistication. It's very important to grasp that the third definition, although it looks just like a mere fact, is actually performing the function of the rule through Prolog's 'natural' pattern matching unification with the variable `Element`.

% first(Element, List) means : some Element is the first element of a List.

% Pascal hacker

```
first2(Element, List) :- List = [Head | Tail], Head = Element.
```

% match Element

```
first1(Element, List) :- List = [Element | Tail].
```

% Prolog power!

```
first(Element, [Element | Tail]).
```

Clearly we could define second, third etc in the same way, but the real power of the list guillotine is that it provides us with a way of handling lists of any length.

Tutorial Appendix 1.6   Recursion

Hofstadter's Law.

Everything takes longer than you expect, even when you allow for Hofstadter's Law.

(Hofstadter, 1979)

Apx 1.6.1 Introducing recursion

Recursion is one of the major techniques of AI research, especially for declarative and functional languages, and is particularly suited to list manipulation. It is normally contrasted with a computing technique called iteration that allows operations to be repeated many times. A simple iterative loop in some procedural language might look like this line: REPEAT 6 TIMES say(hello) NEXT. This line might be used to execute the instruction "say(hello)" 6 times. Recursion is a much more powerful concept than this but is very much harder to follow.

Definition: A recursive relation is one that is defined in terms of itself.

Whilst at first it may seem rather odd to suggest that self-reference of this sort can be useful there are circumstances where it is entirely natural to refer to a definition from within that definition. Eg.

X is a Roman citizen if X's father was a Roman citizen

In general it is never adequate to have just a recursive definition - you also need a stopping condition, since otherwise the definition recurses endlessly referring to itself. The stopping conditions must be a simple check which indicates a clear case of success. So for Roman citizens:

X is a Roman citizen if X was born in Rome

is a clear case for the definition which can be combined with the above recursive case to provide a complete definition of Roman citizenry.

X is a Roman citizen if X was born in Rome

X is a Roman citizen if X's father was a Roman citizen

You can be Roman if you were born in Rome; OR if your father was Roman. Now your father can be Roman by having been born in Rome; OR by his father being Roman. His father could be Roman by having been born in Rome or by having a Roman father; and so on! Recursion can be tricky to keep track of but is often short, elegant and complete whilst not limiting the problem to which it applies. It can also be useful for more procedural examples such as these:

- To tidy a room

    A room is tidy if nothing is on floor OR
    A room is tidy if 1 untidy item is put away and then you tidy the room.

- Climbing a ladder

    A ladder is climbed if there are no rungs left to climb OR
    A ladder is climbed by climbing one rung then climbing the ladder.

Recursion works as a technique where there is a simple success condition that can act as a stopping check and where the problem that is recursed upon gets simpler or more complete via the recursion. In tidying a room and climbing a ladder the problem is simpler because the recursive condition insists that something is put away or a rung is climbed before it recurses. In the Roman citizen example (so long as there are a finite number of fathers known) then this too gets simpler – as you run out of fathers to inherit citizenry from. The catch with the Hofstadter example with which we began is that there is no stopping condition and the problem gets no simpler by the recursion!

You may have noted that in the above examples the stopping checks were given as the first condition in the definitions – this is not just a convention but an essential feature of using recursion in Prolog. Whilst logically both conditions are true and independent, because of the way that Prolog works its way down definitions, trying one clause at a time, it is essential that the stopping condition is attempted before the recursive one. In recursion Prolog effectively jumps out of the current definition and starts again at the top of the definition with some new (recursive) thing to prove. If the recursive condition is first, Prolog would dive back in on itself just in this one clause and never get on to the stopping part to see if it had ever succeeded.

Apx 1.6.2 A recursive predicate for the family database program.

One interesting feature of family trees is that they can be extended back in time through generations of ancestors. It can become difficult to keep track of the exact name for the relationship between distant individuals.

Tutorial Appendix Figure 1.5   Ancestors via Parents

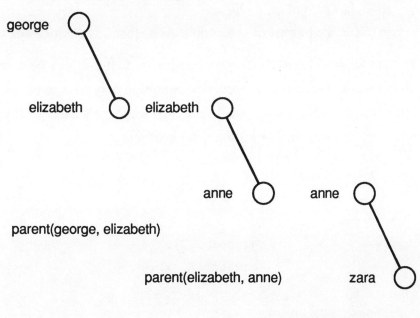

So here we will consider the relationship **ancestor/2** which simply proves any direct link between two individuals in the tree. If we extend the Royal Family tree back just a little to include Elizabeth's father George we can quickly see that there is a link between George and the blood relatives below him through the relationship that we have called **parent**/2. Figure 1.5 illustrates the ancestral connection, via three parent/2 clauses, between George at one end and Zara at the other. Now from Zara's point of view, all the individuals above her to whom she can be connected via the parent relationship are her ancestors – starting with her own parents. A plausible definition for ancestor therefore would be to prespecify all the possible multiple connections of parent relationships. Eg.

```
(i)         ancestor(A, B):-
                        parent(A, B).
(ii)        ancestor(A, C):-
                        parent(A, B),
                        parent(B, C).
(iii)       ancestor(A, D):-
                        parent(A, B),
                        parent(B, C),
                        parent(C, D).
        ...
```

In the above definition we give the first three clauses of this plausible definition. This will work for our example, but would clearly have to be extended with one extra clause for every one higher link that we included in the family tree. If you have grasped the idea of recursion you may be able to see a much more powerful and elegant definition for this problem – where just two clauses will cover any size of tree (see the Roman citizen example).

The two clauses are of course, the stopping check and recursive loop with a declarative meaning as follows:

X is an **ancestor** of Y if

   (i) X is a **parent** of Y OR

   (ii) X is the **parent** of someone S AND that S is an **ancestor** of Y.

The stopping check is the most basic condition of ancestry, that you can be someone's ancestor simply by being their parent. However the recursive condition may take some thinking about as it suggests that even if not their direct parent, you may still be someone's ancestor if you are the parent of someone else who is their ancestor. The Prolog version of this is:

```
(i)         ancestor(X, Y):-
                        parent(X, Y).
(ii)        ancestor(X, Y):-
                        parent(X, S),
                        ancestor(S, Y).
```

Apx 1.6.3 Recursion in Processing Lists

List processing recursion has a very similar structure to all other recursive definitions. Only in list processing definitions what usually happens is that the list guillotine is used to divide the list and the recursive call is on the (now shorter) Tail of the guillotined list. Consider the simple example of room tidying which was introduced above and which can be seen as the logical flavour of a very procedural operation.

(i)   A room is tidy if nothing on floor.

(ii)   Tidy room by putting away 1 item then Tidy room

The contents of the room can be represented as a list of items which need to be put away, and we will imagine that there is a simple predicate put_away/1 which does something useful to its single argument. The stopping check is simply a list which contains no items – equivalent to an empty floor.

```
(i)       tidy_room([]).
(ii)      tidy_room([X|Tail]) :-  put_away(X), tidy_room(Tail).
```

The recursive loop requires that we guillotine the list so that we know about one specific item X and whatever is left in the list (after X is guillotined out) is called Tail. This second condition is only true where it can be proved that X is 'put_away' and that the tail of the list is true of a recursive call to 'tidy_room'. This guillotining of lists is a crucial feature of list-processing recursion as it provides the mechanism whereby the problem for the recursion becomes simpler. That is that the list handed on to the recursive call gets shorter each time around.

Apx 1.6.4 Defining a List Membership Definition

We have already made use of the predicate **member/2** for checking list membership, but it is important to realise that most of the built-in predicates like member can actually be defined themselves in Prolog. So let's define list membership ourselves:

Declarative definition

Element is a member of List
either (i) if Element is the head of the list   [stopping condition]
or   (ii) if Element is a member of the tail of the list.   [recursive condition]

Procedural definition

To find whether Element is a member of the List
(i) extract the first element of the list and if that matches Element we have succeeded
otherwise

(ii) see whether Element is a member of the rest of the list
(with the head guillotined and discarded)

Prolog definition

```
(i)        member(X, [X | Rest]).                    %  stopping condition
(ii)       member(X, [Y | Rest]) :- member(X, Rest).  %  recursive condition
```

Note the astonishing brevity and elegance of the Prolog definition. The stopping check is actually a rather unusual but handy special case in which we don't need to do very much work. The recursive condition does more work on a slightly simpler problem.

Clause (i) says in effect: extract the head of the list - call it variable X, checking whether the element matches this X. If so, succeed (if not, go on to clause 2).

Clause (ii) says: extract the head of the list, call it Y, and forget about it (we know that it can't match the element since otherwise clause 1 would have succeeded). Call the tail of the guillotined list Rest and then check to see whether the 'if' part of the rule is true. The 'if' part of the rule requires that the element X be a member of the list Rest. The problem has become slightly simpler as the Rest list is shorter than the original list (by one element Y).

You need to be familiar with how your version of Prolog handles tracing. Most Prologs have a set of relations that are to do with 'Spypoints'. These are the times that Prolog will alert you about a particular call to a particular predicates definiton. In most Prologs you execute a query to the definition **spy/1** with its argument being the name of the definition that you want to trace. So you would run the query (?) **spy(member)**. In LPA MacProlog you first select 'Spypoints' from the Evaluation menu, click on 'member' then click on 'set spypoints'.

In either case, this will cause Prolog to output a message every time that the predicate member is accessed. Note that "call" means 'try to solve' whereas "exit" means 'a call that has succeeded'. Redo means 'try to find a further solution' for this call and "fail" means that a solution could not be found for the current set of definitions.

NB When Prolog uses Variables internally it does not make use of the specific variable names you give it, like List or X. Instead it converts all variables into unique numbers which are preceded by and underscore '_' character, eg. _1879. In tracing what Prolog is doing, all the variables used are normally in this (hard to read) form.

If you were to try these queries, you would get these results

```
(? i)   member(1, [1,2,3]).        YES.
(? ii)  member(2, [1,2,3]).        YES.
(? iii) member(3, [1,2,3]).        YES.
(? iv)  member(4, [1,2,3]).        NO.
```

Can you work out what is happening from the program trace?

Here is a suitably indented and annotated printout of a program trace for the query above.

```
C0    :member(3, [1, 2, 3])
C1            call: member(3, [1, 2, 3])              (clause 1 fails but clause 2 succeeds)
C2                 call: member(3, [2, 3])            (clause 1 fails but clause 2 succeeds)
C3                      call: member(3, [3])          (clause 1 succeeds)
C3                      exit: member(3, [3])          (so call C3 succeeds)
C2                 exit: member(3, [2, 3])            (so call C2 succeeds)
C1            exit: member(3, [1, 2, 3])             (so call C1 succeeds)
C0    Yes                                             (so call C0 succeeds)
```

Exercises 1.3 Screen Output and Pretty-Printing

E 1.3.1 Built-in screen output primitives

There are three built-in primitives called write, nl and tab which are used for screen output.

Work out what format they use by trying these clauses as queries (see it as detective work - it's what one has to do without a manual!).

(? i) `write(hello), nl.`

(? ii) `tab(8), write(hello_george), nl.`

(? iii) `write(hello), nl, tab(5), write(george).`

(? vi) `write('hello george').`

(? v) `write(George), nl.`

(? vi) `write(hello, george).`   % think - why doesn't it work?

(? vii) `write([hello, nl, George]).`

What do you think `nl` stands for?

Once you've cracked that, we can move on to more flexible methods of writing out results.

E 1.3.2 Itemising a list. This will be the first list-processing recursive predicate you write! Write a predicate with the following specification:

`itemise_list(List)` writes out each member of the List on a separate line. eg.

```
      (?)   itemise_list([one,element,per,line]).
one
element
per
line
```

Hints :

(1) this is a natural problem for the stopping condition / recursive condition duo

(2) if in doubt, think how you would do it by hand.

E 1.3.3 Combining a list

Write a predicate with the following specification: `combine_list(List)` writes out all elements of
the List on the same line separated by single spaces. eg.

```
    (?)  combine_list([useful, for, creating, 'English', from, lists]).
useful for creating English from lists
```

E 1.3.4 Pretty-printing a list

Try to work out what the following predicate does:

```
pretty_print([], Tab) :- nl.
pretty_print([X | Rest], Tab) :-
     tab(Tab), write(X), nl, Tab1 is Tab + 4, pretty_print(Rest, Tab1).
```

Hint : try a query like:

```
(?) pretty_print([each, element, printed, further, across, the, page],  0).
```

NB. this is much harder to understand as it involves the use of a more complex recursion. You
might like to try doing a trace on it.

E 1.3.5 Defining the predicate `last/2`

You have seen that it is trivial to define the predicate `first/2` to get the first element of a list because
this is what the list guillotine does itself. But what about its opposite? The predicate `last/2` will
take two arguments. The second argument will be a list, with any number of elements in it. The first
argument will be bound to the last element of that list. So, `last(X, L)` should mean that X is the
last element of the list L.

Tutorial Appendix 1.7   Summary

Prolog is a programming iceberg. Unlike programming in many languages which gets easier as you
get deeper into their details and mechanism, Prolog can get harder. This appendix should be viewed
as a crash survival course on this iceberg. Pattern matching, the list guillotine, the logical variable,
recursion and backtracking are concepts that appear throughout the projects and which you should
recognise.

The major learning advantage is that you can use Prolog to represent and perform substantial symbol
processing problems as soon as you begin to use it. The major learning problem is that there is a lot
of Prolog that is submerged beneath the water and which can take some time to master. Our assertion
is that one powerful learning method is to tinker with some code to see how it works. Even if you
never really get a full understanding of how the following projects work via Prolog then at least you
will have experienced some working Cognitive Science. If on the other hand you do ... then build it
better.

Glossary

This glossary section provides a short definition of some of the Prolog terminology that we will use in this book. Further explanations and examples are provided in the Prolog tutorial appendix and at the relevant places in the projects.

AND : Conjunction in Prolog is expressed using the comma operator ',' which takes two arguments and is normally written in between the terms to be conjoined. Eg. the definition

```
a:- b, c.
```

can be read as meaning that a is true if b AND c can be proved to be true.

Anonymous variable : The underscore character on its own is referred to as the anonymous variable in that it is a variable which is given no name. Where a variable appears only once in any clause (and can thus not share its value with anything else) or where you do not care what value becomes bound to a variable then it is best to make it anonymous using the underscore. Any number of underscores can appear in one clause and still refer to possibly different things.

Arity : The number of arguments taken by a predicate in a definition, (see Argument).

Argument : The domain of some predicate. Arguments usually appear in a Prolog term surrounded by the round brackets which are dominated by a predicate.

Atom : (also known as Constant) A single word in Prolog beginning with a lower-case alphabetic character a-z. Atoms cannot contain spaces or characters that are not alphanumeric. However the effect of psuedo-spaces is often achieved by using the underscore character in a long word. An atom is normally used to refer to some individual entity or thing which exists in the world we are considering in our Prolog program. Unusual atoms beginning with upper-case or numeric characters or containing spaces must be enclosed in single quotes.

Backtracking : When the Prolog inference engine matches a query term and a database term in some definition it succeeds and may go on to attempt to match and thereby prove some further terms. If any of the further inference fails for whatever reason then the Prolog engine can return to this match to try any alternatives which may be available. This "returning to try alternative solutions" is called backtracking. So, for example, in attempting to prove the terms (?) a, m, n. and where a succeeds Prolog must then prove m and then n. If say m fails to be proved from its database definition then Prolog could return to a to see if there is an alternative way of proving it. The most obvious alternatives are provided via disjunctions in definitions (see OR). In principle, proving a in some other way might cause m to be true under the new conditions. The user can often force Prolog to backtrack when it reports success to a query by asking for more solutions. When we refer to the number of solutions that any query will provide we mean what happens when backtracking returns to a definition to attempt to prove it in another way. So when a definition has "Just One" solution this means that it will succeed once but if Prolog returns to it with backtracking, then it will fail. Some predicate definitions may provide a number of alternative solutions to any single query. This is often referred to as the predicate's ability to *resatisfy* (ie succeed again) on backtracking.

Binding : (of variables) The values that named variables have been given via the matching process are said to be bound to them. Prolog variables can match with either a constant, list or term binding the name of the variable to this specific value. Unbound variables can match with any one thing. Once a variable is bound to some value then it retains this value (within the clause) until the query terminates or backtracking unbinds it. Backtracking unbinds the values given to variables if it returns to before the clause in which the first match of the variable to that value took place. Once a variable is bound to a value any other variables that have exactly the same name in the current clause (until the full stop) will "share" this value. Indeed the only point in giving variables a name at all is to force variables with the same name to share the same value.

Clause : A Prolog term or collection of terms followed by a period (full stop '.') character. A clause normally appears in the database singly as a fact or in a collection as a rule. Normally facts and rules in the database must have at least a one space or new-line after their terminating full-stop. We typically start new clauses on new lines.

Comments : Anything enclosed within special markers which you wish the Prolog program to ignore. The typical markers are the percent character used to ignore anything following it on the same line (until the next line). Or the enclosing slash-star and star-slash combination to 'comment-out' a number of lines. eg /* ... */

Constant : (see Atom).

Conjunction : (see AND).

Declarative definition : A way of reading any Prolog representation which emphasises its meaning independent of how that meaning is to be proved as a sequence of actions. So one might read the rule a :- b, c. declaratively as it is the case that a is true if b and c are also true.

Definition : A collection of facts and rules with the same predicate or relation name. Many Prologs will insist that any single definition is contiguous and that all its clauses must be collected together. When referring to a definition either of the user or built-in we will use the convention of giving the predicate name followed by a slash and then a number referring to the number of arguments that the predicate takes.

Disjunction : (see OR).

Element : (of a list) A member of the set which is a list which can itself be either an atom, a term of any complexity, a variable or even another list.

Fact : A single clause in the database.

Falsity : In Prolog means that terms cannot be proved to be true by the current database definitions.

Guillotine : (of a List) The name that we give to the vertical bar operator 'I' that is used in lists to separate the head from the tail of the list. eg. the variable structure [H | T] is a single list where the head is the first element of the list H and the tail T is the list of what remains without H. Depending how it is used the guillotine can remove things from the front of lists or to add them.

Head : (of a List) The element or elements to the left of the guillotine in a list.

IF : Implication in Prolog is expressed via the colon-dash operator ':-' which appears in rules and takes two arguments. The first argument (normally to the left of the operator) is the consequent and the second (normally written to the right of the operator) is the antecedent of the rule. In Prolog there can only be one consequent to each rule but there can be any number of antecedents (joined by the AND and OR operators). Eg the rule a:- b. can be read as meaning that a is true IF b can be proved to be true. When the query term being proved by Prolog matches the a term the 'IF' in the rule causes the Prolog theorem prover to treat the b term as the new 'query' term to be proved.

Inference Engine : (also known as Theorem Prover) The built-in mechanism that Prolog uses for matching query terms with database definitions to prove the user's queries or internally generated queries required to prove the antecedents of rules.

List : a collection of elements separated by commas and surrounded by one pair of square brackets.

List Processing : Many interesting operations in Prolog work on sets of individuals which are usually represented in lists.

Matching : (also known as Pattern Matching) Matching is the process used by the Prolog inference engine to establish truth or falsity (success or failure). The Prolog engine compares two terms - succeeding if they match and failing if they do not. Normally one term is a query term (to be proved true) and the other is a database term (which is considered to be true). If they match then the query is also considered to be true. If they do not then (unless another match can be made - see Backtracking) it is false. The inference engine matches query terms with facts directly by comparing the values of the predicate and its arguments. It matches rules by comparing the query term with the rule's consequent term but only permitting the match if it can also prove the antecedent terms (see IF). In matching Prolog compares each individual word in the two terms. Variables can match with any one thing where they appear ie an atom, term or list.

Operator : In Prolog any predicate may be declared to be an "operator" which permits the term that it makes to use a special syntactic form, for instance without the requirement for the brackets which must normally surround its arguments. It is done via the built-in predicate op/3. If the predicate takes two arguments it is written in operator form between its arguments. Hence the built-ins like IF ':-', AND ',', OR ';', etc should be seen as operators defined in this way. Operator form should be seen as a sort of syntactic sugar that makes terms easier to read. With the exception of the DCGs parsing project we will avoid its use in our book programs.

OR : Disjunction is normally expressed in Prolog implicitly as the number of separate clauses in the same definition. This is because of the way that Prolog's built-in theorem prover attempts to match query terms to database definitions, ie one at a time, starting with the first and then returning to the next upon failure. Disjunction may also be expressed explicitly in Prolog using the semi-colon operator ';' within rules. However, in this book we will avoid this as the meaning of the implicit form is usually much clearer. Eg.

```
a:- b ; c.
```

means that a is true if b or c can be proved to be true, but we will use the implicit form

```
a:- b.
```

```
a:- c.
```

which means the same thing.

Pattern Matching : (see Matching)

Predicate : (also known as Relation) An atomic word that is the first part of a Prolog term. It can have zero or more arguments. Predicates are also referred to as relations as they often represent the relationships between their arguments.

Procedural definition : A way of reading any Prolog representation which emphasises how Prolog will prove it as a sequence of actions or calls. So one might read the rule a :- b, c. procedurally as Prolog will prove that a is true by first proving that b is true and then proving that c is true.

Query : Prolog is a database language that is made to perform inferences by being issued with queries. A query is a single term or a set of terms (joined with conjunction or disjunction operators) that Prolog is required to prove. It may also generate further query terms for itself as a result of the need to prove the antecedents of rules. Our convention for indicating terms that are intended to be queries is to precede them with a question mark in round brackets. Many Prolog environments provide the user with a query interface that is prompted with a queston mark and hypen '?-' which could be read the same.

Recursion : This refers to a powerful inference device very commonly used in Prolog which involves defining some operation in terms of itself. Normally it involves some definition making a problem slightly simpler in some way and then handing on this simpler problem to the same definition. This will then make the problem simpler and hand it on to itself, and so on. Recursion is normally only useful where there is a clear means of checking whether the problem is solved (see Stopping Check) before invoking recursive inference again.

Relation : (see Predicate)

Rule : A single clause in the database which is followed by the IF ':-' operator and then a collection of one or more clauses.

Sharing : (of variables) Prolog variables which share a name in a single clause will also share the same value as soon as any one of them is bound via matching to something specific such as an atom, term or list. When two variables with different names are matched together then these different names will also share the same value when any one is bound.

Stopping check : (in recursion) This is some simple check for success which prevents a recursive definition form calling itself infinitely. Normally it is present in a clause which is matched before any recursive clauses. In list processing definitions the most usual stopping check is the empty list [ ]. So the recursive call will work by making the list progressively shorter until finally it is empty and can terminate.

Tail : (of a List) The single variable to the right of the guillotine in a list which will be bound to the contents of the list minus the guillotined head element(s). The tail is always one thing and always a variable that will be bound to a list in matching.

Term : A single predicate followed by an optional number of arguments which must be enclosed by round brackets (unless the predicate is declared to be an operator). Prolog will insist that there must be no space between the predicate and the opening bracket of its arguments. Where a predicate has no arguments it should have no brackets - as empty round brackets are normally syntactically illegal.

Theorem Prover : (see Inference Engine)

Truth : In Prolog a term is true if it can be successfully matched with a database clause. Rules can only be successfully matched if the antecedent terms of the rule are proved to be true.

Variable : A single word of Prolog beginning with an uppercase alphabetic character A-Z, or with the underscore character. Prolog usually renames variables to its own internal format (an underscore followed by a unique number) before "working" with them itself. A variable is normally used to refer to any thing in the world that our program represents whose identity is not yet known. (See Binding and Sharing)

A selection of important built-in predicates

append/3 : A list processing predicate that is not normally built-in to most versions of Prolog. It takes three arguments all of which must be lists (or variables that may become bound to lists during its call). The call append(As, Bs, AsBs) means that the lists As and Bs can be appended together to make the single list AsBs. For example the call append([a,b], [c,d], [a,b,c,d]) will be true with just one solution.

assert/1 : A built-in predicate that takes one argument and adds it to the database as a new clause to some definition. This can dynamically change database definitions by adding new clauses to them. It does not resatisfy on backtracking.

call/1 : A built-in predicate that takes one argument and treats it as though it were a query executed by the user. Essentially it calls it using the Prolog inference engine to see if it is true according to the database definitions.

fail/0 : This is a call which will automatically fail.

member/2 : A list processing predicate not normally built-in to most versions of Prolog. It takes two arguments the first of which is an element and the second of which must be a list, and will be true if the element is a member of (can be matched with an element in) the list. So for example `(?) member(c, [a,b,c,d]).` will be true with just one solution.

nl/0 : A built-in predicate with no arguments that moves subsequent printing output (via write/1 or whatever) on to a new line.

not/1 : The negation predicate which is also an operator and may therefore be written without argument brackets in situations where there is no ambiguity about that to which it refers. So the query `(?) not a.` will be true if the call to `a` fails.

retract/1 : A built-in predicate that takes one argument that it will attempt to match with a clause of a database definition which it will then retract. This can dynamically change database definitions by deleting clauses from them. It is quite a dangerous predicate because it may resatisfy on backtracking.

true/0 : This is a call which automatically succeeds. It will not succeed again if backtracking returns to it.

write/1 : A built-in predicate that takes one argument which it prints out, normally to the computer screen for the user to see.

!/0 : The cut operator can be useful but is usually avoided by logic programmers because it has no declarative semantics in a program. It always succeeds and is does not resatisfy on backtracking. However, its important side effect is that it prevents remaining clauses in the definition in which it has succeeded from being attempted via backtracking. It therefore "fixes" the interpretation of the definition by the Prolog engine as being the current one.

=../2 : The equals-period-period operator normally called "univ". It is written between its arguments such that the left hand side argument is a term and the right hand side argument is a list where the first element is the term's predicate and subsequent elements are the term's arguments. eg. `(?) a(b, c) =.. [a, b, c].` is true. This is used because terms in Prolog must usually have a known predicate and a known number of arguments. Using univ the programmer can construct a term from a list in which these things are only determined after univ is called.

Answers to Exercises

In the following we present answers to the exercises presented in this book. All the exercises are presented in order of increasing difficulty. In all cases you should try to solve at least the first few entirely on your own before reading our suggestions.

Answers to Exercises in Tutorial Appendix 1

Answers to Exercises 1.1 The Royal Family Tree

A 1.1.1 Queries to the family database.

    (? i)   `male(philip).` – means is philip in the database as a male?

    (? ii)   `female(philip).` – is philip in the database as a female?

    (? iii)   `male(rod).` – is rod in the database as a male?

    (? iv)   `parent(charles, philip).` – is charles a parent of philip?

A 1.1.2 Logical variables

(a) 'All solutions' to these queries

    (? i) `parent(Someone,william).`

Someone = each of william's parents.

    (? ii) `parent(X,william), female(X).`

X = each of williams female parents. (There should only be one!)

    (? iii) `parent(elizabeth, Person), parent(Person, Child).`

Person = every individual who recieves the parent relationship from elizabeth AND where that Person is also the parent of some Child. So, knowing the structure of the database and the implications of human relationships we can say that all solutions will yield Child = each of elizabeth's grandchildren.

(b) Constructing queries. We will use X to refer to the individual we are seeking.

    (i) who are the children of charles?   (?)   `parent(charles, X).`

    (ii) who was the grandfather of zara?   (?)   `parent(X, S), parent(S, zara).`

    (iii) who is the wife of mark?   (?)   `husband(mark, X).`

A 1.1.3   Defining Rules

(i) mother(M, C) means that M is a mother of C where M is a parent of C and M is a female.

```
mother(M, C):- parent(M, C), female(M).
```

(ii) grandfather(G, C) means that G is a grandfather of C if G is a parent of someone S who is a parent of C and where G is a male. Note that you could also just use grandparent to cover the two parent terms.

```
grandfather(G, C):- parent(G, S), parent(S, C), male(G).
```

(iii) wife(Woman, Man) can be defined as the inverse of an already represented fact husband/2.

```
wife(Woman, Man):- husband(Man, Woman).
```

(iv) sibling(Child1, Child2) : siblings are individuals that share the same parents. So this rule might do the job.

```
sibling(Child1, Child2):- parent(S, Child1), parent(S, Child2).
```

As regards getting all the right answers and only the right answers - you will note here that the sibling rule given will deliver twice the number of sibling relationships that you want, because it allows individuals to be siblings via both parents in turn. So you could reduce this to one set of solutions by defining 'siblingship' only along either the male or female parent line. You may also note that sibling in this form permits an individual to be a sibling of themselves. Because whilst Prolog's use of variables insists the two Ss must be the same there is nothing *stopping* Child1 and Child2 being the same! To exclude this you will need to use a Prolog built-in called **not**/1. This predicate takes one argument as a goal to be queried - and it only succeeds where the goal fails to succeed! So in combination with the Prolog matching operator = 'equals' we could require that Child1 = Child2 is not true.

```
sibling(Child1, Child2):-
              parent(S, Child1),
              parent(S, Child2),
              male(S),
              not( Child1 = Child2 ).
```

You will note that this rule does not cope with divorce - or many other features of families. Also you could use the Prolog built-in not-equals \= which is a more direct counterpart of equals, instead.

(v) cousin(Person1, Person2) : cousins are individuals who have parents who are themselves siblings - so you might try this definition for size.

```
cousin(Person1, Person2):-
              parent(X, Person1),
              parent(Y, Person2),
              sibling(X, Y).
```

Answers to Exercises 1.2 Elementary Lists

A 1.2.1 Finding Shopping

```
shopping_list( [carrots, potatoes,milk, eggs, butter,soap, shampoo] ).
shopping_list( [ [spuds, carrots], [butter, milk], [oranges, lemons] ] ).
```

With these two shopping list clauses in the database – these queries will match as follows:

(? i) `shopping_list( X ).`

Yes.   Where X = [carrots, potatoes, milk, eggs, butter, soap, shampoo]

        OR

        Where X = [[spuds, carrots], [butter, milk], [oranges, lemons]]

(? ii) `shopping_list( [X, Y, Z]  ). Yes.  Where :`

Yes. Where :   X = [spuds, carrots]

                       Y = [butter, milk]

                       Z = [oranges, lemons]

(? iii) `shopping_list( [C, P, M, E, B, So, Sh]  ).`

Yes. Where :   C = carrots

                       P = potatoes

                       M = milk

                       E = eggs

                       B = butter

                       So = soap

                       Sh = shampoo

If you just used S, S instead of So, Sh for the last two elements then the query would fail because Prolog would require that the last two elements of the list be the same thing. As soap and shampoo are quite different atoms then Prolog would fail to find a matching clause in the database and would say No.

A 1.2.2 Matching more words in lists

With this definition for **sentence**/1 into the Prolog database:

```
sentence([[ the, hippy ],  [[ kissed, the, debutante ], [ in, the, park ]]]).
```

Then, so long as you have typed in all the brackets correctly the variables will match with the respective elements of the list. As noted this is cheating terribly – by relying on the meaning of the variable names – which are interpreted by us – and have no special meaning to Prolog.

A 1.2.3   List Processing with member

(? i)   `member(X, [albert, mike, susan, fred]).`

means what X is a member of the list `[albert, mike, susan, fred]`. Procedurally it will cause member to generate a member of the list and bind it to X. Backtracking will cause member to generate each element of the list in turn as a binding for X.

(? ii)   `member( X, [carrots, potatoes, milk, eggs, butter, soap, shampoo]).`

means much the same as (i) above and will generate members of the new list it is given.

(? iii) `shopping_list(List), member(X,List).`

So long as you still have shopping_list/1 defined in the database from a previous exercise, then the first part of the conjunction will succeed binding List to a shopping list. When the second part of the conjunction is called member has a specific list List to generate members from.

A 1.2.4   List Processing with append/3

(? i) `append( [humpty, dumpty], [sat,on,a,wall], X).`

means that the result of appending the first list to the second list is the new appended list X.

(? ii) `append( [humpty, dumpty], Y, [humpty,dumpty,sat,on,a,wall]).`

This asks what list Y can be appended with `[humpty, dumpty]` to make the list `[humpty,dumpty,sat,on,a,wall]`. Now clearly there is only one list for which this is true.

(? iii) `append( [], [fred], List).`

This will return `List = [fred]`   because the result of appending an empty list on to another list is to leave it unchanged.

Answers to Exercises 1.3

A 1.3.1   Built-in screen output primitives

Most of the parts of these queries are to do with simple screen output. In (?v) you may note the underscore notation for the variable – George – does not stand for any known individual. It is just a variable name whose internal underscore-number format your Prolog may print out. In (?vi) the write predicate is given two arguments to write out - and as write expects only one argument this call will probably fail. If it does something odd then it may be that your version of Prolog has a definition of write with two arguments to mean something rather unusual. Now query (?vii) gives write just one argument which it will happily print out - but that argument is quite complex itself as it is a list containing three things. So you may have been able to work out the following from your experiments:

The predicate `nl/0` writes out a newline to the current output stream - normally the computer screen. This puts all subsequent text on the next line. The predicate `write/1` takes its one argument and writes it out - so unless your version of Prolog has some unusual definition for `write/2` the two argument call will fail - as it will be undefined. The predicate `tab/1` prints out the number of spaces given as its argument.

A 1.3.2   Itemising a list

```
itemise_list([]).

itemise_list([H | T]):- write(H), nl, itemise_list(T).
```

This definition has two parts - of course. The stopping check states that a list is itemised if it is empty. Otherwise, the main body of the program guillotines the list handing the head H on wo `write/1` to print out, before it prints out a new line and hands on the remainder of the list T to a recursive call.

A 1.3.3   Combining a list

```
combine_list([]).

combine_list([H | T]):- write(H), tab(1), combine_list(T).
```

The definition for `combine_list/1` is almost identical to itemising a list but it prints out spaces rather than a new line.

A 1.3.4   Pretty-printing a list

```
(1)        pretty_print([], Tab) :- nl.
(2)        pretty_print([X | Rest], Tab) :-
(i)             tab(Tab),
(ii)            write(X), nl,
(iii)           Tab1 is Tab + 4,
(iv)            pretty_print(Rest, Tab1).
```

This definition is a touch more complex because it prints out a different number of spaces each time it prints something. What it should do is take a list and print each element of the list on a separate line with each element further accross the page. If it is given a list to print and a number as arguments, then the number is bound to the variable Tab. This number of spaces is printed out (i); and the head element of the list is written (ii) followed by a new line. Next, (iii) the arithmetic here causes the new variable Tab1 to be bound to the result of adding 4 to the value of Tab. This bigger number is handed on to the recursive call, along with the tail of the list. The recursion continues until the list is empty, with the Tab getting larger each time, until the list is empty and the stopping check (1) is matched with (executing a new line before succeeding).

A 1.3.5   A definition for last/2

Giveaway Hint. One specification of the predicate definition may look something like this :

(i) X is the **last** element of a list where it is the only element in a list.

Otherwise,

(ii) X is the **last** element of a guillotined list whose tail is Y

(we don't care about the head of the list)

if it is the **last** element of this smaller list Y.

If you still can't get it from this hint – by just directly transcribing the words into code then here is the definition.

```
last(X, [ X ] ).
last(X, [ _ | Y ]):- last(X, Y).
```

Don't you feel ashamed – having to look at this answer now? The stopping condition is a useful special case which states that it is trivially true, that if something is the only thing in a list then it is certainly the last thing in the list. The second clause states that X could still be the last element of a (longer) list if it is true that it is the last element in the tail of this (now shorter) list. Procedurally, this definition involves throwing away elements from an arbitary length list until there is only one thing in it.

Answers to Exercises in Chapter 2

Answers to Exercises 2.1

A 2.1.1   (i) Is a canary an animal?

(ii) Is a canary a shark?

(iii) Is a canary a what? Or what is a canary?

(iv) Is a what a bird? Or what is there that is a bird?

A 2.1.2   (i) Can a canary sing?

(ii) Can a canary swim?

(iii) What properties does a canary have?

(iv) What creatures have a known size?

(v) What creatures breathe?

A 2.1.3   (i) `subclass(robin, bird).`

(ii) `property(bird, lays_eggs).`

(iii) `subclass(mammal, animal).`

(iv) `property(mammal, bear_live_young).`

(v) `subclass(dolphin, mammal).` And `subclass(rat, mammal).`

A 2.1.4   (i) You will almost certainly have to slow the program down in a uniform way to see interesting numbers that look like the time categorisation graph given as Figure 3.3. But see the note on functional equivalence below. The times given here should give you a rough idea of the relative differences we might expect.

(?) is a canary a bird.	YES.	Eg.	Time = 1
(?) is a canary an animal.	YES.		Time = 2
(?) is a canary a living thing.	YES.		Time = 3
(?) is a canary a shark.	NO.		Time = 4
(?) has a canary the property yellow.	YES.		Time = 2
(?) has a canary the property breathes.	YES.		Time = 3
(?) has a canary the property swims.	YES.		Time = 4

(ii)   The functional equivalence problem shows that the use of timings can be rather misleading. In this case we need to be looking for a similar **shape** of relationship over the set of timings regardless of the size of the numbers themselves. A less misleading measure than times might simply be to note how many nodes the search must traverse before it finds a value. Explicit values traverse 0 nodes; values inherited direct from a parent node traverse 1, etc; and negative replies will have to traverse the whole tree before they can fail. We have used clock times because they are actually easier to implement (even though you must do some low-level work with your computer) and they can deliver results which are much less boring to plot - property searches will be slower than simple 'isa' queries, as in people for example.

(iii) You should be able to predict timings on any queries by considering how far the program will have to search to find an answer.

A 2.1.5   There are quite a few things wrong with the model as section 2.4 goes on to discuss. The problem of breathing fish is that we really just need to refine what we mean by the word breathe. Fish breathe by consuming oxygen from water rather than from the air as mammals and birds do. The latter problem (ii) is rather more serious, because the ostrich has an explicit entry for not being able to fly and can inherit flying because it is a bird. So it can end up with two completely contradictory values. Clearly we need a way of ruling out inherited values that contradict explicit ones.

Answers to Exercises 2.2

A 2.2.1 Repeating the Collins and Quillian exercises is easy. All the queries are now in a very similar format. Here are a few to get you started.

```
(?)   has_value(canary, a_kind_of, animal).
(?)   has_value(canary, a_kind_of, shark).
(?)   has_value(canary, a_kind_of, X).
(?)   has_value(X, a_kind_of, bird).

(?)   has_value(canary, makes_noise, sings).
(?)   has_value(canary, swim, yes).
(?)   has_value(canary, Property, Value).
(?)   has_value(X, size, Value).
(?)   has_value(X, breathes, Value).
```

A 2.2.2 - Z inheritance.

The simplest solution that looks simiar to the Z inheritance idea involves simply shifing the inheritance clause from (2) to the end (4). This means that for any Object frame you will look for explicit, if_needed, and then default values before moving up the hierarchy to look again.

```
(1)  has_value(Object, Slot, Value):-
            value(Object, Slot, Value).
(2)  has_value(Object, Attribute, Value) :-
            if_needed(Object, Attribute, Value).
(3)  has_value(Object, Attribute, Value) :-
            default(Object, Attribute, Value).
(4)  has_value(Object, Slot, Value):-
            inherits(Object, Slot, Relation),
            value(Object, Relation, SuperClass),
            has_value(SuperClass, Slot, Value),
            not_explicit(Object, Slot).
```

This is noticable for queries like `has_value(tweety, P, V)` which will report the `P = age` of tweety much faster than the old version which only got to calculate `if_needed` links after it had gone right up the hierarchy and started again.

A 2.2.3 Adding a Reason.

The definition given here simply flags each clause with a fourth argument. In the second clause inheritance is flagged, but the value of the recursive call (which must also have four arguments) is not used. The 'inherited' value means that inheritance was required - but without giving any indication of how much or how far it went.

```
has_value(Object, Slot, Value, explicit):-
       value(Object, Slot, Value).
has_value(Object,Slot, Value, inherited):-
       inherits(Slot, Relation),
       value(Object, Relation, SuperClass),
       has_value(SuperClass, Slot, Value, _),
       not_explicit(Object, Slot).
has_value(Object, Slot, Value, calculated):-
       if_needed(Object, Slot, Value).
has_value(Object, Slot, Value, default):-
       default_value(Object,Slot,Value).
```

A 2.2.4 Explanation of properties.

The definition of explain/3 given here basically runs the has_value/4 query and prints out prettily the Reason that the new version of has_value/4 produces.

The writel/1 predicate is a simple utility that is just generally handy. It takes one argument - which is a list and prints out each element of the list in turn. If it encounters the word nl in the list it prints out a new-line rather than the word. This saves us writing a whole series of write statements in the definition and makes it easier to read. So this definition is simplicity itself to understand. It runs the has_value query with the arguments given; then it writes out the introduction to the reasons; and finally it uses write_reason/1 to take the list of reasons provided by has_value and print them out appropriately.

```
explain(Object, Property, Value):-
     has_value(Object, Property, Value, ReasonList),
     writel([Object, ' ', Property,  ' ', Value, nl, '     because', nl]),
     write_reason(ReasonList).
```

The new version of has_value is quite tricky in that the fourth argument Reason has now to be flagged so that it collects enough information (particularly in the second clause for inheritance) to tell you where it has been for explain/3 to print. Now we have noted that write_reason/1 is expecting a list - so all the reasons must be in list format. Clauses 1, 3 & 4 are quite easy in that they simply state (as before) how the value was found. The only new aspect is that each single Reason is now a pair of elements where the first is the reason mechanism and the second is the Object of the value. So if has_value finds what it is looking for at the bird frame node then it returns Reason bound to [explicit, bird]. Clause 2 is only harder in that it must return not only which frame it is going to for the inheritance but also what it is to find when it gets there. So this pair is not so much a reason as the relation that it is using to inherit (usually a_kind_of) plus the SuperClass frame to which it points. This is guillotined on to whatever other reasons are dug up during the recursive call on line (iv).

```
(1)          has_value(Object, Slot, Value, [explicit, Object]):-
                 value(Object, Slot, Value).
(2 i)        has_value(Object,Slot, Value, [Relation, SuperClass | Rs]):-
   ii)           inherits(Slot, Relation),
   iii)          value(Object, Relation, SuperClass),
   iv)           has_value(SuperClass, Slot, Value, Rs),
   v)            not_explicit(Object, Slot).
(3)          has_value(Object, Slot, Value, [calculated, Object]):-
                 if_needed(Object, Slot, Value).
(4)          has_value(Object, Slot, Value, [default, Object]):-
                 default_value(Object,Slot,Value).
```

The definition of write_reason is correspondingly simple. If there is only one pair of elements left in the reason list (1) then this is the final reason to print - first the reason and then the name of the frame. If however (2) the list is longer than two things then some inheritance must have been involved so print out the first pair which will be the property and then the frame name and recurse on the remainder of the list.

```
(1)      write_reason([Reason, Frame]):-
             tab(5),
             writel(['the property is ', Reason, ' for ', Frame, nl]), !.
(2)      write_reason([Property, Frame | Tail]):-
             tab(5),
             writel(['it is ', Property, ' ', Frame, ' and', nl]),
             write_reason(Tail).
```

A 2.2.5 All that can be known about a concept. If your version of Prolog has a built-in setof/3 then this will find all solutions for a query and collect the bindings of any specified variables in the query returning them as a list. This list is ordered alphabetically and any duplicates will be removed.

So setof(V, Q, Vs) means that the query Q will be executed with backtracking forcing all solutions to be found. If the variable V appears in the query and is bound during the query's call then this binding will appear in the list of all these bindings Vs. Most versions of setof insist that you specify in the call which variables you are not interested in.

```
all_info(Object, AllVals):-
     setof((Slot,Value), R^has_value(Object, Slot, Value, R), AllVals).
```

So in the above we would call (?) all_info(fish, All) and expect All to be returned with a list of pairs of the (Slot, Value)'s that are all possible values for the fish frame. The setof/3 query will run the query (?) has_value(fish, Slot, Value, R) and collect up all the bindings for

Slot and Value and return them in AllVars. The caret operator used with R^ *Query* effectively means that we do not care about what R is bound to ie. it is some/any R.

Answers to Exercises in Chapter 3

Answers to Exercises 3.1

A 3.1.1 If you give this simple definition "i feel that noone is really listening" and "i am sick of computers" it should come back with "why do you say that you feel that noone is really listening" and "why are you sick of computers" respectively. If you want to trick it – easy – you could try "i am sure you hate me". As it is, it should reply "why are you sure you hate me", which is not quite right.

A 3.1.2 The pattern suggested : [i, need | X] will cope with things like "i need help" and "i need lots of chocolate" quite well, giving back "what would it mean to you to get help" and "what would it mean to you to get lots of chocolate".

If you want to see the limits of this you could try "i need to get help" which would give "what would it mean to you to get to get help" (read it carefully).

A 3.1.3 A definition for member is given in the Code Appendix as Defn 1.1.

A 3.1.4 Trivially simple – extend the pat/2 definition of ELIZA with a rule like :

```
pat(List, ['Tell me about these feelings of depression.']):-
        member(depressed, List).
```

or

```
pat(List, ['Do you think computers are intimidating?']):-
        member(computers, List).
```

A 3.1.5 One definition might read:

```
family_member(X):- member(X, [father, mother, brother, sister]).
```

It states that X is a family_member if X is a member of the list [father, mother ...]. Clearly you could add further family members into this list for member to test. This may be used in a pattern such as the following:

```
pat(Input, ['Do you get on with your family?']):-
                                        member(X, Input),
                                        family_member(X).
```

The full prototype program solves this in a completely different way using the predicate important/2.

A 3.1.6 See the full prototype Definition 3.12 in the Code Appendix for the `badword/1` definition. You might use it in the `pat/2` definition in a way like this:

```
pat(Input, ['Dont be so unpleasant!']):- member(X, Input), badword(X).
```

This states that this pat reply is appropriate where there is a word X that is a member of the Input list and that the word X is classified in the database as a badword.

Answers to Exercises 3.2

A 3.2.1 The new patterns are generally quite easy to read. The biggest problem you may have is with the addition of some cunning `append/3` parts to the definitions. These rely on append's ability to stick two lists together, to make a third, and to take a third list and tear it apart to make two sublists.

The following pattern actually matches with any list that begins "you ..." but only if the remainder of that list `Rest` can be broken up (by append) into two lists - the second of which begins with "me". So in effect this pattern only matches "you ... me ..." inputs.

```
pattern(x, [you | Rest], ['What makes you think I' | Reply]):-
      append(R, [me | _ ], Rest),
      append(R, ['you ?'], Reply).
```

As you know, the underscore _ in the first append just means "don't care" what this is, ie it could be any list of words that comes after "me ...". We don't care, because we aren't going to use it for anything in the pattern. We are going to use the list of words in `Rest` that comes before "me" because it is called R and the second append sticks "you ?" on to the end of it – `Rest` that is – before it is given to the output pattern to be guillotined on to the end of the output. So the pattern is actually looking for "you Xs me ..." patterns, such as "you *hate* me dont you" so that it can reply "What makes you think I *hate* you?".

In this next pattern a single append cunningly takes the tail of the input list and adds "do you?" on to the end of it before it is guillotined on to the tail of the output list.

```
pattern(60, [it, is | Rest], ['So, you feel that it is' | Rest1]):-
      append(Rest, ['do you?'], Rest1).
```

Unfortunately, this pattern only copes with inputs that begin "it is ...". To handle " ... it is ..." patterns like "she told me that it is ..." would need an earlier append to find something in the middle of the input and a more general reply pattern. You might try this:

```
pattern(61, Input, ['So, is it' | Rest1]):-
      append(_, [it, is | Rest], Input),
      append(Rest, [', really?'], Rest1).
```

Take your time to work this one out. The more cunning appending that you do the harder it is to work out for sure what is happening. The second append here just sticks a question marked ending on to the end of the output.

A 3.2.2 This is the core of one implementation of a "context" program:

```
change_context(New):- retract(context(Old)), assert(context(New)), !.
```

It simply deletes the old entry for this clause and asserts the new one given as its argument. Its probably easiest to insert a call to it in the 'important' definition eg.

```
important(X):- important(X, C), change_context(C).
```

It will then be used via the important call from the pattern chosen. The definition says that if something from the user's input is provably important in some known context then we should change whatever the old context entry was to some new one.

NB. Don't forget that you will also now need to change the 'tidy' definition so that it tidies up the contexts resetting it to whatever you want it to be at the start of the conversation.

So the definition of tidy must include some lines like the following which will delete any context left over from an old conversation and make ELIZA predisposed to start talking about (say) families:

```
...,
retractall(context(_)),
assert(context(family)),
...
```

A well-written context mechanism makes a very big difference to how plausible ELIZA can seem, in that it allows ELIZA to direct the conversation to her strengths. If you have a number of context-dependent patterns then the conversation will be strongly directed to talk about these - especially when the user is attempting to converse outside of ELIZA's therapeutic sphere.

Answers to Exercises in Chapter 4

Answers to Exercises 4.1

A 4.1.1 Pronoun and Adverb rules.

(a) A pronoun rule would add this rule to the existing definition of noun_phrase:

```
noun_phrase  -->  pronoun.
```

Where some dictionary entries for pronouns were also included somewhere such as:

```
pronoun  -->  [she].
pronoun  -->  [he].
pronoun  -->  [we].
```

(b) The relevant rules for adverbs might include a change to both verb_phrase and verb_phrase2. Possible whole new rules are given here:

```
(i)      verb_phrase   -->  adverb,  verb_phrase .
(ii)     verb_phrase   -->  verb_phrase2,  prepositional_phrase .
(iii)    verb_phrase   -->  verb_phrase2 .

(iv)     verb_phrase2  -->  verb,  adverb .
(v)      verb_phrase2  -->  verb,  noun_phrase .
(vi)     verb_phrase2  -->  verb,  noun_phrase,  adverb .
(vii)    verb_phrase2  -->  verb.

(viii)   adverb  -->  [quickly].
(ix)     adverb  -->  [slowly].
(x)      adverb  -->  [quietly].
```

Of the additions to the basic rules: (i) covers cases such as "quickly walked" in an example like "she quickly walked to the shops"; (iv) covers the case such as that posed in the question "walked quickly"; and finally (vi) covers the tricky case such as "she walked to the shops quickly".

You cannot use: `verb_phrase2      -->   verb_phrase2,  adverb .`

since you'll get infinite recursion! This says that a verb_phrase2 will rewrite to itself and an adverb. The first thing that the rewrite will need to find is a verb_phrase2 before looking for the adverb. Now this rule refers it to itself in an endless way because the first thing the recursive call will need to find is a verb_phrase2, and a verb_phrase2 is a verb_phrase2 ... and so on endlessly.

A 4.1.2 There are many different sorts of sentences that this grammar is incapable of parsing. The first sort of thing it can't cope with are simply specific words that it doesn't know. The next problem is with classes of words that it doesn't know about, like conjunctions such as "and". A third problem is with constructions of phrases that it doesn't know about. However the most disturbing limitation to the current rules is the number of **illegitimate** parses that they **will allow**. Consider for example:

* The dog slept the man

* A dogs ran away

NB. Restrictions to the parser to exclude these particular problems are the subject of the later exercises 4.3.2 & 4.3.3.

Answers to Exercises 4.2

A 4.2.1 Parse Trees. The first two trees are of course very similar.

a) the dog bit the man

b) the man hated the cat

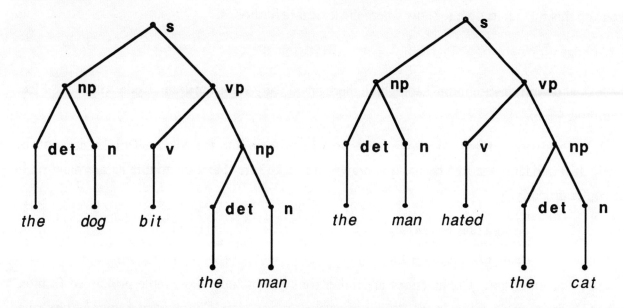

c) he took the big red
   kite from the store

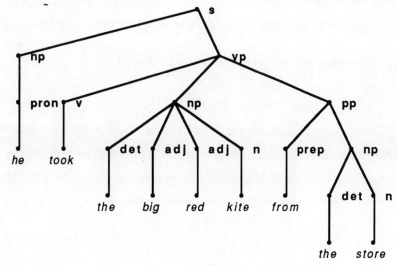

d) the colourless green
   ideas sleep
   furiously

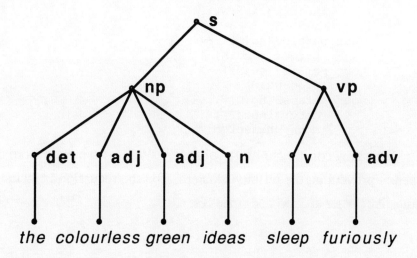

A 4.2.2 The proper-noun rules. You must add a rule like the following to the definition of noun_phrase.

```
noun_phrase(np(N))  -->  proper_noun(N).
```

Then add this rule on its own to show where the lexical definition is.

```
proper_noun(propernoun(N))  -->  [N], { pn(N) }.
```

The lexical definitions are in **pn**/1 for which there are already some entries in Code Appendix 4 (see Definition 4.3.5).

A 4.2.3 Condensing trees. Adding the condense predicate into the parse definition couldn't be easier. Just condense the tree before it is drawn and make sure that the variable names hand-on to each other properly.

```
parse(X):-
      phrase(sentence(T), X),
      condense(T, T1),
      draw_tree(T1), nl.
```

A 4.2.4 Conjunctions. Conjunctions are rather tricky to include in a simple principled fashion. To handle the example given in (a) "rod **and** peter drowned slowly" you need a noun phrase rule. The first suggestion will **not** work because if falls immediately into a deep pit of infinite recursion.

```
noun_phrase(np(np(N1), C, N2)) -->
      noun_phrase(N1),
      conjunction(C),
      noun_phrase(N2)
```

You simply cannot have a definition call itself without consuming some constituents to make the problem become simpler as it continues. The simplest solution to this problem is a rather ad-hoc one - create a new class of constituent - call it noun_phrase3. This new constituent will have exactly the same definition as noun_phrase except without the one mentioning conjunctions. Eg.

```
noun_phrase(np(N1, C, N2)) -->
      noun_phrase3(N1),
      conjunction(C),
      noun_phrase(N2)  .

noun_phrase3(np(N))-->
      proper_noun(N).
noun_phrase3(np(N))-->
      pronoun(N).
noun_phrase3(np(D,N))-->
      determiner(D),
      noun_phrase2(N)  .
```

This new constituent **noun_phrase3** is will be removed from the parse before the recursion happens - preventing the infinity problem. But the recursion is included at the end - to allow noun phrases like "peter and rod and suzie" etc.

For the example in (b) "rod and peter drowned slowly **but** shouted loudly" you need a verb phrase rule. The verb_phrase rule has a very similar problem - but you should be able to work it out yourself by now.

E 4.2.5 An Optional Verb Auxiliary. Clearly you need a rule somewhere amongst the verb phrase rules - but how far down? All that you need to decide is the cases that you would like to allow. So if you want "was running to the bank"; but not "was running the dog", you could pop this in the verb_phrase2 definition to see how it manages.

```
verb_phrase2(vp2(Au, V))  -->  aux(Au), verb(V).
```

If you want "was running away" as well, you may have to add a rule like:

```
verb_phrase2(vp2(Au, V, Ad))  -->  aux(Au), verb(V), adverb(Ad).
```

Whatever rules you try don't forget a lexical rule.

```
aux(aux(A))  -->  [A], { aux(A) }.
```

Answers to Exercises 4.3

A 4.3.1 Some hints for improving the interface. As we have noted a good interface is a very open-ended commitment - it could as sophisticated as you please. The simplest improvement would at least have a preprocessing predicate that checks that each word in the input has a lexical definition somewhere. If it came across an unknown word it could then abort the parse - and force the user to add it to the database by hand. A more sophisticated system would take the set of unknown words and for each one: ask the user to state its class; check that the user has replied a legitimate class word (verb, noun etc); and then assert the word into the lexical definition for that class. An interface to add new rules would be a very advanced project indeed!

A 4.3.2 Hints for Verb restrictions. Transitive verbs can take an object noun phrase and intransitive verbs cannot. The parser can take account of this by the addition of extra arguments to the rules which provide flags for one sort of verb or another. Consider the lexicon and how we might simply mark these two verbs:

```
v(sleeps, intrans) .
v(hit, trans) .
```

Next we must augment the lexical rule to pass on the extra argument:

```
verb(v(X), T) --> [X], { v(X, T) } .
```

Next we must rewrite the verb phrase rules so that they look for the two argument definition of verb. A verb phrase with a following noun_phrase will be marked as requiring a 'trans' verb and one without a following noun_phrase will be marked as 'intrans'. If we decide that both forms can accept a prepositional phrase then the only changes will be in the verb_phrase2 definition.

```
verb_phrase2(vp2(V, A))  -->  verb(V, intrans),  adverb(A) .
verb_phrase2(vp2(V,N))  -->  verb(V, trans),  noun_phrase(N) .
verb_phrase2(vp2(V, N, A))  -->
     verb(V, trans),
     noun_phrase(N),
     adverb(A) .
verb_phrase2(vp2(V))  -->  verb(V, intrans) .
```

You can decide what to do about verbs preceded by auxiliaries from the exercise above.

A 4.3.3 Agreement Hints. To have phrases agreeing with one another you can clearly add extra arguments as with transitivity. The phrase "a dogs" is wrong because the determiner "a" is singular and so its noun must also be singular "dogs". The determiner "the" can be either singular or plural.

Eg.
```
det(the, _) .
det(a, sing) .

n(dog, sing) .
n(dogs, plural) .
```

Do not forget to update the lexical rules to take note of this new argument.

```
determiner(det(X), Agree)  -->  [X], { det(X, Agree) } .

noun(n(X), Agree) -->  [X], { n(X, Agree) } .
```

Next we have simply to add an argument to the noun phrase rules insisting that one the Agreement of the determiner is known - then the Agreement of the noun must be the same.

```
noun_phrase(np(N))  -->  pronoun(N).
noun_phrase(np(D,N))  -->  determiner(D, Agree), noun_phrase2(N, Agree) .

noun_phrase2(np2(A,N), Agree)  -->  adjective(A), noun_phrase2(N, Agree) .
noun_phrase2(np2(N), Agree)  -->  noun(N, Agree).
```

Now clearly not only must phrases agree within themselves, but they must agree with other phrases. So something like "the dogs run" and "the dog runs" are OK, whilst "the dogs runs" and "the dog run" are not. Once the subject noun phrase's agreement is known it dictates the agreement of the verb in the verb phrase. By now you should have the hang of this and be able to do it yourself.

Answers to Exercises in Chapter 5

Answers to Exercises 5.1

A 5.1.1 Hand parsing into CDs. As already noted the degree of 'intelligence' you ascribe to the parser is tricky to decide. eg should 'drink' in (f) automatically imply a 'to' slot of the 'actor' herself?

	Act	Actor	Obj	From	To
a) john walked to table	act(_, ptrans,	[john,	john,	_,	table])
b) john walked from door to table	act(_, ptrans,	[john,	john,	door,	table])
c) the waiter took john's coat	act(_, atrans,	[waiter,	coat,	john,	waiter])
d) john ordered beef	act(_, mtrans,	[john,	beef,	_,	_])
e) john left for pub	act(_, ptrans,	[john,	john,	_,	pub])
f) mary had drink of beer from mug	act(_, ingest,	[mary,	beer,	mug,	mary])
g) waiter brings food from kitchen	act(_, ptrans,	[waiter,	food,	kitchen,	_])

A 5.1.2 A CD Story. "Zaphod went to Milliways, the restaurant at the end of the universe. After having a steak, he tipped the waiter one Arcturan mega-dollar and teleported to Betelgeuse." as Prolog CDs:

	Act	Actor	Obj	From	To
[	act(A, ptrans,	[zaphod,	zaphod,	_,	milliways]),
	act(B, ingest,	[_,	steak,	_,	_]),
	act(C, atrans,	[_,	tip,	_,	_]),
	act(D, ptrans,	[_,	_,	_,	betelgeuse])
]					

Again, there is quite a bit of flexibility in this parse. Note that we have lost the extra detail about Milliways being the restaurant at the end of the universe. This may be added as a set of extra qualifiers in Schank's notation. Also, we have described the tipping event as an ATRANS of a 'tip' to save typing. It could quite possibly have been a PTRANS of the hard currency if you preferred.

Answers to Exercises 5.2

A 5.2.3 The Waiter. To include the waiter bringing the food you would have to add a line like the following in between acts 3 & 4.

```
act(3.5,  ptrans, [Waiter, Food, Kitchen, Table]),
```

A 5.2.4 A simple shopping trip script. You must be able to do better than this.

```
%                     Act       Agent       Object     From        To

script(  shopping,
       [    act(1, [ptrans, Agent,      Agent,     From,       Shop      ]),
            act(2, [atrans, Shopkpr,    Purchase,  Shopkpr,    Agent     ]),
            act(3, [atrans, Agent,      Money,     Agent,      Shopkpr   ]),
            act(4, [ptrans, Agent,      Agent,     Shop,       To        ])
       ]).
```

You may note that as it is this is a very vague script that actually does not capture shopping very well. Not only are there many shopping events that this cannot cope with and which would be difficult to include but (even worse) there are many non-shopping events which this would also cope with! Indeed as it is it is highly unconstrained and needs to have a lot added to it to make it more specific to the acts it is intended to contextualise.

A 5.2.5 A shopping story. "Suzie went to the bakers, the baker gave her some bread and she came home".

```
story(shop1,
     [    act(A, [ptrans, suzie, suzie, _,      bakers]),
          act(B, [atrans, baker, bread, baker, _      ]),
          act(C, [ptrans, _,     _,     _,      home  ])
     ]).
```

In this interpretation of the story we are assuming that the parser cannot disambiguate to whom 'her' and 'she' in the story refer. This will require a trigger like `trigger(baker, shopping).` or some such to be in the database.

A 5.2.6 The definition of `test_sam1` simply runs the sam1 predicate on a named story. It picks up the story and hands it on to be understood, printing out what is happening as it goes along. You will note that it prints out the value of the variable `story` twice. The output is different because the variable is bound to the original story to begin with and any empty slots are printed out as unbound variables. Later on, after **match/2** has had a chance to 'understand' the story some of these unbound variables will have a specific value - so it is printed out again.

Answers to Exercises in Chapter 6

Answers to Exercises 6.1

A 6.1.1 If you examine the trace of an execution of Figure 6.5's rules that is given as Figure 6.6 you will note that the young seriator blithely succeeds in putting the blocks on the table, but that they are not in any particular order! They should be in this order { dddd >> ccc >> bb >> a } but from an initial arrangement given as [ccc, a, dddd, bb] they end up in a table line as { ccc >> a >> dddd >> bb }. Clearly what has happened is that the blocks have just been picked up and put down in a line on the table as they appeared in the heap. The system makes no attempt to check the results of its work.

A 6.1.2 Changing the start state of the production system run by changing heap/1 definition asserted via initialise/0 will cause the seriator to pick up the "nearest" block from the heap in the order that they appear in heap/1. So starting with [dddd, ccc, bb, a] will make the seriator get it right - but simply because it "randomly" picks the right blocks. Whereas the initial heap of [a, bb, ccc, dddd] will cause the seriator to get it exactly seriated the wrong way!

A 6.1.3 You should really have got this from the strong hint! Rule **f3** should read as follows.

```
rule(f3, [ top_goal(add_first_block), not(heap_empty) ],
        [ pick_up_biggest_block ]).
```

A 6.1.4 The predicate flag/0 is in the Code Appendix as D 6.4.2. In fact, Figure 6.8 in Chapter 6 gives you an example of what happens when complex output is printed out for the performance of the competent seriator rules. It essentially allows display_status/4 (D 6.4.1) to print out even more diagnostic information for each rule firing (in apply_productions/1 - D 6.3.2).

If you find both sorts of output helpful you might like to add an extra definition to help you switch between them. Something like this might help - it should just toggle between the two flag settings.

```
switch_flag:- retract(flag(complex_output)),
              assert(flag(simple_output)),
              write('*** simple output set ***'), nl, !.
switch_flag:- retract(flag(simple_output)),
              assert(flag(complex_output)),
              write('*** complex output set ***'), nl, !.
```

Answers to Exercises 6.2

A 6.2.1 The output of the competent seriator. The printout produced for the seriate query, and with 'complex' trace switched on should look very much like the trace given in Figure 6.8. The first thing to note is that it takes rather longer - when the system is troubling to check that it is doing it correctly. With the rules given and [ccc, a, dddd, bb] on the heap the program will pick up the biggest block available, and then each of the rest as they come. So 'dddd' and 'ccc' will go down in the right places straight off - but the system still takes time to check that they are ok. Next 'a' is placed and is relatively OK. But eventually at about rule firing 17, 'bb' is picked up and when it is placed, found to be in the wrong place. So it must be swopped and the new configuration checked before success is noted.

Troubleshooting. The first thing to check is that the rules are ok and to make sure that you have deleted the old seriation rules. You should "reconsult" the new rules - which automatically over-writes the old ones; or on the Macintosh "Reinitialise" the Window and Code concerned. To ensure that these are the only rules in the database you might try the query (?) listing(rule). If this is OK, then the next likely problem is with the way your Prolog may handle sorting. Some Prologs will let you compare atoms with the arithmetic operators > and <, but some require that you use @> and @< or some others. If you need to change it, it is used in the swap in the bubble sort utility as well as the bigger_than test. A final possibility is that your version of Prolog might be using the assert and retracts in an unusual way.

A 6.2.2 A missing rule. The effect of ommitting rule e3 will be to disable the systems ability to swop blocks that have been placed incorrectly. When a block is put down in the wrong place the system will get stuck - as it is not able to shift it. The simulated child stares for a while at the problem on the table and then bursts into tears - unable to continue.

A 6.2.3 A buggy rule. If rule 'e3' has the new state as `checked(ok)` rather than `new_arrangement` it will make the system only do one switch. This models a child who understands that when a block is placed incorrectly - being bigger than the block to its left - then it must be switched. However when the child switches the block with the one on its left it is satisfied that the problem is fixed and will continue placing further blocks. You can see this in any arrangement of blocks that will lead to a need for two switches. For example, starting with [dddd, bb, a, ccc] a seriator will place these blocks in the very same order on the table. The system will note that ccc is checked as wrong and the buggy rule will tell it to switch it - making [dddd, bb, ccc, a] - but it will consider this to be checked ok and finish. To anthropomorphise again you can see the child turning triumphantly to the experimenter with a grin - confident that it has been through all the appropriate motions for success.

Answers to Exercises 6.3

A 6.3.1 Production composition. This could be done with any productions that appear together in the same sequence repeatedly. The 'tiny hint' of the next exercise suggests that you try the 3 productions a1, a3 & a2. Try to do this without looking at the hints - you will feel much better for solving it alone! The new production must be placed before the old ones or replace them entirely.

A 6.3.2 The 3 productions a1, a3 & a2. Try to solve this yourself, but if you really can't then here is a version of a 'composed' rule a0.

```
rule(a0,
        [ top_goal(seriate), not(heap_empty) ],
        [ pick_up_nearest_block, holding(B), push_goal(place_block(B)) ]).
```

It says that if you are seriating and there are still blocks in the heap then pick up the nearest one and looking to see which one it is (it is named B); make the new goal to be to put this block B down appropriately.

A 6.3.3 Modifying a0 to absorbs production p1. You should have the hang of production composition now - here is a suitable version of production 'm1'.

```
rule(m1,
        [ top_goal(seriate), not(heap_empty) ],
        [ pick_up_nearest_block, holding(B), push_goal(place_block(B)),
          put_block_at_right, new_state(new_arrangement) ]).
```

A 6.3.4 Adding a new block eeeee. All that you need to do is to change the initialise definition. Place the new block in the heap assertion; give the table an extra place; and then update the message printed.

```
initialise :-
      retractall( goal_stack(_) ),
      retractall( state(_)       ),
      retractall( hand(_)        ),
      retractall( heap(_)        ),
      retractall( table(_, _)    ),
      assert( goal_stack([seriate])    ),
      assert( state(just_started)      ),
      assert( hand(empty)              ),
      assert( heap([ccc, a, dddd, bb, eeeee]) ),
      assertz( table(1, free) ),
      assertz( table(2, free) ),
      assertz( table(3, free) ),
      assertz( table(4, free) ),
      assertz( table(5, free) ),
      write_list([ 'initial arrangement on heap:
                 [ccc, a, dddd, bb, eeeee],
                 nl]), !.
```

A 6.3.5 If you try hard - with a child who always picks the right block up and doesn't bother to do any checking - you should be able to get the number of production firings under 6 or so.

Answers to Exercises in Chapter 7

Answers to Exercises 7.1

A 7.1.1 Legal moves from this state [upon(a, c), upon(b, pile2), upon(c, pile3)]

```
Action =   move(a, c, b)

Action =   move(a, c, pile1)

Action =   move(b, pile2, a)

Action =   move(b, pile2, pile1)
```

A sketch of the block positions is most helpful here – to work out for yourself if this is right.

A 7.1.2 'All solutions' to the `legal_action` query should yield the moves given in the last question.

A 7.1.3 The definition `legal_action/2` actually works by binding the values in its first argument given the `State` which is its second argument. Firstly, it must be true that `Block` is on somewhere x in the state. This gets a value for the `Block` and inital location x – if no specific one was already known. Next it must check that this block `is_clear` before it can be moved and then that there is some destination that `is_clear` in the state for this block to move to.

```
legal_action(move(Block, X, Destination), State) :-
    upon(Block, X, State),          % find a Block in the State
    is_clear(Block, State),         % check that Block is clear
    is_clear(Destination, State),   % find first clear place/block to go to
    Block \= Destination.
```

The purpose of the restriction: `Block \= Destination` actually simply says that the block `Block` cannot be the same thing as the block-or-place `Destination`. This prevents the second `is_clear` predicate finding the block that it is trying to move as a possible destination and thus moving the block onto itself!

A 7.1.4 The predicate `piles(State, Piles)` says that `Piles` is a list of lists which is a more visually appealing representation of the block locations in `State`. So a query like the following:

```
(?)   piles([ upon (a,c), upon (b,pile2), upon(c, pile3) ], Ps).
```

Should yield `Ps = [[], [b], [a, c]]` because a is on c which is on `pile3`; b is on `pile2` and `pile1` is empty. The definition of the predicate itself is not terribly well written – see if you can improve it.

Answers to Exercises 7.2

A 7.2.1 In terms of our earlier analogy, the drunkard gets into an endless cycle repeating exactly the same circuit of the maze. This is exactly the situation described in Figure 7.1 where the second move chosen on the leftmost path is returning the problem back to its original state. As the system has no way of checking for this problem, it is going to keep committing itself to the same set of moves in an infinite loop!

A 7.2.2 No, `test2` is no better! The system may indeed stumble across the right answer if it starts off with the right arrangement of blocks - but it is much more likely that it is eventually strike an infinite loop and be lost!

A 7.2.3 Prolog always takes the first (top) clause in a predicate definition first, so look at the definition of the `block` predicate.

Answers to Exercises 7.3

A 7.3.1 The query `test_df1(test3)` was harder to achieve than 2 because although it has the same start state it is required to build its block tower on `pile1` rather than on `pile3`. The `pile3` is easier simply because the base block `c` is already there and does not need moving!

```
test_states(test3,
        [ upon(a,c), upon(b,pile1), upon(c,pile3) ],
        [ upon(a,b), upon(b,c),     upon(c,pile1) ] ).
```

A 7.3.2 To get **df1** to print out the list of states visited all you have to do is modify the message given in the first clause of `df1` so that it prints out the value of the third argument to the clause which is the list of all stated `visited`. Eg. Clause 1 of `df1` could look as follows:

```
df1(N, State, State, Visited) :-
    write('** success **'), nl, nl,
    write(Visited), nl, nl.
```

Answers to Exercises 7.4

A 7.4.1 The heuristic `suggest/3` is actually rather simple. It only covers one specific legal move that is generally quite useful in building block towers. The first clause (i) will only ever suggest one move in any search - all the other moves will be suggested as the default - a "merely legal" move by clause (ii). Nevertheless, when asked to suggest a move this definition will always try to make one specific move which helps to build a tower.

```
(i)      suggest(TargetState, CurrentState, move(Block, _, Place)) :-
             upon(Block, Place, TargetState),
             place(Place),
             legal_action(move(Block, _, Place), CurrentState).
(ii)     suggest(_, CurrentState, Move) :-
             legal_action(Move, CurrentState).
```

It is given the TargetState which has a list of all the upon's which make up the systems 'goal' tower. It will find a block that is on a "Place" in the target state and that Place must be a 'place' (rather than a block). It will always suggest a move that involves moving this block onto that place - and so long as this suggestion is legal then the move will be returned. Now, as the goals for this problem are all to do with building block towers, and there is only one block at the base (on a 'place' rather than another 'block') this heuristic always suggests the establishing of the base of the tower.

If you think about it – if this move is not done as soon as possible many other moves may be wasted or need undoing. So in the search - if the 'base-block-establishment' move is ever legal from the current state then it should be done!

A 7.4.2 Obviously `test3` is so much shorter than `df1`'s attempt at `test3` because of this sensible heuristic which gets the base block right as soon as possible. If you want to make it shorter still - try to think of other heuristic ways of suggesting a possibly advantageous move and add a new clause to the suggest definition between the 'base-block-establishment' heuristic and the legal default clause.

Answers to Exercises 7.5

A 7.5.1 The `is_clear` predicate definition contains a good example of an **implicit heuristic**.

```
(i)      is_clear(B, S)  :- block(B), not(member(upon(_, B), S) ).
(ii)     is_clear(P, S)  :- place(P), not(member(upon(_, P), S) ).
```

Clause one (i) says that something 'is clear' in some state S if it is a 'block' B and if there is nothing in the current state which is upon block B. Clause two (ii) states that something 'is clear' if it is a 'place' P and there is nothing in the state S which is recorded as being upon P. Now in the search the is_clear predicate is actually called from within legal_action definition to find an action that is legal. This means that when looking for candidates for being clear it will look first at blocks, and secondly for places. So the first legal moves that it will tend to find will tend to involve moving blocks onto other blocks. The **implicit heuristic** here is to 'stack up blocks whenever possible'. In a world whose goals typically involve producing stacks of blocks this is quite a useful rule of thumb.

If you change the order of the clauses in the is_clear definition :

```
(i)      is_clear(P, S)  :- place(P), not(member(upon(_, P), S) ).
(ii)     is_clear(B, S)  :- block(B), not(member(upon(_, B), S) ).
```

then it will tend to move blocks into empty places. The implicit heuristic involved by swopping the clauses as we have just done would mean 'always move blocks into free spaces whenever possible' which is conceivably less constructive.

A 7.5.2 The effect of changing the order of the block predicate will very much depend upon the definitions that call it. Consider the first clause of the normal `is_clear/2` definition which we discussed above. It is always given a list of upon's in a state and it succeeds for blocks which have nothing on them in this state.

```
        is_clear(B, S)  :- block(B), not(member(upon(_, B), S) ).
```

If the block argument B is bound - to some known block - then the use of `block/1` just amounts to a check that the name given is a block's name rather than a place's name. If however the variable B is unbound (as from a blind call to `legal_action/2` - meaning generate any legal move) then this call gives the name of the first block that it will check for being clear (and hence for moving). So, if the order of block names in the definition is b, c, a then the blocks will be moved in this order - all other things being equal.

A 7.5.3 To introduce a fourth block d all that is required is to add a further clause to the block/1 definition.

```
block(a).
block(b).
block(c).
block(d).
```

Naturally enough adding another block will greatly increase the search time.

A 7.5.4 Implement the **towers of hanoi** game. This uses four discs of different sizes, which can only be piled so that smaller blocks go on top of larger ones. Assuming a<b<c<d (ie a is smallest etc) modify the definition of legal_action so that the hanoi rule applies.

```
%    The Action will be bound to a 'move' of a Block from somewhere X to a Destination.
%    Remember that State is a list of upon/2's stating which blocks are upon what.

legal_action(move(B, X, D), S) :-
        upon(B, X, S),          % find a Block in the State
        is_clear(B, S),         % check that Block is clear
        is_clear(D, S),         % find first clear place or block to go to
        B < D.
```

The restriction states that the block to be moved B must be smaller than the destination block D. Here we use the numeric comparison operator '<' which can also be used to compare characters. So in most Prolog systems word 'b' will be less than word 'c'. This simple change means that all legal moves are now only ones in which a 'smaller' block is moved on to a 'larger' destination. No prizes for guessing that the effect of this restriction is to make the solution time rather longer.

Answers to Exercises 7.6

The new operators with the unknowns filled in are as follows.

```
can( push_to(Box, point(N), Room),

/* if  */       [ pushable(Box), location(point(N), Room), in_room(Box, Room),
                  next_to(robot,Box), on_floor ],
/* del */       [ at(robot, _), at(Box, point(_)), next_to(Box, _) ],
/* add */       [ at(Box, point(N)), at(robot, point(N)) ]).

can( push_next_to(Box, BoxOrDoor, Room),

/* if  */       [ pushable(Box),  in_room(Box, Room),
                  in_room(BoxOrDoor, Room),next_to(robot,Box), on_floor ],
/* del */       [ at(Box, _), at(robot, _),  next_to(Box, _) ],
/* add */       [ next_to(Box, BoxOrDoor), next_to(BoxOrDoor, Box),
                  next_to(robot, BoxOrDoor) ]).

can( push_through(Box, Door, Room1, Room2),

/* if  */       [ connects(Door, Room1, Room2), in_room(Box, Room1),
                  in_room(robot, Room1), next_to(Box, Door),
                  next_to(robot, Door), on_floor ],
/* del */       [ in_room(robot, Room1), in_room(Box, Room1) ],
/* add */       [ in_room(robot, Room2), in_room(Box, Room2) ]).
```

Answers to Exercises 7.7

The complete definition of **can**/4 is given in Code Appendix 7.3, but the four problem ones are given here for you to check. Our interpretation of these operators is certainly open to question and we would encourage you to experiment with them and others yourself. For example, we have insisted that the robot must be next_to a box before it climbs upon it - but have not added that it is next_to the box when it climbs off. There is infact a very great deal of refinement to these operator definitions that you could untertake.

```
can( turn_on( switch(S) ),

/* if  */      [ at(switch(S), Point), at(box(N), Point ), on(robot, box(N) ) ],
/* del */      [ status(switch(S), _) ],
/* add */      [ status(switch(S), on) ]).

can( turn_off( switch(S) ),

/* if  */      [ at(switch(S), Point), at(box(N), Point ), on(robot, box(N) ) ],
/* del */      [ status(switch(S), _) ],
/* add */      [ status(switch(S), off) ]).

can( climb_on( box(B) ),

/* if  */      [ next_to(robot, box(B)), on_floor ],
/* del */      [ on_floor ],
/* add */      [ on(robot, box(B)) ]).

can( climb_off( box(B) ),
/* if  */      [ on(robot, box(B)) ],
/* del */      [ on(robot, box(B)) ],
/* add */      [ on_floor ]).
```

Answers to Exercises 7.8

7.8.1 When given two or more goals, STRIPS does one at a time, and blithely assumes that the first goal state still holds true after the second goal has been achieved, thus leading to some rather human errors. While test(9) asks the robot to climb on a box at point(6) does not actually specify that they should both be achieved together and we have no obvious mechanism for doing so. If you scrutinise the printout you will see that with this goal order, the robot climbs on the first box it can find, then gets off again and walks casually on to point(6). In fact, STRIPS knows nothing about **goal interaction** and assumes that all of its goals are **independent**. As it is, achieving the second goal undoes the achievement of the first. Should try harder!

```
**   Complete Plan is
        walk_next_to(box(1), room(1))
        climb_on(box(1))

        climb_off(box(1))
        walk_next_to(door(1), room(1))
        walk_through(door(1), room(1), room(5))
        walk_next_to(door(4), room(5))
        walk_through(door(4), room(5), room(4))
        walk_to(point(6), room(4))
```

7.8.2 You might guess that test(10) (the same as test(9) but with the two goals re-ordered) would solve the previous problem. Clearly, from our intelligent perspective, if one must be at a point and on a box, then one must push the box there and get on it. Now our planner does actually work this out, but only after some **gross inefficiency**. In fact, given the problem climb on box(1) at point(6), first the poor robot trundles all the way to point(6) and then goes all the way back back to where it started and pushes the box through to point(6) so that it can climb on top of it Still, it got there in the end! This is another aspect of *goal interaction*. However, here there is a beneficial interaction between the goals that we would expect an intelligent agent to spot and take advantage of. In this case, the plan for one goal could be efficiently absorbed into the plan for another.

```
**   Complete Plan is
        walk_next_to(door(1), room(1))
        walk_through(door(1), room(1), room(5))
        walk_next_to(door(4), room(5))
        walk_through(door(4), room(5), room(4))
        walk_to(point(6), room(4))

        walk_next_to(door(4), room(4))
        walk_through(door(4), room(4), room(5))
        walk_next_to(door(1), room(5))
        walk_through(door(1), room(5), room(1))
        walk_next_to(box(1), room(1))
        push_next_to(box(1), door(1), room(1))
        push_through(box(1), door(1), room(1), room(5))
        push_next_to(box(1), door(4), room(5))
        push_through(box(1), door(4), room(5), room(4))
        walk_next_to(box(1), room(4))
        climb_on(box(1))
```

Now what you should be asking is why - given the above exercise where we found that the robot planner treats its goals entirely independantly - does the robot push the box at all? Why does it simply not do the opposite of test(9) and walk back to the room and get on the box where it stands? If you look at the printout and the operators you should be able to work it out.

```
2: >>>> Trying to achieve : next_to(robot, box(1))
             Action : walk_next_to(box(1), _4866)
             Conditions :   in_room(robot, _4866)
                          & in_room(box(1), _4866)
                          & on_floor
```

In this segment of the planning output the robot has walked into room(4) so as to be at the point of its first goal and finds that it must be next to the box before it can get on to it for its second goal. It decides that the best means to achieve this end is to walk_next_to the box in some unknown room. Now its preconditions for walking next to something is that the thing and the robot both be in the same room and the robot be on the floor. Now, the first precondition to be achieved is that the robot be in a room and we dont know which one yet (ie it is _4844). This is trivially true because the robot is already in room(4). So _4844 is bound to the value room(4) which means that when we come to the precondition for the box location we will require that it be in room 4 also! The apparent intelligence of the robot in 'understanding' our intent compared to test(9) is illusory - simply a side-effect of the ordering of the preconditions in the walk_next_to operator! Had the preconditions been around the other way then the robot would have simply walked back and got on the box wherever it was located. Try swopping the preconditions to see if this is so - you may notice that this causes some other problems in other places.

A Note on the Code Appendices

The following appendices contain the code which supports the project chapters. There is an appendix for each of the projects given and the number of the appendix corresponds with the number of the chapter involved. The definitions given in these appendices are accompanied by some little comments which may assist the reader to understand them - but the definitions which must be understood to make the project sensible are all documented in the main text of the chapters. Also it will be noted that some of the definitions given here are slightly more complex looking than their main-text chapter equivalents. This is becuase we have added further complexities here so that the programs will print out more extensive diagnostic information about their progress etc. In the main text we have tended to discuss only the essence of the definition - stripping away the inessential and distracting parts to make them more clear. Where we ask the user to build parts of a system through the exercises we have provided an incomplete toy version and a further more complete version for when the exercises are done.

To save the reader excess typing you can send a small sum to the publishers and they will send a copy of the software for these programs to you on a disc. A suitable order-form is enclosed in the book. In providing these definitions we are assuming that the reader has access to a 'standard' version of Prolog - often referred to as "Edinburgh" or "Quintus" standard Prolog. We actually work in a Prolog for the Apple Macintosh™ micro called Logic Programming Associates MacProlog™. So the disc software is available in these two versions. The MacProlog disc contains extra features - available on the Macintosh™ that are not documented here, including rather more sophisticated input and output facilities and the graphics tree-drawing program used in the parsing project.

Summary:

Code Appendix 1 : General Utilities
Code Appendix 2 : Semantic Nets & Frames
Code Appendix 3 : Pattern Matching & ELIZA
Code Appendix 4 : Parsing using DCGs
Code Appendix 5 : Semantics & SAM
Code Appendix 6 : Production Systems & Seriation
Code Appendix 7 : Search, Planning & STRIPS

Code Appendix 1
General Utilities

Almost all of the programs in these appendices use the definition **member**/2 and some use **append**/3. So if your version of Prolog does not include them built-in we include them here.

For most of the appendix programs which output results to the screen, different output predicates have been given which print out the appropriate thing in the appropriate style. Where long sequences of write statements would be required we have normally supplied a simple recursive definition which takes the things to print in a list and does them - treating new lines and calls to tab etc appropriately. One simple development of the book might be to standardise all these different output calls into your own style/format. To help you in this we also include a simple version of the predicate **writel**/1 here.

Definitions D 1.4 to D 1.10 are input/output predicates that are written from a standard Prolog perspective. Your own Prolog may have its own specialist input/output relations that you may more effectively use. These are primarily used in project in Chapter & Appendix 4, but may also be used in Chapter 5 and some of the other advanced exercises.

```
% D 1.1 : member/2
%          X is a member of a list if it is at the head of the list or a member of the tail of the list

member(X, [X | _]).
member(X, [_ | Y]):- member(X, Y).
```

```
% D 1.2 : append/3
%          append( L1, L2, L3) says that L3 is the list which is made up of appending
%          together of the two lists L1 and L2.

append([], L, L).
append([X | Xt], Y, [X| Zt]):- append(Xt, Y, Zt).
```

```
% D 1.3 : writel/1
%          write each element out using write/1 recursing on the tail of the list.
%          Unless the element is the word nl or the term tab/1 in which case call these first.

writel([]).
writel([nl | T]):- nl, !, writel(T).
writel([tab(S) | T]):- tab(S), !, writel(T).
writel([H | T]):- write(H), writel(T).
```

```
% D 1.4 : talk/2
%           talk(Output, Input) prints out the list that is Input as a prompt for the user.
%           Then it reads in the users reply and returns this as a list of the individual
%           words bound to Input. writel/1 prints out the message Output. Then readline/1
%           takes in a sequence of characters from the keyboard. And finally chars_to_words/2
%           turns the characters into a list of words.

talk(Output, Input):-
    writel(Out),
    readline(Line),
    chars_to_words(Line, Input).
```

```
% D 1.5 : readline/1
%           readline(Chars) reads a line as a sequence of characters terminated by a return.
%           The get0/1 call gets a character from the current input stream (usually the keyboard -
%           but could just as well be a file or whatever). It then hands this on to readline1/2.
%           NB. In this we throw away all the punctuation. (See definition D 1.10).

readline(Chars):-
    get0(Char), !,
    readline1(Char, Chars).
```

```
% D 1.6 : readline1/2
%           readline1(Char, Chars) does some work for readline/1
%           it adds byte Char to the list of Chars until it reaches the new line 13 char
%           - ie normally the user will hit the 'return' keyboard key.

readline1(13, []).
readline1(X, [X | T]):-
    readline(T).
```

```
% D 1.7 : chars_to_words/2
%           chars_to_words(Chars, Words) takes a list of chars and returns a list of words.
%           Clause 1 says that if an empty list of chars has an empty list of words.
%           Clause 2 says that if the first character is an interesting one ie alphanumeric
%               then find the first word and return it as a Word - after recursing on the remainder
%               of the list
%           Clause 3 says that if the first char cannot be part of a word then throw it away
%               and just look at the remainder of the list of characters.

chars_to_words([], []).
chars_to_words([Char|R], [Word|Ws]):-
    alphanum(Char, _),                    % could be start of a word
    do_a_word([Char|R], Word, Remains),   % make a word from the list
    chars_to_words(Remains, Ws).
chars_to_words([Char | T], List):-
    not(alphanum(Char, _)),
    chars_to_words(T, List).              % Throw away any rubbish
```

% D 1.8 : **do_a_word**/3
```
%              do_a_word(Cs, W, Rs) takes a list of chars Cs and returns a the first word W and what
%              remains Rs after the word W is removed from the list Cs.  The call to word_chars/3 does
%                 most of the actual work.
%              The built-in name/2 relates the ascii value of a list of characters to an atomic word.
%                 It turns the list of WordAscii characters into the atom Word.
```

```
do_a_word(List, Word, Remains):-
    word_chars(List, WordAscii, Remains),
    name(Word, WordAscii).
```

% D 1.9 : **word_chars**/3
```
%              word_chars(Cs, W, Rs) does the work for do_a_word/3.
%              Clause 1 is the stopping check - ie if the next character cannot be part of the word then stop.
%                 This returns the whole of the remaining list.
%              Clause 3 is a special case that states that a list with no character in should return an empty
%                 list. (eg. for when a word is right at the end of a list of words - followed by nothing).
%              Clause 2 recurses on itself if it sees a useful, alphanumeric char - putting that char into the
%                 list which is its second argument.
```

```
word_chars([Char|R], [], [Char|R]):-
    not(alphanum(Char, _)).
word_chars([Char|R], [Char1|Cs], C0):-
    alphanum(Char, Char1),
    !,
    word_chars(R, Cs, C0).
word_chars([], [], []).
```

% D 1.10 : **alphanum**/2
```
%              alphanum(C, C1) dictates which ascii characters can form part of a word.
%              It has two arguments only for the second clause which converts upper case letters
%              A-Z to lower case letters a-z.  So these and numbers and a very few special characters
%              can form words.  NB  In this we throw away all the punctuation.
```

```
alphanum(C, C):- C > 96, C < 123.   % lowercase a-z
alphanum(C, L):- C > 64, C < 91, L is C + 32.   % Uppercase - convert to lower
alphanum(C, C):- C > 47, C < 58.
alphanum(39, 39).   %  single quote ' for apostrophes
alphanum(45, 45).   %  hyphen -
alphanum(95, 95).   % underscore _
```

Code Appendix 2
Semantic Nets & Frames

Definitions 2.1   Semantic memory

```
%  D 2.1.1 : subclass/2
%  subclass(Thing, Class) means that
%    Class is the superordinate category for Thing.

subclass(tweety, canary).
subclass(canary, bird).
subclass(ostrich, bird).
subclass(bird, animal).
subclass(fish, animal).
subclass(shark, fish).
subclass(salmon, fish).
subclass(animal, living_thing).

%  D 2.1.2 : property/2
%  property(Thing, P) means that a class of Thing has the immediate property P
%  the clauses are clumped together for tidiness.

property(animal, breathes).
property(animal, has_skin).
property(animal, eats).
property(animal, can_move).

property(bird, warm_blooded).
property(bird, has_feathers).
property(bird, can_fly).
property(bird, has_wings).

property(canary, can_sing).
property(canary, size(small)).
property(canary, colour(yellow)).

property(ostrich, size(tall)).
property(ostrich, cannot_fly).

%  D 2.1.3 : Isa/2
%  Isa(Thing, Class) means that Class is a superordinate category for Thing.
%  If (i)  Thing has an immediate superclass,
%      (ii) Thing has a superclass and the superclass isa thing itself.

isa(X, Y):- subclass(X, Y).
isa(X, Z):- subclass(X, Y), isa(Y, Z).
```

```
%  D 2.1.4 : has_property/2
% has_property(Thing, P) means
%   that a Thing has the property P
%   and these properties can be inherited via the 'isa' relation.

has_property(Thing, P):-
    property(Thing, P).
has_property(X, P):-
    isa(X, SuperClass),
    property(SuperClass, P).
```

Definitions 2.2 Timing

The timing exercises rely on the Prolog implementation's use of the computer's system clock. Two versions of the predicate **speed**/3 are given here. Both of them take a time, run the query they were given, take another time and work out how much time has elapsed.

The first relies on your version of Prolog having a predicate which measures elapsed time - usually from when you "started up". So **ticks**(X) will reply YES with X = 1234 etc, with a larger number each time you execute it. The second version **time**(Hrs, Mins, Secs) uses a predicate which looks at the 'system clock' and gives the time of day in hrs/mins/secs. It must clearly do extra calculation to work out the total time this is in seconds.

YesNo is bound to 'yes' if the query succeeds, 'no' if it fails.

TimeTaken will be in ticks in version 1 (eg @1/60 sec for LPA MacProlog™); or in seconds in version 2 (eg ESI Prolog™).

NB. One possible problem with this timing measure - especially the **time**/3 one which can only return the number of seconds elapsed is that on many computers the queries we suggest will be over far too quickly - before 1 second has been registered! If this is the case then you must consider means of getting real timings. Remember that you are looking for the relative timings between different types of query - so one solution would be to make Prolog call each query a number of times over in succession. So if for example you might alter the definition of **test_query**/2 given below so that instead of calling call(X) just the once it called it 10 times. Eg. call(X), call(X), call(X) ... etc. Unfortunately, whilst this should work for calls that succeed but will make the calls that fail seem much too fast - as they will not get past the first **call**/1. A better solution would be to use Prolog's **repeat**/0 and **fail**/0 built-ins to construct something that iterated for however many times required - doing the query again whether it succeeds or fails. We leave this problem for the reader.

You should also note that these timings are not very accurate - they only give a rough guide to how long the query took.

% **D 2.2.1a** : **speed**/3
% **Version 1** for ticks/1 - an elapsed time predicate

```
speed(Query,TimeTaken,YesNo):-
      ticks(StartTime),
      test_query(Query,YesNo),
      ticks(FinishTime),
      TimeTaken is FinishTime - StartTime.
```

% **D 2.2.1b** : **speed**/3
% **Version 2** for time/3 - a system clock predicate

```
speed(Query,TimeTaken,YesNo):-
      time(Hrs1, Min1, Sec1),
      test_query(Query,YesNo),
      time(Hrs2, Min2, Sec2),
      to_secs(Hrs1, Min1, Sec1, Hrs2, Min2, Sec2, TimeTaken).
```

% **D 2.2.2** : **test_query**/2
% **test_query**(Q, YN) calls a query Q and YN indicates its sucess or failure
%   It is used by speed/3 as you might want to know how long a failed query
%   took as much as a sucessful one

```
test_query(Query, yes):- call(Query), !.
test_query(Query, no).
```

% **D 2.2.3** : **to_secs**/7
% to_secs(Hrs1, Min1, Sec1, Hrs2, Min2, Sec2, TimeTaken)

```
to_secs(Hrs1, Min1, Sec1, Hrs2, Min2, Sec2, TimeTaken):-
      StartSeconds is Hrs1 * 60 * 60 + Min1 * 60 + Sec1,
      EndSeconds is Hrs2 * 60 * 60 + Min2 * 60 + Sec2,
      TimeTaken is EndSeconds - StartSeconds.
```

Definitions 2.3   Frames

% **D 2.3.1** : **has_value**/3

```
has_value(Object, Slot, Value):-
      value(Object, Slot, Value).
has_value(Object,Slot, Value):-
      inherits(Slot, Relation),
      value(Object, Relation, SuperClass),
      has_value(SuperClass, Slot, Value),
      not_explicit(Object, Slot).
has_value(Object, Slot, Value):-
      if_needed(Object, Slot, Value).
has_value(Object, Slot, Value):-
      default_value(Object,Slot,Value).
```

% **D 2.3.2** : **not_explicit**/2
/* The first two clauses are cut (the exclaimation mark after the if) so that backtracking won't let the same entry (especially has_as_part) be true again in the third clause. It would be true again in the third clause for some frames - but not all - which is why we need the second clause which makes it an exception for all frames. If it was not cut then it would be true twice in this definition and produce two solutions on backtracking */

```
not_explicit(_, a_kind_of):- !.
not_explicit(_, has_as_part):- !.
not_explicit(Object, Slot):- not(value(Object, Slot)).
```

% D 2.3.3 : value/3

```
value(living_thing, slot, energy_source).      value(animal, slot, food_source).
value(living_thing, slot, reproduction).       value(animal, slot, locomotion).
value(living_thing, slot, size).               value(animal, slot, habitat).
value(living_thing, slot, age).                value(animal, slot, skin_covering).
value(living_thing, slot, colour).             value(animal, slot, weight).
value(living_thing, slot, date_of_birth).      value(animal, slot, family_name).
                                               value(animal, slot, breathes).
value(dog, slot, breed).                       value(animal, slot, circulation).
value(dog, slot, owned_by).

value(living_thing, a_kind_of, thing).

value(animal, a_kind_of, living_thing).        value(mammal, a_kind_of, animal).
value(animal, energy_source, food).            value(mammal, breathes, air).
value(animal, has_as_part, head).              value(mammal, reproduction, placental).
value(animal, has_as_part, body).              value(mammal, skin_covering, fur).
value(animal, has_as_part, eyes).              value(mammal, circulation, warm_blooded).
value(animal, has_as_part, tail).              value(mammal, fly, no).
                                               value(mammal, has_as_part, legs).

value(bird, a_kind_of, animal).                value(fish, a_kind_of, animal).
value(bird, breathes, air).                    value(fish, breathes, water).
value(bird, reproduction, egg).                value(fish, reproduction, egg).
value(bird, circulation, warm_blooded).        value(fish, circulation, cold_blooded).
value(bird, skin_covering, feathers).          value(fish, skin_covering, scales).
value(bird, fly, yes).                         value(fish, fly, no).
value(bird,swim,no).                           value(fish, swim, yes).
value(bird, has_as_part, legs).                value(fish, has_as_part, fins).
value(bird, has_as_part, wings).               value(fish, has_as_part, gills).

value(dog, a_kind_of, mammal).                 value(whale, a_kind_of, mammal).
value(dog, habitat, land).                     value(whale, habitat, sea).
value(dog, makes_noise, barks).                value(whale, size, huge).
value(dog, size, medium).                      value(whale, food_source, plankton).
value(dog, run, yes).
value(dog, food_source, carnivore).

value(ostrich, a_kind_of, bird).               value(canary, a_kind_of, bird).
value(ostrich, size, big).                     value(canary, makes_noise, sings).
value(ostrich, fly, no).                        value(canary, size, small).
value(ostrich, run, yes).                      value(canary, colour, yellow).

value(shark, a_kind_of, fish).                 value(salmon, a_kind_of, fish).
value(shark, size, big).                       value(salmon, size, medium).
value(shark, bite, yes).                       value(salmon, colour, pink).
value(shark, habitat, sea).                    value(salmon, habitat, sea_and_rivers).

value(lassie, a_kind_of, dog).                 value(lara, a_kind_of, dog).
value(lassie, breed, collie).                  value(lara, breed, labrador).
value(lassie, coat, long_haired).              value(lara, colour, yellow).
                                               value(lara, name, lara).
                                               value(lara, weight, 20).
                                               value(lara, date_of_birth, 1985).
value(tweety, name, tweety).
value(tweety, a_kind_of, canary).
value(tweety, owned_by, joe).
value(tweety, date_of_birth,1989).

value(X, part_of, Y):- has_value(Y, has_as_part, X, _).
```

% D 2.3.4 : **inherits**/2
% inherits(S, V) means that slot S can be inherited via slot V

```
inherits(S, a_kind_of):-
       member(S,[age, a_kind_of, bite, breathes, breed, circulation, coat,
colour,date_of_birth, disposition, energy_source, fly, food_source, habitat,
has_as_part, likes, makes_noise, owned_by, reproduction, run, size,
skin_covering, slot, swim, weight]).
inherits(S, part_of):-
       member(S, [ part_of, age, colour, owned_by ]).
       %  only a few slots may be inherited by a part of the concept
```

% D 2.3.5 : **If_needed**/3
% A simple if_needed demon.

```
if_needed(Object, age, A) :-
      value(Object, date_of_birth, DoB),
      current_year(CY),
      A is CY - DoB.
```

% D 2.3.6 : ·**default_value**/3
% some simple default values for a frame.

```
default_value(dog, disposition, friendly).
default_value(dog, likes, fetching_sticks).
```

% D 2.3.7 : **current_year**/1
% This is simply a database flag that is used by one of the contents of an if-needed slot

```
current_year(1990).
```

Code Appendix 3
Pattern Matching & ELIZA

```
%  D 3.1  : eliza/0
%  eliza parodies a conversation with a non-directive
%  "Rogerian" therapist  It asks a lot of reflective questions.
%  This is basically just the predicate that tidies up and calls therapy/1.

eliza :-
    tidy,
    therapy(['Welcome to ELIZA.  What seems to be worrying you ?']).
```

```
%  D 3.2  : therapy/1
%  therapy(Input) takes an Input from the user and attempts to find
%   an appropriately "therapeutic" reply using the database of patterns.
%  It is recursive.  If the input is just 'bye', then it finishes with a message.
%  Otherwise it goes through each doable pattern attempting to match the input.
%  When a match is found it is given to talk/2 which prints it out and gets a
%   further input to hand recursively to 'therapy'.

therapy([bye]) :-
    writel(['Goodbye.', nl,
          'I hope you feel better !', nl,
          'Have a nice day.']).
therapy(Output):-
    talk(Output, Input),
    match(Input, Reply), !,
    exchanges(Reply, Reply1),
    therapy(Reply1).
```

```
%  D 3.3  : match/2
%  match(Input, Output) generates an Ouput given the Input

match(Input, Output):-              % picks up empty list and multi-word matches
    pattern(P, Input, Output),      % picks up empty list and [i,am | Rest] etc
    doable(P),
    add(P).                         % flag that pattern P has been used
match([_ | T], Output):-           % otherwise throw away first word
    match(T, Output).               % and recurse on the tail
```

```
%  D 3.4  : add/1
%  add(N) is a predicate which adds a database flag to say that a pattern has
%   been 'done'.  It states that there is no need to add a pattern marked with
%   an 'x'; otherwise assert its numeric flag.

add(x).
add(N):- integer(N), asserta(done(N)).
```

% **D 3.5** : **doable**/1
% **doable**(N) is a predicate which checks that a pattern has not already
%   been flagged in the database as having been 'done'. Patterns marked with
%   an 'x' are always 'doable'; otherwise failure to find an appropriate flag
%   in the database means that it is doable. Its argument is always an atom.

```
doable(x).
doable(N):- integer(N), not(done(N)).
```

% **D 3.6** : **tidy**/0
% **tidy** is a simple bookkeeping predicate that is invoked at the beginning
%   of an interaction to 'tidy' up the database - resetting all the flags.

```
tidy:-
      retractall(done(X)),
      asserta(done(seed)), !.
```

% **D 3.7** : **exchanges**/2
% **exchanges**(In, Out) is a predicate that will take a stream of words in the
%   list In and return the list Out with all the words that match with
%   exchange/2 exchanged. eg. (?) exchanges([i, am, unhappy], X). YES. X = [you, are, unhappy].

```
exchanges([], []).
exchanges([X, Y | T], [X1, Y1 | T1]):-
      exchange([X, Y], [X1, Y1]),
      exchanges(T, T1), !.
exchanges([X | T], [X1 | T1]):-
      exchange([X], [X1]),
      exchanges(T, T1), !.
exchanges([X | T], [X | T1]):-
      exchanges(T, T1), !.
```

% **D 3.8** : **exchange**/2
% **exchange**(Old, New) states that the sequence of words in Old
%   should be exchanged for the sequence of words in New.

```
exchange([i, am], [you,are]).
exchange([you, are], [i, am]).
exchange([are, you], [am, i]).
exchange([am, i], [are, you]).
exchange([i, was], [you, were]).
exchange([you, were], [i, was]).
exchange([was, i], [were, you]).
exchange([were, you], [was, i]).
exchange([i], [you]).
exchange([me], [you]).
exchange([you], [me]).
exchange([my], [your]).
exchange([your], [my]).
exchange([us], [you]).
exchange([you], [us]).
```

% **D 3.9** : **pattern**/3
% **pattern**(N, In, Out) means that the "therapeutic" reply Out is appropriate to the user input
% which matches the pattern In. Patterns are numbered N (integer or 'x').

% First the 'quit' pattern

```
pattern(x, [X], [bye]):- member(X, [bye, stop, halt, finish, cheerio]).
```

% echoing patterns - will not be repeated

```
pattern(10, [i, X, my | Rest], ['Do you have these feelings of ', X,
        ' towards your ', Rest, ' often ?']):-
    feelings(X).
pattern(20, [i | Rest], ['Why do you say that you ' | Reply]) :-
        append(R, [you | Rs], Rest), append(R, [' me ?'], Reply).
pattern(30, [they | Rest], ['Why makes you say that they ' | Reply]):-
        append(R, [me | _], Rest),
        append(R, [' you ?'], Reply).
pattern(40, [this, is | Rest], ['Why do you say that this is' | Rest]).
pattern(50, [my | Rest], ['Your' | Rest]).
pattern(60, [it, is | Rest], ['So, you feel that it is' | Rest1]):-
        append(Rest, ['do you?'], Rest1).
```

% general patterns with some echoing - can be repeated

```
pattern(x, [i, am | Rest], ['How long have you been' | Rest]).
pattern(x, [you | Rest], ['What makes you think I' | Reply]):-
        append(R, [me | _ ], Rest),
        append(R, ['you ?'], Reply).
pattern(x, [i, like | Rest], ['Does anyone else you know like' | Rest]).
pattern(x, [i, feel | Rest], ['Do you often feel that way ?']).
```

% Patterns triggered by just one word - not to be repeated

```
pattern(100, [X | _], ['Cut the foul language, slimeball !']):-
        badword(X).
pattern(110, [X | _], ['Why do you feel the need to be so hostile?']):-
        badword(X).
pattern(120, [help | _], ['What sort of help do you think you need?']).
pattern(130, [X | _], ['Do you like animals, I mean pets and suchlike ?']):-
        animal(X).
pattern(140, [prolog | _], ['Prolog is hell, wouldnt you say?']).
pattern(150, [L | _], ['Would you say programming was difficult?']):-
        member(L, [lisp, pascal, basic, cobol, fortran, c, compiler]).
pattern(160, [X | _], ['You seem rather unsure of yourself ?']):-
```

```
        uncertain(X).
pattern(170, [X], ['Dont be so short with me!',
        'What does', X,' mean here?']):- yesorno(X).
pattern(180, [X | _], ['Do computers frighten you ?']):-
        important(X, computers).
pattern(190, [X | _], ['How close are you to your', X, ?]):-
        important(X, family).
pattern(200, [X | _], ['Is your', X, 'very important to you as a friend?']):-
        important(X, friends), not((X = friend; X = friends)).
pattern(210, [X | _], ['How do you get on with friends in general ?']):-
        important(X, friends).
pattern(220, [X | _], ['Please try to be more positive about things!',
        'Tell me something good that has happened recently.']):-
        badfeelings(X).
pattern(240, [X | _], ['Cheer up you miserable wretch !']):- badfeelings(X).
pattern(250, [], ['Tell me about your family']).
pattern(260, [], ['I am still listening ...']).
pattern(x, [X], ['What do you mean,', X, '?']).
```

        % General Catchall pattern that will always work if all else fails

```
pattern(x, [], ['Tell me more ... ']).
```

% D 3.10 : Important/2
% Important(W, C) means that the word W is important in the context of C.

```
important(mum, family).
important(dad, family).
important(father, family).
important(mother, family).
important(sister, family).
important(brother, family).
important(son, family).
important(daughter, family).
important(family, family).
important(boyfriend, friends).
important(girlfriend, friends).
important(friend, friends).
important(friends, friends).
important(lover, friends).
important(mate, friends).
important(mates, friends).
important(byte, computers).
important(prolog, computers).
important(computers, computers).
important(computer, computers).
```

% **D 3.11** : **question**/1
% **question**(Q) means that the word Q is a 'question' word.

```
question(why).
question(what).
question(when).
question(who).
question(how).
question('?').
```

% **D 3.12** : **badword**/1
% **badword**(B) means that the word B is bad.
% Use your imagination to extend this one ...

```
badword(bastard).
badword(sod).
badword(bloody).
```

% **D 3.13** : **badfeelings**/1
% **badfeelings**(B) means that the word B is a "bad-feeling".

```
badfeelings(dislike).
badfeelings(dislikes).
badfeelings(despise).
badfeelings(unhappy).
badfeelings(hate).
badfeelings(hates).
badfeelings(depressed).
badfeelings(suicidal).
badfeelings(suicide).
badfeelings(kill).
badfeelings(murder).
badfeelings(death).
```

% **D 3.14** : **goodfeelings**/1
% **goodfeelings**(G) means that the word G is a "good-feeling".
% Fewer than the "bad" ones - so you can see what Eliza wants to talk about!

```
goodfeelings(like).
goodfeelings(likes).
goodfeelings(happy).
goodfeelings(love).
goodfeelings(loves).
```

% **D 3.15** : **feelings**/1

```
feelings(X):- goodfeelings(X).
feelings(X):- badfeelings(X).
```

% **D 3.16** : **yesorno**/1
% **yesorno**(YN) defines the words yes and no.

```
yesorno(yes).
yesorno(no).
```

% **D 3.17** : **uncertain**/1
% **uncertain**(U) defines "uncertain" words.

```
uncertain(may).
uncertain(might).
uncertain(perhaps).
uncertain(maybe).
uncertain(possibly).
uncertain(probably).
```

% **D 3.18** : **negative**/1
% **negative**(N) defines "negative" words.

```
negative(not).
negative(no).
negative(wont).
negative(cant).
negative(dont).
```

% **D 3.19** : **done**/1
% **done**(X) meaning X is a number of a pattern that has been used

```
done(0).
```

Code Appendix 4
Parsing using DCGs

The grammar rule parser program is divided into four main sections. The first §4.1 is included for the benefit of those readers whose own version of Prolog cannot cope directly with the grammar rule syntax. It may also be of general interest to show how simple it is to write compilers for Prolog in Prolog itself. What it actually does is take a high level set of commands in one syntax and "compile" them into another (lower) set of commands. In one way or another this is just what all computer language compilers do. Nevertheless we have not sought to explain fully this process or the code for the tranlator here. The grammar rule translator given here is adapted from Clocksin & Mellish (1981) and Sterling and Shapiro (1986). If you need to use it you may well have to adapt it slightly to suit your system. Hopefully most readers can skip directly on to the next sections which have the listings for a simple and then a more complex English language parser. The final section provides some interface predicates.

Definitions 4.1   A Grammar Rule Translator

```
%%%   <New Operator>   %%%

?-  op(200, xfx, '-->').
```

/* **phrase**/2 is needed by the parser definitions in the next section. When you have changed the grammar rules in any way you will have to :

    i) reconsult the grammar rules to replace the old ones in the database

    ii) retract all the old definitions (of s, verb_phrase, noun, etc)

    iii) run the translate/0 program to turn the '-->' rules into Prolog clauses that can be called directly.

*/

% **D 4.1.1** : **phrase**/2 is taken from Clocksin & Mellish (1981)

```
phrase(Ptype, Words) :-
     Ptype =.. [Pred | Args],
     append(Args, [Words, []], NewArgs),
     Goal =.. [Pred | NewArgs],
     call(Goal).
```

% **D 4.1.2** : **translate**/0
% Effectively means "forall rules --> translate and assert Prolog version"


```
translate:-
     (Lhs --> Rhs),
     translate((Lhs --> Rhs), PrologRule),
     assertz(PrologRule),
     fail.
translate:-  write('translation complete'), nl.
```

% **D 4.1.3** : **translate**/2 & 3
% **translate**(GrammarRule, PrologClause)
% translates a single DCG GrammarRule into a single PrologClause
% by using translate/3 to turn the left-hand-side of the rule into the Head
% and the right-hand side of the grammar rule into the Body of the Prolog clause


```
translate((Lhs --> Rhs), (Head :- Body)):-
     translate(Lhs, Head, Xs, Ys),
     translate(Rhs, Body, Xs, Ys), !.

translate((A, B), (Ap, Bp), Xs, Ys):-
     translate(A, Ap, Xs, Xs1),
     translate(B, Bp, Xs1, Ys).
translate({ X }, X, S, S).
translate(A, Ap, S, S1):-
     non_terminal(A),
     A =.. List,
     append(List, [S, S1], NewList),
     Ap =.. NewList.
translate(Xs, true, S, S1):-
     terminals(Xs),
     sequence(Xs, S, S1).
```

% **D 4.1.4** : **non_terminal**/1
% the opposite of terminal - ie not lists.

```
non_terminal(A):-not(terminals(A)).
```

% **D 4.1.5** : **terminals**/1
% terminals are the parts of rules (on the rhs) that are just lists with terminal words in them.

```
terminals([X|Xs]).
```

% **D 4.1.6** : **sequence**/1
% used to strip off a sequence of terminals.

```
sequence([X|Xs], [X|S], S0):-sequence(Xs, S, S0).
sequence([], Xs, Xs).
```

Definitions 4.2   A simple phrase structure grammar parser

% **D 4.2.1** : **parse**/1
% **parse**(List) calls the built-in primitive phrase on the List
%   phrase knows about the database grammar rule format
%   the actual call asks if List is a 'phrase' of type 'sentence'

```
parse(List):-
     phrase(sentence, List).
```

% **D 4.2.2a** : The Grammar Rules

```
sentence -->  noun_phrase,  verb_phrase .

noun_phrase -->  determiner ,  noun_phrase2 .

noun_phrase2 -->  adjective ,  noun_phrase2 .
noun_phrase2 -->  noun .

verb_phrase -->  verb_phrase2 , prepositional_phrase .
verb_phrase -->  verb_phrase2 .

verb_phrase2 -->  verb .
verb_phrase2 -->  verb ,  noun_phrase .

prepositional_phrase -->  preposition ,  noun_phrase .
```

% **D 4.2.2b** : The Lexical Rules

```
verb --> [hit] .
verb --> [sat] .
verb --> [bit] .

adjective --> [big] .
adjective --> [lazy] .
adjective --> [green] .

determiner -->  [the] .
determiner -->  [a] .

noun --> [dog] .
noun --> [man] .
noun --> [tree] .

preposition--> [on].
preposition--> [by].
```

Definitions 4.3 : PARSER-1 : A Definite Clause Grammar parser

% D 4.3.1 : **parse**/1
% **parse**(X) calls the built in predicate phrase/2 to see if X is a sentence with tree T
%   if it is then it uses draw-tree/1 to print it out to the screen
%   followed by a new-line, nl.

```
parse(X):-
    phrase(sentence(T), X),
    draw_tree(T), nl.
```

% D 4.3.2a : The Grammar Rules

```
sentence(s(N, VP))   -->   noun_phrase(N),  verb_phrase(VP) .

noun_phrase(np(N))   -->   pronoun(N).
noun_phrase(np(D,N))   -->   determiner(D), noun_phrase2(N) .

noun_phrase2(np2(A,N))   -->   adjective(A), noun_phrase2(N) .
noun_phrase2(np2(N))   -->   noun(N) .

verb_phrase(vp(VP, PP))   -->   verb_phrase2(VP),
    prepositional_phrase(PP) .
verb_phrase(vp(VP))   -->   verb_phrase2(VP) .

verb_phrase2(vp2(V, A))   -->   verb(V),   adverb(A) .
verb_phrase2(vp2(V,N))   -->   verb(V),   noun_phrase(N) .
verb_phrase2(vp2(V, N, A))   -->
    verb(V),
    noun_phrase(N),
    adverb(A) .
verb_phrase2(vp2(V))   -->   verb(V).

prepositional_phrase(pp(PREP,NP))   -->
    preposition(PREP),
    noun_phrase(NP) .
```

% D 4.3.2b : The Lexical Rules

```
verb(v(X))   -->   [X], {v(X)}.

adjective(adj(X))   -->   [X], {adj(X)}.

determiner(det(X))   -->   [X], {det(X)}.

noun(n(X))   -->   [X], {n(X)}.

pronoun(pron(X))   -->   [X], {pron(X)}.

preposition(prep(X))   -->   [X], {prep(X)}.

adverb(adv(X))   -->   [X], {adv(X)}.

conjunction(conj(X))   -->   [X], {conj(X)}.

relative_pronoun(relpron(X))   -->   [X], {relpron(X)}.
```

Definitions 4.3.3 to 4.3.14 : The lexicon

% D **4.3.3** : **det**/1
% **det**(Determiner)

```
det(the).
det(a).
det(all).
det(an).
det(any).
det(each).
det(every).
det(no).
det(some).
```

% D **4.3.4** : **n**/1
% **n**(Noun)

```
n(program).
n(professor).
n(book).
n(ideas).
n(cat).
n(mat).
n(time).
n(man).
n(woman).
n(world).
n(thing).
n(years).
n(house).
n(hill).
n(dog).
```

% D **4.3.5** : **pn**/1
% **pn**(Propernoun)

```
pn(terry).
pn(mary).
pn(shrdlu).
pn(rod).
pn(peter).
```

% D **4.3.6** : **adj**/1
% **adj**(Adjective)

```
adj(long).
adj(clever).
adj(trivial).
adj(colourless).
adj(green).
adj(lost).
adj(one).
adj(many).
adj(high).
adj(big).
```

% D **4.3.7** : **v**/1
% **v**(Verb)

```
v(bit).
v(bites).
v(bitten).
v(took).
v(sleep).
v(sleeps).
v(slept).
v(sits).
v(sat).
v(halt).
v(halts).
v(halted).
v(lives).
v(live).
v(lived).
v(write).
v(writes).
v(wrote).
v(have).
v(has).
v(had).
v(hit).
v(hits).
v(give).
v(gives).
v(gave).
v(builds).
v(built).
```

% D **4.3.8** : **prep**/1
% **prep**(Preposition)

```
prep(as).
prep(at).
prep(by).
prep(from).
prep(in).
prep(into).
prep(near).
prep(of).
prep(on).
prep(through).
prep(to).
prep(towards).
prep(under).
prep(with).
prep(within).
prep(upon).
prep(except).
prep(for).
prep(up).
```

% D **4.3.9** : **adv**/1
% **adv**(Adverb)

```
adv(quickly).
adv(happily).
adv(furiously).
adv(once).
adv(there).
```

% D **4.3.10** : **conj**/1
% **conj**(Conjunction)

```
conj(and).
conj(but).
conj(or).
```

% D **4.3.11** : **aux**/1
% **aux**(Auxiliary)

```
aux(could).
aux(is).
aux(was).
aux(have).
aux(have).
aux(has).
aux(been).
aux(be).
```

% D **4.3.12** : **relpron**/1
% **relpron**(RelativePronoun)

```
relpron(that).
relpron(who).
relpron(whom).
```

% D **4.3.13** : **whpron**/1
% **whpron**(Wh_Pronoun)

```
whpron(who).
whpron(whom).
whpron(what).
```

% D **4.3.14** : **pron**/1
% **pron**(Pronoun)

```
pron(he).
pron(him).
pron(you).
pron(it).
pron(she).
pron(her).
pron(i).
pron(me).
pron(they).
```

Definitions 4.4 : Parse Tree Pretty Printing

```
%  D  4.4.1 : print_tree/1
%              print_tree(T)  prettily prints out a tree T starting from tab of zero

print_tree(Tree) :- print_tree(Tree, 0).
```

```
%  D  4.4.2 : print_tree/2
%              print_tree(TreeOrLeaf, Tab) :  prints out the parse tree
%              The argument Tab takes care to indent it properly accross the screen
%              Clause 1 prints the leaves of the tree - ie 'atoms' - not trees themselves
%              Clause 2 breaks up a clause (indicating a tree) using univ '=..'
%                     it uses the predicate as the root node and its arguments as branches

print_tree(Leaf, Tab) :-
        atomic(Leaf),
        tab(Tab), write('| '),
        write(Leaf), nl.
print_tree(Tree, Tab) :-
        Tree =.. [H | T],
        tab(Tab), write('| '),
        write(H), nl,
        Tab1 is Tab + 5,
        print_list(T, Tab1).
```

```
%  D  4.4.3 : print_list/2
%              print_list(L, T)  prints the branches of a tree in List L at tab Tab
%              the branches are elements in a list L where each is given to print_tree/2
%              one at a time to be printed.  Tab maintains each at the same 'print depth'.

print_list([], _).
print_list([H | T], Tab) :-
        print_tree(H, Tab),
        print_list(T, Tab).
```

```
%  D  4.4.4 : condense/2
%              condense(Tree1, Tree2) means that Tree2 is a more condensed tree than Tree1
%                 actually it has all the 'spare' np2 & vp2 branches pruned out
%              Clause 3 does all the real work turning a clause into a list
%                 handing the list on to condenseL/2 where the clause arguments can be condensed
%                 and then turning the product back into clause-form again.
%              The call to flatten/2 in clause 3 ensures that any
%              Clauses 1 & 2 effectively 'throw away' a specific node if it is np2 or vp2

condense(X, L) :-
    X =.. [np2 | T],
    condenseL(T, L).
condense(X, L) :-
    X =.. [vp2 | T],
    condenseL(T, L).
condense(X, Y) :-
    X =.. [P | T],
    condenseL(T, T1),
    flatten(T1, T2),
    Y =.. [P | T2].
```

```
%  D 4.4.5 : condenseL/2
%            condenseL(ListIn, ListOut)  does the work for condense/2
%            don't need to condense atoms but do need to condense non-atoms

condenseL([], []).
condenseL([H | T], [H | T1]):-
    atom(H), !,
    condenseL(T, T1).
condenseL([H | T], [H1 | T1]):-
    condense(H, H1),
    condenseL(T, T1).
```

Code Appendix 5
Semantics & SAM

Definitions 5.1 : The Full SAM 1 Program Listing

```
%  D 5.1.1 : test_sam1 /1
%           test_sam1(N) says pick a named story N and "SAM Understand" it.

test_sam1(Name):-
    story(Name, Story),
        nl,write('Input Story = '), write(Story), nl, nl,
    sam1(Story, Understood_Story),
        write('Matched Story = '), write(Story), nl, nl,
        write('Matched Script = '), write(Understood_Story), nl.
```

```
%  D 5.1.2 : sam1 /2
%           sam1(IS, FS) means that filled script FS describes input story IS.

sam1(InputStory, ScriptEvents):-
    find(InputStory, ScriptName),
    script(ScriptName, ScriptEvents),
    match(ScriptEvents, InputStory).
```

```
%  D 5.1.3 : find /2
%           find(InputStory, ScriptName) means trigger a ScriptName for the InputStory.

find(InputStory, ScriptName):-
    member(act(_, _, Slots), InputStory),
    member(Word, Slots),
    nonvar(Word),
    trigger(Word, ScriptName).
```

```
%  D 5.1.4 : match /2
%           match(InputStory, ScriptEvents)  means that InputStory is a sub-sequence of ScriptEvents.

match([], _).
match([Ln | RStory], [Ln | RScript]) :- match(RStory, RScript).
match(Story, [_ | RScript]):- match(Story, RScript).
```

```
%  D 5.1.5 : script /2
%           script(Name, List) means that the List is the set of CD acts for a script called Name.

script(restaurant,
    [    act(1, ptrans, [Actor, Actor,   PlaceX,   Restrnt]),
         act(2, ptrans, [Actor, Actor,   Door,     Seat   ]),
         act(3, mtrans, [Actor, Order,   Actor,    Waiter ]),
         act(4, ingest, [Actor, Food,    Plate,    Actor  ]),
         act(5, atrans, [Actor, Money,   Actor,    Waiter ]),
         act(6, ptrans, [Actor, Actor,   Restrnt,  PlaceY ])  ]).
```

```
%  D 5.1.6 : trigger /2
%           trigger(Filler, Script) means that the Filler triggers the named Script

trigger(pizza_hut, restaurant).
trigger(waiter, restaurant).
```

```
%  D 5.1.7 : story /2
%             story(N, List)  this means that a story called N is the list of events represented in List.
%             test1 : john went to pizza_hut, ate a pizza, and left

story(  test1,
        [    act(A, ptrans, [ john, john,  _, pizza_hut]),
             act(B, ingest, [ _,    pizza, _, _         ]),
             act(C, ptrans, [ _,    _,     _, _         ]) ] ) .
```

Definitions 5.2 : The Full SAM 2 Program Listing

```
%  D 5.2.1 : test_sam2 /1
%             Given a named story (Eg  test1, test2, etc) this will organise the "SAM Understanding" of it
%             It uses the primitives 'write'  and 'nl' to "pretty print" the results and
%             uses 'paraphrase_cd' to create English-like output sentences

test_sam2(Name):-
      story(Name, Story), nl,
      write('Input story named '), write(Name), write(' was:'), nl,
      write(Story),
      sam2(Story, ScriptName, Understood_cds),
      write('Script triggered was: '), write(ScriptName), nl, nl,
      write('SAMs CDs are'), nl, write(Understood_cds), nl, nl,
      write('****************'), nl,
      paraphrase_cd(Understood_cds, Understood_Story),
      write('SAMs understanding is : '), nl, nl,
      write(Understood_Story).
```

```
%  D 5.2.2 : sam2/3
%  sam2(InStory, SName, FilledScript) says FilledScript describes InStory according to script SName
%             (i)  'find' the name of a suitable script to help parse the story
%             (ii)  get the contents of this 'script'
%             (iii) 'match' the script contents with the story contents
%             (iv) 'name_defaults' will fill in any unfilled slots with appropriate script defaults

sam2(InputStory, ScriptName, ScriptEvents):-
      find(InputStory, ScriptName),
      script(ScriptName, ScriptEvents, Defaults),
      match(InputStory, ScriptEvents),
      name_defaults(Defaults).
```

```
%  D 5.2.3 : find/2
%  find(InputStory, ScriptName) says trigger a ScriptName for the Story.
%             Works by  finding any constant in the InputStory which can perform as a trigger to a script.
%             Enhanced to look for strong triggers first

find(InputStory, ScriptName):-
      member(TriggerStrength, [strong, medium, weak]),
      member(act(_, _, Slots), InputStory),
      member(Word, Slots),
      nonvar(Word),
      trigger(Word, TriggerStrength, ScriptName).
```

% D 5.2.4 : match/2
%   **match**(InputStory, ScriptEvents) means that InputStory is a sub-sequence of ScriptEvents.

```
match([], AnyScript).
match([Line | Story], [Line | ScriptEvents]) :- match(Story, ScriptEvents).
match(Story, [Line | ScriptEvents]):- match(Story, ScriptEvents).
```

% D 5.2.5 : name_defaults/1
%   **name_defaults**(Variable_DefaultPairs) unifies each Variable in the default pairs
%   with its default if it is still uninstantiated.

```
name_defaults([]).
name_defaults([[(N), (N)] | L]):- name_defaults(L).
name_defaults([[N1, N2] | L]) :- N1 \= N2, name_defaults(L).
```

%%% SAM 2 Restaurant Script %%%
% D 5.2.6 : script/3
% **script**(ScriptName, ScriptEvents, DefaultPairs) The scripts here are much fuller than in the main text

```
script(restaurant,
[    act(1,   ptrans, [Actor, Actor, EarlierPlace, Restaurant]),
     act(2,   ptrans, [Actor, Actor, Door, Table]),
     act(3,   atrans, [WineWaiter, WineList, WineWaiter, Actor]),
     act(4,   mtrans, [Actor, Wine, Actor, WineWaiter]),
     act(5,   atrans, [Waiter, Menu, Waiter, Actor]),
     act(6,   mtrans, [Actor, Order, Actor, Waiter]),
     act(7,   ptrans, [WineWaiter, Wine, Cellar, Table]),
     act(8,   ingest, [Actor, drink(Wine), Glass, mouth(Actor)]),
     act(9,   ptrans, [Waiter, Food, Kitchen, Table]),
     act(10, ingest, [Actor,food(Food), Plate, Actor]),
     act(11, ptrans, [Waiter, Plates, Table, Kitchen]),
     act(11, ptrans, [Waiter, Waiter, Kitchen, Table]),
     act(12, mtrans, [Actor, Coffee, Actor, Waiter]),
     act(13, ptrans, [Waiter, Coffee, Kitchen, Actor]),
     act(14, ingest, [Actor, drink(Coffee), Cup, mouth(Actor)]),
     act(15, atrans, [Waiter, Bill, Waiter, Actor]),
     act(16, atrans, [Actor, Money, Actor, Waiter]),
     act(17, atrans, [Actor, Tip, Actor, Waiter]),
     act(18, ptrans, [Actor, Actor, Restaurant, NextPlace])
        ],
[    [Actor, customer],
     [EarlierPlace, place1],
     [Restaurant, restaurant],
     [Door, door],
     [Table, table],
     [WineWaiter, wine_waiter],
     [WineList, wine_list],
     [Wine, wine],
     [Waiter, waiter],
     [Menu, menu],
     [Order, order],
     [Glass, glass],
     [Cellar, cellar],
     [Food, meal],
     [Kitchen, kitchen],
     [Plate, plate],
     [Plates, dirty_plates],
     [Coffee, coffee],
     [Cup, cup],
     [Bill, bill],
     [Tip, tip],
     [Money, money],
     [NextPlace, place2] ]).
```

```
script(fast_food,
[   act(1,   ptrans, [Actor, Actor, EarlierPlace, Restaurant]),
    act(2,   ptrans, [Actor, Actor, Door, Table]),
    act(3,   atrans, [Hostess, Menu, Hostess, Actor]),
    act(4,   mtrans, [Actor, Order, Actor, Hostess]),
    act(5,   ptrans, [Hostess, Food, Kitchen, Table]),
    act(6,   ingest, [Actor, food(Food), Plate, mouth(Actor)]),
    act(7,   ptrans, [Actor, Actor, Table, Checkout]),
    act(8,   atrans, [Hostess, Bill, Hostess, Actor]),
    act(9,   atrans, [Actor, Money, Actor, Hostess]),
    act(10, ptrans, [Actor, Actor, Restaurant, NextPlace])
    ],
[   [Actor, customer],
    [EarlierPlace, place1],
    [Restaurant, mcdonalds],
    [Door, door],   [Table, table],
    [Menu, menu],   [Hostess, hostess],
    [Order, order],
    [Food, meal],    [Kitchen, kitchen],
    [Checkout, checkout],
    [Plate, plate],
    [Bill, bill],
    [Money, money],
    [NextPlace, place2]
]).
```

% D 5.2.7 : trigger/3
% **trigger**(T, St, ScrN) the trigger word T triggers the script name ScrN with strength St
%   the last clause copes with labelled slots like drink(X), allowing X to act as a trigger word
%   (if it is bound to something specific - ie. not a variable)

```
trigger(waiter, strong, restaurant).
trigger(pizza_hut, weak, restaurant).
trigger(hamburger, strong, fast_food).
trigger(pizza_hut, weak, fast_food).

trigger(Clause, Strength, Name) :-
    Clause =.. [Label, Trigger],
    nonvar(Trigger),
    trigger(Trigger, Strength, Name).
```

% D 5.2.8 : story/2
% **story**(Name, CD_Story) is a sample story in conceptual dependency
% story test1 reads as : "John went to mcdonalds, had a hamburger and left"
% story test2 reads : "John went to a restaurant, had a steak and went home"

```
story(test1,
[   act(One,   ptrans, [ john,  john,                _, mcdonalds] ),
    act(Two,   ingest, [ _,     food(hamburger)., _, _         ] ),
    act(Three, ptrans, [ Actor, Actor,               _, _         ] ) ] ).

story(test2,
[   act(One,   ptrans, [ john,  john,                _, restaurant] ),
    act(Two,   ingest, [ _,     food(steak), _, _          ] ),
    act(Three, ptrans, [ Actor, Actor,               _, home       ] ) ] ).
```

```
% D 5.2.9  : paraphrase_cd/2
% paraphrase_cd(CDs, English) means
%           Declaratively : Take a list of CDs and return a list of English paraphrases
%           Procedurally : Take the head of the CDs list, translate it; and paraphrase the tail of the CDs list

paraphrase_cd([], []).
paraphrase_cd([act(_, CD, Slots) | As], [Engl | Bs]):-
     translate_cd(CD, Slots, Engl),
     paraphrase_cd(As, Bs).
```

```
% D 5.2.10  : translate_cd/3
% translate_cd( CD, [Agent, Object, From, To], EnglishText)
%           translates a CD into English sentence format -  only works for a few key restaurant-type CDs!

translate_cd(ptrans, [A, A, S, D], [A, went, from, S, to, D]).
translate_cd(ptrans, [A, O, S, D],
     [A, brought, the, O, from, the, S, to, the, D]):- A \= O.

translate_cd(mtrans, [A, Message, A, P], [A, told, the, P, the, Message]).

translate_cd(ingest, [A, food(Food), Plate, Mouth], [A, ate, the, Food]).
translate_cd(ingest, [A, drink(Drink), Glass, Mouth], [A, drank, the, Drink]).
translate_cd(ingest, [A, Food, Plate, Mouth], [A, consumed, the, Food]).

translate_cd(atrans, [A, Obj, A, Recip], [A, gave, the, Obj, to, the, Recip]).
```

```
% D 5.2.11  : output/1
%           output(Term) writes a series of Terms to the current output channel.
%           If Term is a list prints each item separated by space.  Otherwise uses standard 'write' form.
%           Can incorporate nl as an item

output([])  :- nl.
output([X|Xs])  :- output1(X), output(Xs).
```

```
% D 5.2.12  : output1/1
%           output1(Term) does all the work for the recursive shell of output/1.

output1([])  :- nl.
output1(nl)  :- nl.
output1([X|Xs]):- write(X), write(' '), output1(Xs).
output1(A):- write(A).
```

Code Appendix 6
Production Systems & Seriation

Definition 6.1   Production Rules for a Naive Seriator

```
rule(f1, [top_goal(seriate), state(just_started)],
             [push_goal(add_first_block), new_state(adding_blocks)]).
rule(f2, [top_goal(add_first_block), holding(Block)],
             [put_block_at_far_left, pop_goal_stack]).
rule(f3, [top_goal(add_first_block), not(heap_empty)],
             [pick_up_nearest_block]).
rule(s1, [top_goal(seriate), hand_empty, heap_empty],
             [pop_goal_stack, new_state(finished)]).
rule(a1, [top_goal(seriate), state(adding_blocks)],
             [push_goal(add_another_block)]).
rule(a2, [top_goal(add_another_block), holding(Block)],
             [pop_goal_stack, push_goal(place_block(Block))]).
rule(a3, [top_goal(add_another_block), not(heap_empty)],
             [pick_up_nearest_block]).
rule(p1, [top_goal(place_block(Block)), holding(Block)],
             [put_block_at_right, pop_goal_stack]).
```

Definition 6.2   Production Rules for a Competent Seriator

```
rule(f1,    [top_goal(seriate), state(just_started)],
              [push_goal(add_first_block)]).
rule(f2,    [top_goal(add_first_block), holding(Block)],
              [put_block_at_far_left, new_state(new_arrangement), pop_goal_stack]).
rule(f3,    [top_goal(add_first_block), not(heap_empty)], [pick_up_biggest_block]).

rule(s1,    [top_goal(seriate), hand_empty, heap_empty],
              [pop_goal_stack, new_state(finished)]).

rule(a1,    [top_goal(seriate)], [push_goal(add_another_block)]).
rule(a2,    [top_goal(add_another_block), holding(Block)],
              [pop_goal_stack, push_goal(place_block(Block))]).
rule(a3,    [top_goal(add_another_block), not(heap_empty)],
              [pick_up_nearest_block]).

rule(p1,    [top_goal(place_block(Block)), holding(Block)],
              [put_block_at_right, new_state(new_arrangement)]).

rule(e1,    [top_goal(place_block(Block)), state(new_arrangement)],
              [examine(Block, Result), new_state(checked(Result))] ).
rule(e2,    [top_goal(place_block(Block)), state(checked(ok))], [pop_goal_stack]).
rule(e3,    [top_goal(place_block(Block)), state(checked(wrong))],
              [switch_blocks(Block, Left), new_state(new_arrangement)]).
```

Definitions 6.3   Seriation Various

```
% D 6.3.1 : seriate/0
%           seriate attempts to achieve the full seriation task

seriate:-
      initialise,
      apply_productions(1),
      write('Finished'), nl.
seriate:-
      write('Failed!'), nl, fail.
```

```
% D 6.3.2 : apply_productions/1
%           apply_productions(N) is the meta-interpreter for the production rule system
%           N counts the number of times (since the first call) that a production has fired
%           only a toy meta-interpreter since there is no explicit conflict resolution

apply_productions(_) :-
      state(finished).
apply_productions(N) :-
      rule(Identifier, PrecondList, ActionsList),
      call_list(PrecondList),
      call_list(ActionsList),
      display_status(N, Identifier, PrecondList, ActionsList),
      N1 is N + 1,
      !,
      apply_productions(N1).
```

```
% D 6.3.3 : call_list/1
%           call_list(Goals) attempts to prove each element of the list Goals in turn.
%           Succeeds only if each one is true
%           uses the built-in primitive call(X) which has the same effect as the query X

call_list([]).
call_list([Goal | Remains] ) :-
      call(Goal),
      call_list(Remains).
```

```
% D 6.3.4 : Initialise/0
%           Initialise sets all of the micro-world and memory definitions to their starting state
%           For some Prologs you may have to declare the definitions asserted here as dynamic.

initialise :-
      retractall( goal_stack(_) ),
      retractall( state(_)      ),
      retractall( hand(_)       ),
      retractall( heap(_)       ),
      retractall( table(_, _)   ),
      assert( goal_stack([seriate])   ),
      assert( state(just_started)     ),
      assert( hand(empty)             ),
      assert( heap([ccc, a, dddd, bb]) ),
      assertz( table(1, free) ),
      assertz( table(2, free) ),
      assertz( table(3, free) ),
      assertz( table(4, free) ),
      write_list(['initial arrangement on heap:  ', [ccc, a, dddd, bb], nl]), !.
```

```
%  D 6.3.5 : top_goal/1
%           top_goal(G) states that G is the current top goal on the goal stack

top_goal(X):- goal_stack([X|_]).
```

```
%  D 6.3.6 : push_goal/1
%           push_goal(G) changes the current goal stack to have a new top goal G

push_goal(X)  :-
       retract(goal_stack(Stack)),
       assert(goal_stack([X | Stack])), !.
```

```
%  D 6.3.7 : pop_goal_stack/0
%           pop_goal_stack deletes the current top goal on the goal stack

pop_goal_stack  :-
       retract(goal_stack([_|T])),
       assert(goal_stack(T)), !.
```

```
%  D 6.3.8 : new_state/1
%           new_state(S) states that S is to be the new state of the micro-world

new_state(State)  :-
       retract(state(_)),
       asserta(state(State)).
```

```
%  D 6.3.9 : holding/1
%           holding(B) states that the system is currently holding a block in its hand

holding(B)  :- hand(B), not(B = empty).
```

```
%  D 6.3.10 : heap_empty/0
%           heap_empty states that there are no blocks left in the heap

heap_empty :- heap([]).
```

```
%  D 6.3.11 : hand_empty/0
%           hand_empty states that the systems hand is empty

hand_empty :- hand(empty).
```

```
%  D 6.3.12 : pick_up_block/1
%           pick_up_block(B) is an action which deletes a specific block B from the heap and
%           puts it in the simulators hand

pick_up_block(B)  :-
       hand(empty),
       heap(H),
       member(B, H),
       retract(heap(H)),
       retract(hand(empty)),
       del(B, H, NewH),
       assert(heap(NewH)),
       assert(hand(B)).
```

```
%  D 6.3.13 : pick_up_nearest_block/0
%           pick_up_nearest_block is an action which picks up the first block it finds in the heap

pick_up_nearest_block :-
        heap([ Block | _ ]),
        pick_up_block(Block).
```

```
%  D 6.3.14 : pick_up_biggest_block/0
%           pick_up_biggest_block is an action which picks up the biggest block it finds in the heap
%           it uses the predicate bsort/3 to find the biggest block in the heap

pick_up_biggest_block :-
        heap(H),
        bsort(H, [ BigBlock | _ ]),
        pick_up_block(BigBlock).
```

```
%  D 6.3.15 : put_block_at_far_left/0
%           put_block_at_far_left says that if the far left place in the table line is free
%           then put down the block there

put_block_at_far_left :-
        table(1, free),
        put_block_at_right.
```

```
%  D 6.3.16 : put_block_at_right/0
%           put_block_at_right says that if the simulator is holding a block then put it down
%           at the next free position to the right of the current line on the table

put_block_at_right :-
        holding(Block),
        retract(hand(Block)),
        retract(table(N, free)),
        assert(hand(empty)),
        assertz(table(N, Block)).
```

```
%  D 6.3.17 : examine/2
%           examine(B, IsOk) examines the block B relative to the block to its immediate left.
%           IsOk is bound to 'ok' if B is smaller than the block to its left, or 'wrong' if not.

examine(Block, ok) :-
        table(1, Block), !.
examine(Block, IsOk) :-
        table(N, Block),
        N1 is N - 1,
        table(N1, Block1),
        bigger_than(Block1, Block, IsOk).
```

```
%  D 6.3.18 : bigger_than/3
%           bigger_than(B1, B2, IsOk) if B1 greater-than-or-equal-to B2 then IsOk is bound to 'ok'
%           if B1 is less than B2 then IsOk will be bound to 'wrong'.  Does the comparing for examine/2.
%           This works for the blocks because these arithmetic comparison operators should work with
%           the characters a-z with a < z. So dddd > ccc > bb > a.

bigger_than(A, B, ok) :- A > B.
bigger_than(A, B, wrong) :- A < B.
```

% **D 6.3.19** : **switch_blocks**/2
%   **switch_blocks**(B1, B2) will switch the positions of two blocks on the table.
%   It says that B1 is to be changed with the block to its immediate left B2.

```
switch_blocks(Block, _) :-
     table(1, Block), !.
switch_blocks(Block, Left) :-
     table(N, Block),
     N1 is N - 1,
     table(N1, Left),
     retract(table(N, Block)),
     asserta(table(N1, Block)),
     retract(table(N1, Left)),
     asserta(table(N, Left)), !.
```

Definitions 6.4   Input-Output predicates for the Production system

```
% D 6.4.1 : display_status/4
%           display_status(N, Identifier, PrecondList, ActionsList)
%           displays current status - rule just fired, its conditions & the actions, plus the current state of WM
%           can have either 'simple' display (which gives brief details) or a full
%           display (which shows everything) depending on the value of the predicate flag/1

display_status(N, Identifier, _, Actions):-
      flag(simple_output),
      write_list([N,'  From Rule ', Identifier, ' : ']),
      writelts(Actions, ' & '), nl,
      display_blocks, nl, !.
display_status(N, Identifier, PrecondList, ActionsList):-
      flag(complex_output),
      display_rule(N, Identifier, PrecondList, ActionsList),
      display_blocks,
      goal_stack(GS),
      state(St),
      write_list([':  Goal Stack : ', GS, nl,
                  ':  State : ', St, nl
                 ]).
```

```
% D 6.4.2 : flag/1
%           flag is a simple setting that can give either 'complex_output' or 'simple_output'
%           it is used by display_status to affect the detail printed out

flag(simple_output).
```

```
% D 6.4.3 : display_rule/4
%           display_rule(N, Identifier, PrecondList, ActionsList)  <-
%           displays the rule which has just fired, labelling it with N = how many fired up to now

display_rule(N, Identifier, PrecondList, ActionsList) :-
      nl,
      write_list([N, '   By rule ', Identifier, nl,
                  ' IF', tab(8), elts(PrecondList), nl,
                  ' THEN ',   tab(2), elts(ActionsList), nl
                 ]).
```

```
% D 6.4.4 : display_blocks/0
%           display_blocks displays the position of the blocks in terms of table, hand, heap

display_blocks :-
      whole_table(Table),
      hand(Hand),
      heap(Heap),
      write_list([':  Table : { ', elts(Table, ' >> '), ' }', nl,
                  ':   Hand : ', Hand, nl,
                  ':   Heap : ', Heap, nl
                 ]).
```

```
% D 6.4.5 : whole_table/4
%           whole_table(T)  determines the current 'fillers' for the 4 slots on the table

whole_table([B1, B2, B3, B4]) :-
     table(1, B1),
     table(2, B2),
     table(3, B3),
     table(4, B4).
```

```
% D 6.4.6 : write_list/1
%           A specialised form of the writel/1 utility given in appendix 1.

write_list([]).
write_list([X | Xs]):-
     write_element(X), !,
     write_list(Xs).
```

```
% D 6.4.7 : write_element/2
%           write_element(X, Sep) writes element X then Sep
%           with appropriate action for X = nl or tab(N)
%           if element X is a list prints it out with elements separated by Sep

write_element(nl)  :- nl.
write_element(tab(N))  :- tab(N).
write_element(elts(X))  :- writelts(X).
write_element(elts(X, Sep))  :- writelts(X, Sep).
write_element(X)  :- write(X).
```

```
% D 6.4.8 : writelts/1
%           writelts(L) writes out its argument list L with each element joined by the separator &

writelts(X)  :- writelts(X, ' & '), !.
```

```
% D 6.4.9 : writelts/2
%           writelts(L, S)  writes out a list L joined by the separator S

writelts([], _):- write([]).
writelts([X], _)  :- write(X), !.    %  last element of list
writelts([X | Xs], Sep):-
     write(X), write(Sep),
     writelts(Xs, Sep).
```

%%% general utilities %%%

```
% D 6.4.10 : bsort/2
%           bsort(L1, L2) means that L2 is list L1 with all of the elements "bubble" sorted
%           It is not efficient as it just keeps looking for things to.swap in L1 and  keeps recursing
%           on its first clause until it cannot find two things to swap then clause 2 succeeds trivially.

bsort(List, SortedList):- swap(List, List1), !, bsort(List1, SortedList).
bsort(List, List).
```

```
% D 6.4.11 : swap/2
%           swap(L1, L2) attempts to find two elements to swap in L1 returning L2
%           it insists that the bigger elements must come first !

swap([X, Y | Rest], [Y, X | Rest]):- X < Y.
swap([X | Rest], [X | Rest1]):- swap(Rest, Rest1).
```

% **D 6.4.12** : **del**/3
%   Used in defn 7.3.12 to delete a block from the heap list
%   **del**(E, L1, L2) says that L2 is the list L1 with the first element E deleted from it.
%   The first clause is the stopping check - if E is at the head of L1 then just return the tail
%   otherwise clause two says that it E cannot be bound with Y then return Y with the list L
%   after you have successfully deleted E from list L (leaving L1)

```
del(E, [E | L], L).
del(E, [Y | L], [Y | L1]):- E \= Y, del(E, L, L1).
```

Code Appendix 7
Search, Planning & STRIPS

In the following set of definitions: **member**/2 is used.

Definitions 7.1   Depth First Problem Solving

%%% The Blocks World Representation %%%

% **D 7.1.1** : **block**/1
%   **block**(B).states that the thing named B is a block in the blocks-world

```
block(a).
block(b).
block(c).
```

% **D 7.1.2** : **place**/1
%   place(P) states that the thing named P is a place on table of the blocks-world

```
place(pile1).
place(pile2).
place(pile3).
```

% **D 7.1.3** : **legal_action**/2
%   **legal_action**(Action, State) says Action is legal in state State
%   The Action will be bound to a 'move' of a Block from somewhere X to a Destination.
%   Remember that State is a list of upon/2's stating which blocks are upon what.

```
legal_action(move(Block, X, Destination), State) :-
        upon(Block, X, State),           % find a Block in the State
        is_clear(Block, State),          % check that Block is clear
        is_clear(Destination, State),    % find first clear place or block to go to
        Block \= Destination.
```

% **D 7.1.4** : **is_clear**/2
%   **is_clear**(Thing, State) says that Thing is clear in state State
%   where Thing can be a block or a place (pile) and State is a list of upon's.

```
is_clear(Block, State) :- block(Block), not(member(upon(_,Block), State) ).
is_clear(Place, State) :- place(Place), not(member(upon(_,Place), State) ).
```

% **D 7.1.5** : **upon**/3
%   **upon**(X, Y, S) means that block X is on block or place Y in state S
%   It searches through the S state list for upon/2's and re-presents them in this form

```
upon(X, Y, State) :- member(upon(X, Y), State).
```

%%% Brute-force searches %%%

```
% D 7.1.6 : df0/3
%          df0(NDepth, Start, Goal) tries to transform Start state into Goal state
% The df stands for depth-first! This is 0 because it is using "only" left-first depth first search.
% Almost always falls into non-terminating loop.
% NDepth is the index of depth of recursion to make the printout more informative.

df0(_,State, State) :- write('**  success **').        %  stopping condition
df0(N, State, GoalState) :-
     legal_action(Action, State),                      %  find an Action to try
     update_state(Action, State, NewState),            %  find the NewState
     display_states(N, Action, State, NewState),
     N1 is N+1,
     df0(N1, NewState, GoalState).                      %  recurse
```

```
% D 7.1.7 : df1/4
%          df1(NDepth, Start, Goal, Visited) finds a plan to move from Start to Goal state
% An improvement on df0 in that avoids infinite loop by storing states visited in the list Visited
% and forbidding re-visits. NDepth monitors depth of recursion as before.

df1(N, State, State, Visited) :- write('**  success **'), nl,nl.
df1(N, State, Goal, Visited) :-
     legal_action(Action, State),
     update_state(Action, State, NewState),
     not(member(NewState, Visited)),
     display_states(N, Action, State, NewState),
     N1 is N+1,
     df1(N1, NewState, Goal, [NewState | Visited]).
df1(N,_,_,_) :-
     N1 is N-1,
     write('***   Dead end - backtrack over action '),
     write(N1), write(' ***'), nl, fail.
```

```
% D 7.1.8 : df2/4
%          df2(NDepth , State, GoalState, Visited) transforms State into GoalState heuristically
% improvement on df1 in that it uses domain-dependent heuristic to guide search

df2(_, State, State, _) :- write(' ** success **'), nl.
df2(N, State, GoalState, Visited) :-
     suggest(GoalState, State, Action),                %  use a heuristic
     write('*** Suggested action: '),
     write(Action), nl,
     update_state(Action, State, NewState),
     not(member(NewState, Visited)),                   %  prevent loop
        display_states(N, Action, State, NewState),
     N1 is N+1,
     df2(N1, NewState, GoalState, [NewState | Visited]).
df2(N, _, _, _) :-
     N1 is N-1,
     write('***   Dead end - backtrack over action '),
     write(N1), write(' ***'), nl, fail.
```

% **D 7.1.9** : **update_state**/3
% **update_state**(move(X, Y, Z), OldState, NewState) says Action changes OldState to NewState
%   NB. also maintains order of blocks in State

```
update_state(move(X, Y, Z), State, NewState) :-
     list_substitute(upon(X, Y), upon(X, Z), State, NewState).
```

% **D 7.1.10** : **suggest**/3
%   **suggest**(TargetState, CurrentState, Action) attempts to use heuristic knowledge
%   about the blocks world.   Heuristic used is:
%   (i) Action results in correct positioning of a base block in TargetState & is legal from CurrentState.
%   OR
%   (ii) Action is legal from CurrentState.

```
suggest(TargetState, CurrentState, move(Block, _, Place)) :-
     upon(Block, Place, TargetState),
     place(Place),
     legal_action(move(Block, _, Place), CurrentState).
suggest(_, CurrentState, Move) :-
     legal_action(Move, CurrentState).
```

%%%   Testing Depth First search   %%%

% **D 7.1.11-13** : **test_df0**/1 ; **test_df1**/1 ; **test_df2**/1
%   **test_df?**(Name) performs a depth first search to transform Start state into Goal state
%   eg. the query test_df1(test2) tries to 'solve' test2 using search df1
%   In df1 & 2 the first element of the list of visited states is the start state StartS.
%   All searches start off with the print-counter set to 1.

```
test_df0(Name) :-
     test_states(Name, StartS, GoalS),
       piles(StartS, P0),
       write('** Initial State:  '), write(P0), nl,
       piles(GoalS, PG),
       write('** Goal State:     '), write(PG), nl,
     df0(1, StartS, GoalS).

test_df1(Name) :-
     test_states(Name, StartS, GoalS),
       piles(StartS, P0),
       write('** Initial State:  '), write(P0), nl,
       piles(GoalS, PG),
       write('** Goal State:     '), write(PG), nl;
     df1(1, StartS, GoalS, [StartS]).

test_df2(Name) :-
     test_states(Name, StartS, GoalS),
       piles(StartS, P0),
       write('** Initial State:  '), write(P0), nl,
       piles(GoalS, PG),
       write('** Goal State:     '), write(PG), nl,
     df2(1, StartS, GoalS, [StartS]).
```

```
% D 7.1.14 : test_states/3
%           test_states(N, S, G) means that the test named N starts with state S and ends with state G
%    these provide a set of three named test configurations of initial state and goal state.
%    test1 says turn [a, b]  []  [c] into []   []   [a, b, c]
%    test2 says turn [b]  []  [a, c] into []   []   [a, b, c]
%    test3 says turn [b]  []  [a, c] into [a, b, c]  []   []
```

```
test_states(test1,
    [ upon(a,b),  upon(b,pile1),  upon(c,pile3) ],
    [ upon(a,b),  upon(b,c),      upon(c,pile3) ] ).
test_states(test2,
    [ upon(a,c),  upon(b,pile1),  upon(c,pile3) ],
    [ upon(a,b),  upon(b,c),      upon(c,pile3) ] ).
test_states(test3,
    [ upon(a,c),  upon(b,pile1),  upon(c,pile3) ],
    [ upon(a,b),  upon(b,c),      upon(c,pile1) ] ).
```

```
% D 7.1.15 : display_states/4
%           display_states(N, Action, State, NewState) displays effects of Action on the states
```

```
display_states(N, Action, State, NewState) :-
        write('Action '), write(N), write(':  '), write(Action), nl,
      piles(State,[P1, P2, P3]),
        tab(5), write('from state:  '),
        write(P1), write('  '), write(P2), write('  '), write(P3), nl,
      piles(NewState,[Q1, Q2, Q3]),
        tab(5), write('to state:  '),
        write(Q1), write('  '), write(Q2), write('  '), write(Q3), nl.
```

```
% D 7.1.16 : piles/2
%           piles(State,Piles)  shows the given State as the three piles
```

```
piles(State,[P1, P2, P3]) :-
      upon_pile(State, pile1, P1),
      upon_pile(State, pile2, P2),
      upon_pile(State, pile3, P3), !.
      %    the cut prevents upon_pile being re-statisfied
```

```
% D 7.1.17 : upon_pile/3
%           upon_pile(State,Pile,Blocks)  says that Blocks is the list of blocks on  a specific Pile in State
%    eg. upon_pile ([ upon(a,c), upon(b,pile2), upon(c,pile3) ], pile3, [a,c] )
```

```
upon_pile(State, Pile, [B1, B2, B3, B4]) :-
      upon(B1, B2, State),
      upon(B2, B3, State),
      upon(B3, B4, State),
      upon(B4, Pile, State).
upon_pile(State, Pile, [B1, B2, B3]) :-
      upon(B1, B2, State),
      upon(B2, B3, State),
      upon(B3, Pile, State).
upon_pile(State, Pile, [B1, B2]) :-
      upon(B1, B2, State),
      upon(B2, Pile, State).
upon_pile(State, Pile,[B1]) :-
      upon(B1, Pile, State).
upon_pile(State, Pile, []).
```

% D 7.1.18 : list_substitute/4

% **list_substitute**(Old, New, OldList, NewList) says that

% NewList is the result of replacing all occurrences of Old in OldList by New

```
list_substitute(X, Y, [], []).
list_substitute(X, Y, [X|Xt], [Y|Yt]):- list_substitute(X, Y, Xt, Yt).
list_substitute(X, Y, [Z|Zt], [Z|Yt]):- Z \= X, list_substitute(X, Y, Zt, Yt).
```

Definitions 7.2 -- STRIPS

% D 7.2.1 : strips/2

%   **strips**(SS, GS) says generate and output a plan to turn start state SS into the goal state GS.

```
strips(StartState, GoalState):-
    write('** Goals: '), nl,
    write_list(GoalState), nl,
    .plan(1, GoalState,StartState, [], FinalState, Plan),
    nl, write('**  Complete Plan is'), nl, write_list(Plan), nl.
```

% D 7.2.2 : plan/6

%   **plan**(NOps, GList, CState, CPlan, NState, NPlan) plans to achieve a list of goals.

%   NOps refers to the number of operations/actions involved - it is used just for the printout

%   GList is the list of goals; CState refers to the current state whilst and NState is the new one

%   resulting from solve-ing one action.

%   CPlan and NPlan refer to the current and new plans that go along with the states.

%   These are built up so that they can be printed out to the user as it progresses.

```
plan(_, [], State, Plan, State, Plan).
plan(N, [G | Goals], State, Plan, GoalState, GoalPlan):-
    solve(N, G, State, Plan, State1, Plan1),
    plan(N, Goals, State1, Plan1, GoalState, GoalPlan).
```

% D 7.2.3 : solve/6

%   **solve**(NOps, Goal, CurrentState, CurrentPlan, NewState, NewPlan)

%   tries to achieve a single Goal either by checking whether it is currently true

%   or by finding an Action and planning to achieve its list of Preconds

```
solve(_, Goal, State, Plan, State, Plan):-   % solved trivially if Goal always true
    always(TrueFacts),
    member(Goal, TrueFacts).
solve(_, Goal, State, Plan, State, Plan):-    % or if Goal true in current state
    member(Goal,State ).
solve(N, Goal, State, Plan, NewState, [Action|Plan1]):-
        pp1(N, Goal),
    can(Action, Preconds, Dels, Adds),     % look for an appropriate Action
    member(Goal, Adds),                    % which has the Goal in its addlist
    pp2(N, Action, Preconds),
    N1 is N + 1,
    plan(N1, Preconds, State, Plan, State1, Plan1),   % plan to achieve the PreConds
    update_state(Dels, Adds, State1, NewState),       % update the state
    pp3(N, Goal).
```

% **D 7.2.4** : **update_state**/4
%   **update_state**(DeleteList, AddList, State, NewState) says
%   NewState is State minus the delete-list DeleteList plus the AddList

```
update_state(DeleteList, AddList, State, NewState) :-
     del(DeleteList, State, State1),
     add(AddList, State1, NewState).
```

%%% Strips Utilities %%%

% **D 7.2.5** : **del**/3
%   **del**(DelList, List,NewList) says NewList comprises the elements of List which are not in DelList
%   This definition of del/3 is very similar to the one given in D 6.4.12 except that it deletes a list
%   of elements rather than a single one - and all occurrences rather than just the first.

```
del(_, [], []).
del(Del, [X | Xs], [X | Ys]) :-
   non_member(X, Del),
   del(Del, Xs, Ys).
del(Del, [X | Xs], Ys) :-
   member(X, Del),
   del(Del, Xs, Ys).
```

% **D 7.2.6** : **add**/3
%   **add**(AddList, List, NewList) says NewList is List appended to AddList avoiding duplicates

```
add([],List2,List2).
add([X|Xs],List2,[X|Ys]):-
   non_member(X,List2),
   add(Xs,List2,Ys).
add([X|Xs],List2,Ys ):-
   member(X,List2),
   add(Xs,List2,Ys).
```

% **D 7.2.7** : **non_member**/2
%   **non_member**(X, List) if X is not a member of List

```
non_member(X, []).
non_member(X, [Y | Ys]) :-
   X \= Y,
   non_member(X, Ys).
```

% **D 7.2.8** : **test**/1
%   **test**(N) runs the strips program with different goals on the start_state/1 in the database

```
test(1) :-
     start_state(StartState),
     strips(StartState,  [at(robot, point(1) )] ).
test(2) :-
     start_state(StartState),
     strips(StartState,  [at(robot, point(5) )] ).
test(3) :-
     start_state(StartState),
     strips(StartState,  [at(robot, point(6) )] ).

test(4) :-
     start_state(StartState),
     strips(StartState,  [next_to(box(1), box(2) ), next_to(box(3), box(2))] ).
test(5) :-
     start_state(StartState),
     strips(StartState,  [at(box(1), point(3) ) , at(box(3), point(1))] ).
```

```
test(6)  :-
     start_state(StartState),
     strips(StartState,  [in_room(box(1), room(2) )] ).
test(7)  :-
     start_state(StartState),
     strips(StartState,  [at(box(1), point(6) )] ).

test(8)  :-
     start_state(StartState),
     strips(StartState,  [status(switch(1), on)] ).
test(9)  :-
     start_state(StartState),
     strips(StartState,  [on(robot,box(1)), at(robot,point(6))] ).
test(10)  :-
     start_state(StartState),
     strips(StartState,  [ at(robot,point(6)), on(robot,box(1))] ).
```

%%% The Robot World %%%

% **D 7.2.9** : **always**/1
%   **always**(L) gives the list L of all the unchangable facts
%   always true in this STRIPS environment

```
always([
     pushable(box(1)),
     pushable(box(2)),
     pushable(box(3)),
     location(point(1),  room(1)),
     location(point(2),  room(1)),
     location(point(3),  room(1)),
     location(point(4),  room(1)),
     location(point(5),  room(5)),
     location(point(6),  room(4)),
     in_room(switch(1),  room(1)),
     at(switch(1),  point(4)),
     connects(door(1),  room(1),  room(5)),
     connects(door(1),  room(5),  room(1)),
     connects(door(2),  room(2),  room(5)),
     connects(door(2),  room(5),  room(2)),
     connects(door(3),  room(3),  room(5)),
     connects(door(3),  room(5),  room(3)),
     connects(door(4),  room(4),  room(5)),
     connects(door(4),  room(5),  room(4)),
     in_room(door(1),  room(1)),  in_room(door(1),  room(5)),
     in_room(door(2),  room(2)),  in_room(door(2),  room(5)),
     in_room(door(3),  room(3)),  in_room(door(3),  room(5)),
     in_room(door(4),  room(4)),  in_room(door(4),  room(5))
     ]).
```

```
%  D 7.2.10 : start_state/1
%           start_state(L) says that the list L contains the changable facts
%           that make up the start state in this strips environment

start_state([
    at( box(1), point(1) ),
    at( box(2), point(2) ),
    at( box(3), point(3) ),
    at( robot,  point(4) ),
    in_room( box(1), room(1) ),
    in_room( box(2), room(1) ),
    in_room( box(3), room(1) ),
    in_room(robot, room(1) ),
    status(switch(1), off),
    on_floor
    ]).
```

%%% Strips Pretty Print Output Utilities %%%

```
%  D 7.2.11 : write_list/1
%           write_list(L) writes a list of items  L in reverse order, one element per line

write_list([X|Xs]):-
    write_list1(Xs),
    write(X), nl.
write_list([]):- write('Nothing need be done.'), nl.
```

```
%  D 7.2.12 : write_list1/1
%           write_list1(L) does all the work for write_list/1.

write_list1([]).
write_list1([X|Xs]):-
    !,
    write_list1(Xs),
    write(X), nl.
```

```
%  D 7.2.13-5 : pp1 to pp3/2
%           pretty print out messages with the right messages and tabs.

pp1(N, G):-
    write(N), write(': '),
    pin(N),
    write('Trying to achieve : '), write(G),
    nl, !.

pp2(N, A, P):-
    N1 is ((N + 5) * 2),
    tab(N1), write('Action : '), write(A), nl,
    tab(N1), write('Conditions : '), writesp(P), nl, !.

pp3(N, G):-
    write(N), write(': '),
    pout(N),
    write('Achieved Goal : '), write(G), nl, !.
```

```
%  D 7.2.16 : pin/1
%           pretty print out the right number of indented arrows in.

pin(0):-!.
pin(N):- write('>>'), N1 is N - 1, pin(N1).
```

% **D 7.2.17** : **pout**/1
%   pretty print out the right number of indented arrows out.

```
pout(0):-!.
pout(N):- write('<<'), N1 is N - 1, pout(N1).
```

% **D 7.2.18** : **writesp**/1
%   pretty print a list with & between all elements but the last.

```
writesp([]).
writesp([X]):- write(X), !.
writesp([H|T]):- write(H), write(' & '), writesp(T).
```

Definition 7.3   STRIPS Robot world operators -- can/4

% **can**(Action, Preconditions, Del, Add) says
%   Action is possible only if Preconditions are true.
%   After Action is applied the list Del is to be deleted from current state
%   and the list Add is to be added to it
%   NB. This definition is incomplete - you finish it via the exercises!

% the first three operators relate to the robot walking around:
%   walk_to(Place, Room)
%   walk_next_to(BoxOrDoor, Room)
%   walk_through(Door, Room1, Room2)

```
can( walk_to(Place, Room),

/* if  */       [location(Place, Room), in_room(robot, Room), on_floor],
/* del */       [at(robot, _), next_to(robot, Box), next_to(Box, robot)],
/* add */       [at(robot, Place)]).

can( walk_next_to(BoxOrDoor, Room),

/* if  */       [in_room(robot, Room), in_room(BoxOrDoor, Room), on_floor],
/* del */       [at(robot, _), next_to(robot, Box), next_to(Box, robot)],
/* add */       [next_to(robot, BoxOrDoor)]).

can( walk_through(Door, Room1, Room2),

/* if  */       [in_room(robot, Room1), connects(Door, Room1, Room2),
                  next_to(robot, Door), on_floor],
/* del */       [next_to(robot, box(Box)), next_to(box(Box), robot),
                  at(robot, _), in_room(robot, Room1)],
/* add */       [in_room(robot, Room2)]).
```

```
%  now the operators relating to box pushing:
%            push_to(Box, point(N), Room)
%            push_next_to(Box, BoxOrDoor, Room)
%            push_through(Box, Door, Room1, Room2)

can( push_to(Box, point(N), Room),

/* if  */         [pushable(Box), location(point(N), Room),
                     in_room(Box, Room), next_to(robot,Box), on_floor],
/* del */         [at(robot, _), at(Box, point(_)), next_to(Box, _)],
/* add */         [at(Box, point(N)), at(robot, unknown)]).

can( push_next_to(Box, BoxOrDoor, Room),

/* if  */         [pushable(unknown),  in_room(Box, Room),
                     in_room(BoxOrDoor, Room),next_to(robot,Box), on_floor],
/* del */         [at(Box, _), at(robot, _),  next_to(Box, _)],
/* add */         [next_to(Box, BoxOrDoor), next_to(BoxOrDoor, Box)]).

can( push_through(Box, Door, Room1, Room2),

/* if  */         [connects(Door, Room1, Room2), in_room(Box, Room1),
                     in_room(robot, Room1), next_to(Box, Door),
                     next_to(robot, Door), on_floor],
/* del */         [in_room(robot, Room1), in_room(Box, Room1)],
/* add */         [unknown]).

% these four operators relate to turning on light switches:
%            turn_on( switch(S) )
%            turn_off( switch(S) )
%            climb_on(box(B))
%            climb_off(box(B))

can( turn_on( switch(S) ),

/* if  */         [at(switch(S), Point), at(box(N), Point ), on(robot, box(N) )],
/* del */         [status(switch(S), _)],
/* add */         unknown).

can( turn_off( switch(S) ),

/* if  */         [at(switch(S), Point), at(box(N), Point ), on(robot, box(N) )],
/* del */         unknown,
/* add */         unknown).

can( climb_on(box(B)),

/* if  */         [next_to(robot, box(B)), on_floor],
/* del */         [on_floor],
/* add */         [on(robot, box(B))]).

can( climb_off(box(B)),

/* if  */         [on(robot, box(B))],
/* del */         unknown,
/* add */         unknown).
```

Definitions 7.4   A complete can/4 definition

```
can( walk_to(Place, Room),
/* if  */        [ location(Place, Room), in_room(robot, Room), on_floor  ],
/* del */        [ at(robot, _), next_to(robot, Box), next_to(Box, robot) ],
/* add */        [ at(robot, Place) ]).

can( walk_next_to(BoxOrDoor, Room),
/* if  */        [ in_room(robot, Room), in_room(BoxOrDoor, Room), on_floor ],
/* del */        [ at(robot, _), next_to(robot, Box), next_to(Box, robot) ],
/* add */        [ next_to(robot, BoxOrDoor) ]).

can( walk_through(Door, Room1, Room2),
/* if  */        [ in_room(robot, Room1), connects(Door, Room1, Room2),
                    next_to(robot, Door), on_floor],
/* del */        [ next_to(robot, box(Box)), next_to(box(Box), robot),
                    at(robot, _), in_room(robot, Room1) ],
/* add */        [ in_room(robot, Room2) ]).

can( push_to(Box, point(N), Room),
/* if  */        [ pushable(Box), location(point(N), Room), in_room(Box, Room),
                    next_to(robot,Box), on_floor ],
/* del */        [ at(robot, _), at(Box, point(_)), next_to(Box, _) ],
/* add */        [ at(Box, point(N)), at(robot, point(N)) ]).

can( push_next_to(Box, BoxOrDoor, Room),
/* if  */        [ pushable(Box), in_room(Box, Room),
                    in_room(BoxOrDoor, Room),next_to(robot,Box), on_floor ],
/* del */        [ at(Box, _), at(robot, _), next_to(Box, _) ],
/* add */        [ next_to(Box, BoxOrDoor), next_to(BoxOrDoor, Box),
                    next_to(robot, BoxOrDoor) ]).

can( push_through(Box, Door, Room1, Room2),
/* if  */        [ connects(Door, Room1, Room2), in_room(Box, Room1),
                    in_room(robot, Room1), next_to(Box, Door),
                    next_to(robot, Door), on_floor ],
/* del */        [ in_room(robot, Room1), in_room(Box, Room1) ],
/* add */        [ in_room(robot, Room2), in_room(Box, Room2) ]).

can( turn_on( switch(S) ),
/* if  */        [ at(switch(S), Point), at(box(N), Point ), on(robot, box(N)) ],
/* del */        [ status(switch(S), _) ],
/* add */        [ status(switch(S), on) ]).

can( turn_off( switch(S) ),
/* if  */        [ at(switch(S), Point), at(box(N), Point ), on(robot, box(N)) ],
/* del */        [ status(switch(S), _) ],
/* add */        [ status(switch(S), off) ]).

can( climb_on( box(B) ),
/* if  */        [ next_to(robot, box(B)), on_floor ],
/* del */        [ on_floor ],
/* add */        [ on(robot, box(B)) ]).

can( climb_off( box(B) ),
/* if  */        [ on(robot, box(B)) ],
/* del */        [ on(robot, box(B)) ],
/* add */        [ on_floor ]).
```

Subject and Selected Definitions
Index

COGNITIVE SCIENCE PROJECTS IN PROLOG
SOFTWARE ORDER FORM

The software described in *Cognitive Science Projects in Prolog* is available on floppy disk for both Apple Macintosh (3.5" disk) and MS-DOS microcomputers (IBM PC compatible, 3.5" or 5.25" disk). In both instances the code is the "Edinburgh" standard dialect of the Prolog language. The disk contains full versions of the code which is presented in the book. Rather than laboriously type out the program code in the relevant book appendix with all the problems and errors that this can produce, you can just directly load it from the single disk.

   The disk includes a text file which explains all the contents and how they relate to the book programs. The programs are provided as simple text files that may be loaded into any standard version of Prolog or into a word processor. In addition the Apple Macintosh version contains a set of program files prepared especially for users of Logic Programming Associates' MacProlog™. These files contain not only all the documented programs in the book, but some further programs which make use of the more sophisticated Macintosh interface. These include for example, a graphics program which produces trees for the language parser and an interface that contains MacProlog™ input-output routines.

Please send me the disk(s) for *Cognitive Science Projects in Prolog* by Scott and Nicolson detailed below.

	Quantity	Price
Apple Mac 3.5" disk (SW0044) @ £50.00.	_____	_____
MS-DOS 3.5" disk (SW0045) @ £50.00.	_____	_____
MS-DOS 5.25" disk (SW0046) @ £50.00.	_____	_____

Prices are inclusive of postage and packing.

Subtotal = _____

Value Added Tax @ 17.5% *(applicable to U.K. orders only)* = _____

TOTAL AMOUNT PAYABLE = _____

Name: _____

Delivery Address: _____

_____

_____

I enclose a cheque for: _____

Cheques must be made payable to Lawrence Erlbaum Associates Limited and drawn on a UK bank. Eurocheques are not accepted.

I authorise you to debit my credit card with the amount of: _____

My Access/American Express/Visa No. is: _____

Expiry Date: _____ Date: _____

Signature: _____

Credit Card address: _____

Please return this form to Lawrence Erlbaum Associates Ltd., 27 Palmeira Mansions, Church Road, Hove, East Sussex BN3 2FA, England.